CRIMINAL JUSTICE ADMINISTRATION IN INDIA

CRIMINAL JUSTICE ADMINISTRATION IN INDIA

DR. SHIV KUMAR DOGRA

University Institute of Laws
Panjab University Regional Centre
Ludhiana (Punjab)

Foreword by

PROF. J.K. CHAUHAN

Professor, Deptt. of Laws
(Former Director, Panjab University
Regional Centre, Ludhiana and Muktsar)
Panjab University, Chandigarh

DEEP & DEEP PUBLICATIONS PVT. LTD.
F-159, Rajouri Garden, New Delhi - 110 027

CRIMINAL JUSTICE ADMINISTRATION IN INDIA

ISBN 978-81-8450-122-3

Printed in India at NEW ELEGANT PRINTERS
A-49/1, Mayapuri, Phase-I, New Delhi - 110 064

Published by DEEP & DEEP PUBLICATIONS PVT. LTD.,
F-159, Rajouri Garden, New Delhi - 110 027 • Phone : 25435369, 25440916
E-mail : ddpubs@gmail.com • ddpbooks@yahoo.co.in
Showroom :
2/13, Ansari Road, Daryaganj, New Delhi - 110 002 • Telefax : 23245122

Contents

Foreword

It is the primary duty of every State to protect rights of every individual as well as the property. The State has provided the Criminal Justice Administration to protect the rights of the innocent and punish the guilty. The Criminal Justice Administration is devised more than a century back. It has become ineffective. A large number of guilty go unpunished in a large number of cases. The system takes years to bring the guilty to punish. It has ceased to deter criminals. Crime is increasing rapidly everyday. The citizens live in constant fear. The quality of justice determines the quality of society of governance.

India has inherited and borrowed from colonial power systems of criminal law and procedures, as well as rules of evidence, courts, police and correctional systems, that fail to fit its current societal needs. Today, cases of murder, rape, theft, assault, robbery, disorderly conduct, and bride burning occur much more than the past. The open violation of laws, bribery of police, presence of professional criminal, intimidation of victims and witnesses are experienced in day-to-day life. Those who are not directly victimized often live in a constant state of fear and victimization. In actual practice, the problem of crime is much more serious than the official figures show. It has been estimated that from one-third to one-half of all serious crimes are not reported due to a variety of reasons, including intimidation and harassment of the victims. It is generally felt that the Criminal Justice Administration in our country is in a very sad state. Hardly six or seven percent cases go up for trial, result in conviction. It means either that too many innocent persons are prosecuted unnecessarily or that a high percentage of guilty persons are being acquitted due to some shortcomings in the system. Either way the position is unacceptable.

Indian judiciary led by the Supreme Court has exhibited a judicial activism in clearing the misconceptions about the concept of the criminal trial under the procedure prescribed in the country which has resulted in the weakening of the Criminal Justice System. Realising such misconceptions, the Hon'ble Supreme Court in the *State of Punjab v. Jagir Singh* AIR 1973 SC, 2407 observed that "a criminal trial is not like a fairy tale where in one is free to give flight to one's imagination and fantasy. It concerns itself with the question as to whether the accused assigned at the trial is guilty of the crime with which he is charged. Crime is an event in real life and is the product of inter-play of different human emotions".

The present book *"Criminal Justice Adminstration In India"* is very relevant and unique work in several aspects done by Dr. Shiv Kumar Dogra. The book covers most important current issues regarding the Criminal Justice Administration in India. The study is divided systematically which starting with introductory of the concept of Criminal Justice Administration to give stepwise development of Criminal Justice Administration in India during different eras.

The study has quite brilliantly examined the philosophical goals and theoretical principles of Criminal Justice Administration. Taking a broad canvas of Criminal Justice Philosophies, the author has defined the concept of crime and compared the Criminal Justice Administration of India with United States of America and United Kingdom. The author highlighted the working system and provisions of present Criminal Justice Administration in India and highlighted the drawbacks. A sincere attempt has been made to throw light on the role played by Indian judiciary to strengthen in present Criminal Justice Administration in India. The book provides a new insight into the working of the police which is most important component of Criminal Justice Administration by going through the detail study of role of police Administration. Dr. Dogra with his competent scholarship and admirable erudition has put forward some important issues and attempted answers to these issues by giving valuable suggestions.

I appreciate the scholarly efforts of Dr. Shiv Kumar Dogra and congratulate him for his interest and valuable contributions to the development and bring out anthology on Criminal Justice Administration in India. I am sure that the book will be useful to Academicians, Judges, Lawyers, Law students, and Administrators. I hope that the hard work of the author will be rewarded by taking into consideration the conclusion and suggestions of the study.

J.K. CHAUHAN
Professor, Deptt. of Laws
(Former Director, Panjab University
Regional Centre, Ludhiana and Muktsar)
Panjab University, Chandigarh

Preface

In every free country, which has adopted a system of governance through democratic principals like our country, the people have their fundamental inalienable rights and enjoy the recognition of inherent dignity and equality, of course subject to reasonable restrictions. The life of man in a society would be a continuing disaster if left unregulated. The principal means for such regulation is the law, which serves as a measure of society's balance of order and compassion and an instrument of social welfare in human rights, liberty and dignity as enshrined in Article 21 of our constitution.

The Criminal Justice Administration consists of three identifiable components. Each operating within its own sphere and communications. These three components can be categorized generally as: (i) Police, (ii) Courts, and (iii) Corrections or Punishments which known in systems terminology as the input process and components. The generic term "Police" includes all investigating agencies directly or indirectly involving, identifying and apprehending the suspects or accused. The expression "Court" includes all courts, namely, from trial court up to the highest court of the land. The corrections or punishment component refers not only to the traditional sentence of imprisonment but also all kinds of Reformations and Rehabilitation as well as Treatment Centers.

It gives me immense pleasure to acknowledge the assistance and cooperation of those persons who have helped me throughout the course of my work.

At the very outset, I would like to thanks Almighty God for having given me valuable opportunity and enough patience to complete my work.

At very first opportunity, out of the profound sense of indebtedness, I take immense pride to heartily acknowledge Prof. (Dr.) Kamaljeet Singh, Director, Panjab University Regional Centres, Ludhiana and Muktsar for his inspiring and valuable guidance.

Constructive suggestions have always soothing and desired effects, hence it's my duty to thank and express to record my gratitude to Prof. Suresh Kapoor (Dean and Chairman, Deptt. of Laws, HPU, Shimla), Prof. A.S. Sankhyan (Former Dean and Chairman, Deptt. of Laws, HPU, Shimla), Prof. P.L. Mehta (Director, School of Legal Study, Shimla), Dr. S.S. Jaswal (Assistant Research Professor, ILI, Delhi), Dr. Devinder Singh (Reader, Panjab University, Chandigarh), Faculty members of Deptt. of Laws, HPU, Shimla, School of Legal Studies, Shimla and Panjab University Regional Centre, Ludhiana specially Mr. Rajneesh Sharma and Ms. Vaishali Thakur.

Whatsoever I deserve for, is solely due to my beloved parents and my family members. They have always inspired and kept my moral in good spirit at every juncture of my life with their blessings, love, affection and inspiration.

Thanks are also due to the staff of Law Library, HPU, Shimla, HPU School of Legal Studies Library, Indian Law Institute Library, Indian Institute of Advanced Studies Library, Panjab University Chandigarh Library and Panjab University Regional Centre Ludhiana Library for their cooperation and help.

I am also grateful to my students of Panjab University Regional Centre, Ludhiana and School of Legal Studies, Shimla for their affectionate cooperation. I also express my immense debt and gratitude to the staff of Panjab University Regional Centre, Ludhiana, especially Cap. A.S. Randhawa, Mr. Gurdev and Mr. Rajmal.

Last but not the least I thank all persons who were directly and indirectly involved with this work and learned authors whose work I have consulted and referred. Also on the same platform I extend my thanks to Deep and Deep Publications (P) Ltd. who agreed to publish this manuscript and gave it present shape.

SHIV KUMAR DOGRA

1

Introduction

"Long ago we made a trust with destiny, and now the time comes when we shall redeem pledge, not wholly or in full measure, but very substantially. At the stroke of midnight hour, when the world sleeps, India will awake to life and freedom. A moment comes, which comes but rarely is lustory, when we step out from the old to new, when an age ends, and when the soul of a nation, long suppressed, finds utterance. It is fitting that at this solemn moment we take the pledge of dedication to the service of India and her people and to the still larger cause of humanity. . . . We end today the period of ill fortune and India discovers herself again. The achievement we celebrate today is but a step, an opening of opportunity, to the greater triumps and achievements that await us. Are we brave enough and wise enough grasp this opportunity and accept the challenges of the future? . . . Freedom and power bring responsibility. This responsibility rests on this assembly a sovereign body represent the sovereign people of India. . . . The service of India means the service of the millions who suffer. It means the ending of poverty and ignorance and disease and inequality of opportunities. The ambitions of greater men of our every eye.

That may be beyond us, but as long as there are tears and sufferings, so long our work will not be over. And so we have to labour and work hard, to give reality to our dream."[1]

Looking back over the years that have rolled by since then, one is apt to question and doubt, whether we have progressed well on the path of democracy and evolved smooth and successful working arrangements for the purposeful functioning of the three important wings of the society of the democratic system, i.e. legislature, executive and the judiciary. While steering the country towards the promise objectives of the secular, socialist and welfare state for its hundred of million people. The government has had to regulate in an increasing degree the conduct and business of different sections of people through present criminal justice system. This has meant increasing exercise of the power by the Government through its widely spread apparatus of the courts and the police in several matters effecting the daily life of the people.

In every civilized society, the primary role of a criminal justice administration is to protect the members of that society. In this respect, it is a formal instrumentality authorized by the people of a nation to protect both their collective and individual rights. Another major duty of any administration of criminal justice is the maintenance of law and order. Since crime and disorder disrupt stability in the society, we have vested the criminal justice administration with the authority to act as the means by which the existing order is maintained.

In addition, to these major roles and duties, there are a number of important functions of criminal justice administration. The prevention of crime, the suppression of criminal conduct by apprehending offenders for whom prevention is ineffective, to review the legality of our preventive and suppressive measures, the judicial determination of guilt or innocence of those apprehended, the proper disposition of those who have been legally found guilty and the correction by socially approved means of the behaviour of those who violate the criminal law are some of them.[2]

---

1. Spoken by Pandit Jawahar Lal Nehru, our First Prime Minister when he addressed the Constituent Assembly in New Delhi on the eve of Independence on 14th August, 1947.
2. See, Robert D. Pursley, *Introduction to Criminal Justice*, (1978), p. 7.

Modern society is reached at its highest point (culmination) of centuries of social interaction, attempts to understand individual and collective behavior, and efforts to find adequate means of social control. This social control began with the family and kinship ties, ethical systems and religious controls and eventually the criminal law and criminal justice administration of the modern state. In present context the crime is defined by legislative action or governmental decree, law enforcement agencies identify suspected offenders, the courts convict those legally found guilty, and correctional systems attempt to rehabilitate offender.[3] The nature and extent of crime in society provides some index as to where the social problems lie in that society and the number of people involved.

The concept of crime therefore, involves the idea of a public as opposed to a private wrong, with the consequent intervention between the criminal and the injured party by an agency representing the community or public as a whole. In this view, the crime is intentional commission of an act or omission deemed socially harmful or dangerous and specifically defined, prohibited and punishable under the criminal law, which shall be in force for the time being. Difficulty arises from this definition because of the practical problems often involved in determining whether or to what degree an act is intentional, because some offences known as 'strict liability offences' are punished as crimes even though they may be unintentional. Legislatures are sometimes influenced by powerful vocal minorities to enact legislation which benefits only a certain group or which reflects only its view of what is right and wrong. Such law may be contrary to general good and opposed to the moral convictions of the general public.[4]

In modern civilized societies only violations of rules promulgated and enforced by agencies of the government technically are crimes. Although crime is sometimes viewed in a very broad way as the violation of any important group standard of as the equivalent of anti-social, immoral and sinful behaviour, much immoral behaviour is not covered by the criminal law and violation of some laws included in the

---

3. See, Venon Fox, *Introduction to Criminology*, (1976), p. 17.
4. See, *Encyclopedia Britannica*, Vol. 6, (1966), p. 754.

criminal code are not regarded as immoral or even anti-social, or are so regarded only by a small portion of the population. Labour unions, professional organisations and many other groups within a society establish rules for their members and provide penalties for infractions but such rules are not part of criminal law. No matter how immoral, disgusting or harmful an act may be, it is not legally a crime unless it is covered by a law which prohibits it and prescribes punishment for it.[5]

The concept of justice was developed in ancient Greece along with the concept of democracy in the fifth century B.C. It had its origin in the ideas of vengeance of primitive and ancient man and is of Old Testament. The concept was to protect the weak from the strong, to keep the strong from using a wrong as license to over react in return. Justice involves the infusion of morality into law. Plato held that justice was a rational principle at the root of moral distinctions that converge in each individual to make a rational society. A rational society was one in which the principle of justice had power as well as manifest authority.[6]

Justice is basically the protection of the weak from the strong and the mitigation of strength with wisdom. While law is generally aimed at the preservation of the *status-quo*, whether the ancient feudal system, the Church, the State, the monarchy, or an economic system, it changes slowly in the direction of morality, wisdom and the protection of the weak from the strong, justice was originally based on the need of the individual for protection.

The criminal justice administration exists because society has deemed it appropriate to enforce the standards of human conduct so necessary to protecting individuals and the community. It seeks to fulfil the goal of protection through enforcement by reducing the risk of crime and apprehending, prosecuting, convicting and sentencing those individuals who violate the rules and laws promulgated by society. The offender finds that the criminal justice administration shall punish him for his violation by removing him from society and simultaneously will try to dissuade him from repeating a social act through rehabilitation.[7]

---

5. *Ibid.*
6. See, *supra* note 3, p. 16.
7. See, Chamelin C. Neil, *Introduction to Criminal Justice*, (1975), p. 5.

Basically, the criminal justice administration is comprised of police, courts and correctional machinery. Each contains varying divisions. The police is responsible for controlling crime and maintaining law and order. The courts are prosecuting agency in criminal justice administration. Finally, the aim of the correction is institutionalizing the activities of the offender and rehabilitating him to full and useful participation in the society.

The role of police in the administration of criminal justice is clearly defined. The legislators enact the law; the police enforce them and lawyers, magistrate and judges conduct the trial with the active participation of the public. The penologists and their associates in the field of extra institutional correction have the responsibility of the treatment and the ultimate disposition of convicted offenders. All the legislators, the police, the prosecutors, the judiciary, the public and the penologists are the part of a team. The attitude and posture of any single member of this team has a direct effect on every other member.[8]

The word police is derived from the Greek word *'politeia'* or its Latin equivalent *'politia'*. The Latin word *'politia'* stands for State or administration.

But the word police today is generally used to indicate the body of civil servants whose duties are preservation of order, prevention and detection of crime and enforcement of laws.[9] Ernst Fround defined police power as *"the power of promoting public welfare by restraining and regulating the use of property and liberty."* In a broad sense, the term police connotes the maintenance of public order and the protection of persons and property from the hazards of public accidents and the commission of unlawful acts.[10]

All societies need some methods and rules to maintain order. Even in the smallest societies, informal sanctions discourage deviation. In the simplest forms of State organisation, informal sanctions are supplemented by agents of the ruler who enforce his decisions. Although the police function is universal in society, it is only the large and more complex States that full-time officials are appointed with special police responsibilities regulated by politics, tradition and law.

---

8. See, S.K. Ghosh, *Police in Fermet*, (1981), p. 20.
9. See, Sanker Sen, *Police Today*, (1986), p. 85.
10. See, *Encyclopedia Britannica*, Vol. 18, (1966) p. 153.

Most police in such societies are enrolled in State, provincial, traffic regulation and preventive patrol. [11]

The function of policing is to control the behaviour of individuals or groups acting against the safety of persons and property. By custom and religion, certain acts are labeled as wrongs against society. These acts are also considered anti-social in nature, classes of crimes, or offences against the State have emerged from the codification of law and regulations.

In police administration, John P. Kenny states, *"It is a folk system for policing which relies on control methods established by the family, the community or a tribal leaders or councils. The prevailing customs prescribe the system."*[12] Thus, the formally and officially, the duties of a police officer are prescribed by legislative or administrative mandate are the protection of life and property, preservation of the peace, prevention of crime, detection and arrest of violators of law, enforcement of laws and ordinances, and safeguarding the rights of individuals.[13]

Police is a service dedicated to the protection of life, liberties and property of citizens and the battle arm of the society to deal with criminals and lawless elements. Powers given to them under the law alone will not enable them to perform these duties to the satisfaction of people. They need the full cooperation and support of the public. The police have a significant role to play in the political development of a society by keeping under check the forces of disintegration and disorder. Indian police had stood a bulwark against all threats to national integrity and acted as island of sanity during communal and caste frenzy.

The concept of police as law and order maintenance agency in one or another form had been developed as accordingly as the society developed. In ancient India the *Rigveda* and *Authurveda* mention certain crimes and punishments in Vedic India. The kings maintained a body of secret advisors and emissaries and personally patrolled the

---

11. See, *The Encyclopedia Britannica*, Vol. 25, (2002), p. 959.
12. See, William B. Mainicoe and Jan C. Menning, *Elements of Police Supervision*, 2nd ed. (1978), p. 8.
13. See, Alen E. Bent and Ralph A. Rossum, *Police, Criminal Justice and Community*, (1976), p. 3.

streets in the nights, in disguise to study and receive first hand information to restore peace and tranquility.[14]

The Mughal rulers also had a well organised police force for maintaining law and order in society. This system was, however, different from the *Vedic* age. The police official called as *'Fauzdar'* was in-charge of the entire police force with a number of subordinate officials called *'Darogas'* or *'Kotwals'* working under him. The policeman called the *'Sipahi'* was the official of lowest rank in the police constabulary of the Mughals. The detective branch of the police was called *'Khuphia'* who assisted the police in criminal investigations. The chief police administrator of the province was called *'Subedar'* or *'Nizam'*.

The modern police force in India, however was created during the British rule in the last quarter of the 19th century and was built up slowly. The British inherited several indigenous police systems from Mughal and their other contemporary predecessors. They re-organised it and developed it on a more or less uniform pattern throughout India. They tried different experiments in different provinces to have a police system suited for their purpose.[15]

The police organisation in Indian States is primarily governed by the Police Act of 1861, which was based on the recommendations of the Police Commission of 1860. Section 4 of the Act lays down the principles, on which organisation of the State force rests till today.

Police is a State subject along with public orders, administration of justice, prisons, reformation and borstal institutions. The Constitution of India clearly amplifies that the legislature of any State had exclusive power to make laws for such State. The Union Government is also indirectly involved in the Police Administration of the country.

In United Kingdom, a police officer is considered an officer of the law and not a servant of any executive or public authority. In Lord Denning's words, the Commissioner of Police is *"answerable to the law and to the law alone"*. In India the police has to first carry out the directions of the political executive and the

---

14. See, S. Mahartaj Begum, *District Police Administration*, (1996), pp. 23-24.
15. See, Giriraj Shah, *Encyclopaedia of Crime, Police and Judicial System*, Vol. 1, (1999), p. 8.

bureaucracy and then only enforce, to the extent possible, the law of the land. The interests of the people to whom according to the National Police Commission, the police should have been primarily responsible, take the backseat. This aberration, is a direct consequence of the wrong priorities assigned in the Police Act of 1861, which has become a milestone around the neck of the police department.

The Police Act, 1861 still continues in statute books without any substantial changes. Does it mean that the police role does not require any redefinition and that what was designed to serve the British imperial interests is fit to be perpetuated even when we are a secular democratic Republic.

The police structure in the States is crumbling. It has become a tool in the hands of unscrupulous, self-seeking politicians. At the central level also, it has started showing cracks. How else can we explain the paralysis of forces, both of the State and the Centre, during the demolition at Ayodhya and riots in Gujarat. How else do we understand the criminal justice system dragging its feet for ten years to punish the guilty men of 1984 riots. It is high time that the basic questions were examined in depth and remedial measures taken before the hollow men . . . the stuffed men plunge the country into chaos.

The presumption that a person acts honestly applies as much in favour of a police officer as of other persons, and it is not a judicial approach to distrust and suspect him without good grounds thereof. Such an attitude could do neither credit to the magistracy nor good to the public. It can only run down the prestige of the police administration.[16]

Hence the police, being an integral organ of the society, has been developed primarily for the preservation of the social order and the protection of the State authority.[17]

Thus, the police represents a mere segment of the administrative sub-system of the wide political universe, but in all political systems it has been and remains the central agency of the criminal justice system. Mr. William Seagle on the American Criminal system emphasised that:[18]

---

16. Aher Raja Khima *v.* State of Saurashtra, (1956) CrLJ 426 at 439.
17. See, Modh. Ashraf, *Police and Administration of Criminal Justice in India : An Appraisal*, C&MLJ, Vol. 36, No. 2, April-June, 2000, p. 139.
18. *Ibid.*

"The whole machinery of criminal justice is designed to facilitate the escape of the person accused of a crime. But the blame for this situation has inescapably with the system itself, rather than with the man who administers it."

The main function of administration of criminal justice is performed by the criminal law courts comprising of Magistracy and the Court of Session. The Supreme Court and the High Courts have only appellate jurisdiction in criminal cases. These courts are generally engaged in dispensing abstract and even handed justice in terms of principles set forth in an absolute law. It, therefore, follows that the court must impart justice within the limits of the law so as to maintain uniformity and impartiality in the determination of guilt and punishment of the accused. Generally, all criminal courts possess in inherent power. All such powers as are necessary to do right and to undo wrong in the course of administration of justice on the principle of common law embodied in the maxim: [19]

"Quando Lex Aliqud Alicue Concedit
Concedere Videtur Id Sine Quo
Res-ipsa Esse Non Protest."

When law gives a person anything it gives him that without which it cannot exist. Whenever anything is required to be done by law and it is found impossible to do that things unless something not authorized in express terms, be also done than that something else will be supplied by necessary intendment.

No legislative enactment dealing with procedure can provide for all the cases that may possibly arise and it is an established principle that courts possess inherent powers apart form the express provisions of the law, which are necessary to their existence and the proper discharge of duties imposed by law. According to Blaise Pascal, *"Justice without power is inefficient, power without justice tyranny. Justice without power is opposed because there are always wicked men. Power without justice is soon questioned. Justice and power must, therefore, be brought*

---

19. See, Sanjay Malik, *Justice Through Inherent Powers of the Court*, CrLJ, Vol. 36, No. 1, Jan.-March (2000), p. 22.

together, so that whatever is just may be powerful and whatever is powerful may be just."

There are basically two systems that society may take in dealing with one who is accused of a crime. Firstly, by presuming his innocence until it has effectively succeeded in proving him guilty under due process of law, or secondly, by presuming his guilt unless he successful disprove that assumption under similar process.[20] These two systems, known as the accusatorial system and inquisitorial system which is followed in different parts of the world in administration of criminal justice. In the accusatorial system followed in common law countries, the burden of proving that an accused person violated some law is on the prosecution while in the inquisitorial system which is followed in some European countries, it is for the accused person to prove that he is not guilty of the crime allegedly committed by him. In India where the accusatorial system is followed, there is a presumption in favour of the accused person that the offence has not been committed by him and presumption continues to be operative until the prosecution is able to prove its case according to the rules of procedure and evidence prescribed by law.[21] The same principle has been incorporated in the Evidence Act:

Whoever desires any court to give judgement as to any legal right or liability dependent on the existence of facts which he asserts must prove that those facts exists.[22]

The doctrine of legal guilt requires more than mere factual guilt. Rather, an accused is guilty if and only if the State can prove, under various procedural restraints dealing with admissibility of evidence, the burden of proof, and the requirement that guilt can be proved beyond a reasonable doubt, that he did in fact commit the crime.[23] As Packer observes, *"none of these requirements has anything to do with the factual question of whether the person did or did not engage in the conduct that is charged as the offence against him; yet favourable answers to any of them will mean that he is legally innocent."*

---

20. See, Harry W. More, *Principle and Procedures in the Administration of Justice*, (1975), p. 297.
21. See, Ahmed Siddique, *Criminology*, (2005), p. 45.
22. See, Law of Evidence Act, 1872, Sec. 101.
23. See, Ralph A. Rossum, *The Politics of the Criminal Justice System*, (1978), p. 185.

Criminal justice system operates in accordance with specific criminal statutes. The penal statutes prescribe the acts of commission or omission and make them punishable. The implicit purpose is to define a crime and its constituent elements, so that a prosecution can be based on it and the violator may be brought under these statutes. Legislatures in democratic societies all over the world have a tendency to over react to crime. But their over enthusiasm to stricter enforcement of criminal law is frequently counter-productive. Strict punishment against aggressive or anti-social offences is what people will normally welcome but offences designed to produce social conformity or to legislate morality will always create problems in the realms of criminal law making and criminal law enforcement. The non-enforceability of these laws ultimately poses a serious threat to the integrity of the entire criminal justice system.[24]

The criminal justice administration is devoted to reduction in imprisonment rates by increasing reliance on fines and community-based programme as alternatives. The correctional institution concentrates on those convicted offenders who are imprisoned and calls for fundamental changes in the organizational features and supporting ideology of the correctional institutions.[25]

Society has a real interest in the release of prisoners, since these individuals have been committed for definite terms by the court and release on parole. Individuals in the general public are frequently skeptical of probation and parole. These persons sometimes assert that both parole and probation are based on compassion for the offender. They point out that in the real world punishment is the fact of life.

Under our criminal justice system, fear of punishment alone prevents the bulk of people from violating the law.[26] Probation and parole seems to be somewhat at variance with these ideas. It should be remembers, though that rehabilitation is as important to society as to the criminals.

---

24. See, P.D. Sharma, *Police and Criminal Justice Administration in India*, (1985), pp. 3-5.
25. See, Elmer H. Johnson, *Crime, Correction and Society*, (1978), p. 360.
26. See, Charles F. Hemphill, *Criminal Procedure the Administration of Justice*, (1978), p. 258.

In modern times it is popularly assumed that the criminal law need not to be applied as a retributive measure nor be applied to procure absolutely deterrent effect, nor to achieve restitutive values, but these laws ought to be applied to correct the offenders with a view to improving the conduct of offenders who are capable to recovery with the intention of law and have a mind capable of receiving guidance for good behaviour.[27] The criminal laws should aim to seek, is not just a change in behaviour but a change of hearts that may lead to the change in behaviour. Rehabilitation is a complex process. It starts from proclamation of offenders by courts, it works through acclamation of offenders in custody and ends with reclamation of offenders in society. As soon as an offender is proclaimed as an offender on conviction, the process of rehabilitation starts.[28]

With the development of the several human behavioural and social sciences the faith in the rehabilitation has been further consolidated in the present century. But the views that the rehabilitative processes should strive to reform, re-socialise, modify or re-make the criminal so that they will refrain from further law-breaking.[29] The sociologists and criminologists have often been in the forefront of the rehabilitation movement, agitating for more professional treatment workers, expansion of correctional services, and improvement in the treatment theory on which correctional ventures are based.

All the criminologists and sociologists through various theories of reformation tried to establish that as the ultimate object of administration of criminal justice is to reduce or prevent crime and as there is no other better way controlling offender than by incarceration, so as to prevent recidivism one should evolve principles and process for reformation of prisoners.

The wars, urbanization, industrialization and the migration of masses form the villages to the urban slums settling have served the magnitude and kinds of problems relating to juvenile. These factors have not only resulted in creation of juvenile delinquents but has also resulted in the

---

27. See, M.A. Ansari, *Tribals and Corrective Justice*, (1988), p. 32.
28. *Ibid.*
29. See, Nitai Roy Chowdhary, *Indian Prison Laws and Correction of Prisoners*, (2002), p. 181.

problems of poverty, destitution, prostitution and various forms of social and economic exploitation directly affecting the children in our society. The children needs to be provided with care, protection, maintenance, education, training, etc., all with the aim of their rehabilitation in the society.[30] The children being an important asset, every effort should be made to provide them equal opportunities for development so that they become robust citizens physically fit, mentally alert and morally healthy endowed with the skills and motivations needed by the society.

All criminal justice systems in the world has three separately organised parts—the police, the courts and the prison or correction. Each agency has its distinct task to perform. However, these tasks are by no means independent of each other. What each one does and how it does, materially affect the quality of work done by other agencies in the criminal justice system. The courts can deal only with those whom the police arrests. The job of correction can be done only with those who are delivered to the agency by the orders of the courts. Moreover, the method by which the criminal justice system deals with individual cases represents a continuum. These are not random action but proceed with an orderly progress of events, some of which like arrest and trial may be visible, but some others of even greater importance may occur outside the public view.

30. See, N.K. Chakrabarti, *Institutional Correction in the Administration of Criminal Justice*, (1999), p. 19.

Genesis of Criminal Justice Administration in India

I. INTRODUCTION

Administration of justice is one of the most important function of the State. If men were Gods and angels, no law courts would perhaps be necessary, though even then the person who doubts the truth (sceptics) might refer the quarrels among Gods, particularly in the context of Goddesses. Though man may be a little lower than the angels, he yet shed-off the brute. To curb and control that brute (cruel like-beast) and to prevent degeneration of society into a State of tooth and claw, which is required, i.e. rule of law. Being human, disputes are bound to arise amongst each other. For the settlement of these disputes, there is a need for guidelines in the form of laws to redress the grievances by courts. Laws and courts have always gone together. There is a close relationship between them, neither courts can exist without the laws nor laws without the courts. The State deals with the administration of the laws through the agency of the courts. The courts are the institutions to which one turn whenever he feel being the victims of a wrong and there arise within him an urge to seek redress or justice. Nothing rankles more in human heart than a broadening sense of injustice. No society can allow a situation to grow where the impression prevails of there being no proper and effective redress for grievances of its members.[1]

II. DEVELOPMENT OF CRIMINAL JUSTICE ADMINISTRATION DURING VARIOUS PERIODS

History of criminal justice administration in India can conveniently be studied under three major periods—Ancient, Medieval and Modern Period. Modern period may be divided in pre-independence period and post-independence period.

Ancient period extends for nearly 1500 years before and after the end of Hindu era and beginning of the Christian era. Medieval period begins with the Muslim era with the first major invasion by Muslims in 1100 A.D. to seventeenth century. Modern period begins with the consolidation of the British era in the middle of the eighteenth century and lasts for nearly two hundred years.

(A) Criminal Justice Administration in Ancient India

In examining the administration of justice in ancient India it is necessary to keep constantly in mind the social structure of that era in which it operated. The social system is a bye-product of the various forces which appears in different forms. Socio-legal culture is a mirror of a people's overall development. The fact that ancient Indian sociology was spiritually oriented is evident from the law Codes of ancient India. Rich philosophical traditions and literature, of which legal culture is only a segment, are the proof that the ancient Indian mind was constantly engaged in the pleasures of understanding, the problems of superior life. Therefore, when we study a judicial concept in ancient Indian jurisprudence it has to be understood in its social and spiritual context.[2]

---

1. See, H.R. Khanna, Judiciary in India and Judicial Process, (1985), p. 4.
2. See, S.D. Sharma, *Administration of Justice in Ancient India*, (1988), p. ix.

The dawn of history was the golden age. In *Satyayuga*, the rules of conduct were strictly observed by all including the king, or the headman of the tribe. Where there was no infringement of any rule or law, there was no question of punishment. Men were not wicked, and they adhered to truth and virtue. They never departed from established customs and traditions. That era was of complete happiness for all because even if anyone erred at all, he ratified his errors by prayers and sacrifices. In fact they were ruled by *Dharma* and they even did not find it necessary to have a king or his laws.

At an unspecified time, the Aryans were possessed with the desire for expansion. This was necessary with the growth of population. They, therefore, left their original home, and passed through many countries till they ultimately settled in India. It appears that while passing through other countries as well, they might have intermingled with different tribes.[3]

Some rules of social conduct were needed to prevent the growth of brutish (rude) instincts in man. To prevent an anarchical state in society, the rules of conduct were promulgated. Then came into existence sin and crime. The administering authority had to punish both after due investigation and enquiry.

The *Rigveda* is the oldest record of intellectual excellence and Rigvedic concept of *Rita* has been the shaping force of the Indian civilization and culture. The date of Rigveda is difficult as well as impossible to determine.

Dr. Radakrishnan subscribes to the view that Vedas embody crude suggestions and elementary moral ideas and spiritual aspirations of the early mind or society.

The other view is represented by Sri Auorbindo that the whole progress of Indian thought has been a steady falling away from the highest spiritual truths of the Vedic hymns.[4]

The important works which have influenced the legal course in ancient India are Dharmasastras, Kautilya's Arthasastra, the Manusmriti and Yajnavalkyasmriti. Probable dates are : Dharmasastras 1000 B.C. to 300 B.C., Arthasastra 325

3. See, Damayanti, Doongaji, "*Law of Crime and Punishment in Ancient Hindu Society*", (1986), p. 7.
4. See, *supra* note 2.

B.C. to 2nd Century A.D., Manusmriti 2nd century B.C. to 2nd century A.D and Yajnavalkyasmriti 100 B.C. to 300 A.D.

(i) Dharmasastras

The Dharmasastras are the earliest types of literature in Sanskrit in which some details of the law in the modern sense of the term are available. It may be presumed that the Dharamasastras were written before the Arthasastra of Kautilya which was undoubtedly written about 300 B.C. Hence, though no clear-cut limit can be fixed to the composition of the Dharamsastra, it will not be very far from the truth if it is said that these works were mainly produced between 100 B.C. and 300 B.C.[5]

In Dharamsastras it is interesting to observe that for them crime principally meant an evil act done with a certain degree of violent attitude. The criminal was said to be a person who without minding the physical or the spiritual effects of his acts was promoted by the absolute spirit of violence and openly engaged himself in causing, suffering to others by his acts such as theft, hurt, adultery, etc. For them offences against the king were the most serious particularly joining hands with the enemy, and they also punished severely those who violated a trust.[6] Such offences could be compared with treason and felony.

All the offences were punishable with fine or imprisonment. Punishments varied according to whether an offence was against the king or the ruling authority, or against a person to whom the offender owed duty or allegiance or amounted to only misdemeanors.[7]

The original conception of crimes in Hindu law have begun with the violation of religious and social rules followed by elaborate enjoinment of *prayaschitta*. A man accusing a Brahmin of a crime was deemed to have been committed a similar crime himself and in case of the Brahmin's innocence, his guilt was regarded as doubly sinful. A man who assaulted a Brahmin with hands or weapon was said to be banished from heaven for one thousand years; and if blood falls from the body

---

5. See, U.C. Sarkar, *Epochs in Hindu Legal History*, 1st ed., (1958), p. 55.
6. See, *supra* note 3, p. 2.
7. *Ibid.*, p. 3.

of a Brahmin, he will lose heaven for a number of years.[8] A
Brahmin who was not otherwise permitted to use weapons and
arms could do so when his life is threatened, in the exercise of
his right of private defence.

If a man who received or retained stolen property, he was
treated as a thief. A woman who committed adultery with a
man of lower caste was caused to be killed by dogs. The
adulterer also was to be killed. If the king did not strike or
punish the guilty person, the guilt fell upon him.[9] It is quite
clear from the above that the earliest conception of criminal
justice administration was blending of religion and law.

(ii) Kautilya's Arthasastra

After the earliest Dharamsastras, the work that deserve the
greatest attention is the famous Arthasastra of Kautilya. There
cannot be any doubt that Kautilya or Chanakaya, the famous
minister of Chandragupta Maurya, was the author of
Arthasastra. Kautilya's Arthasastra was written between 321
B.C. to 300 B.C.[10] Kautilya had a wonderful personality and
genius. He was believed to have responsible for the over-throw
and the destruction of the Nanda kings. Though he was known
as the maker of an Emperor and an empire. His philosophy
could be summarized by the following couplet:[11]

"Asimahi vayam bhiksam asavaso vasimahi
sayi-mahi mahipristhe kurvi mahi kimisvaraih."

Regarding his work, it must be said that quite a new path
was chalked out by him. His subject matter was Arthasastra.
The Arthasastra dealt exclusively with the rights and duties of
the king from the standpoint of actual administration involving
in the creation and regulation of the different departments of the
government including the most important organ of the State,
viz. judiciary.

In Arthasastra, Kautilya devoted two chapters to law. One
is known as the chapter on Dharamsthiya and the other is

---

8. See, *supra* note 5, p. 62.
9. *Ibid.* p. 63
10. See, V.K. Gupta, *Kautilyan Jurisprudence*, (1987), p. 1.
11. See, *supra* note 5, p. 81

known as the chapter on Kantakasodhanam. The former is supposed to deal with civil law and latter with criminal law. But this generalization is not quite tenable in as much as in the chapter on Dharamsthiya, there are many topics which really deserve to be included in the chapter on criminal law.[12]

The last four chapters of Book III in Kautilya's Arthasastra deal with crime such as robbery, defamation, assault, gambling, betting and other miscellaneous offences relating to crime. Robbery or Sahasa has been defined by Kautilya as sudden and direct seizure of person or property and as such it has got to be contrasted with theft which implies only fraudulent or indirect seizure. Kautilya again conceives a truly criminal element in robbery when he says that the fine or punishment shall be in accordance with the gravity of crime[13] rather than to the value of the article involved. For this purpose, Kautilya describes the different kinds of fines—first amercement, middle most amercement and the highest amercement.[14]

For abetment of robbery, an abettor has to be fined twice or four times accordingly as he causes another man to commit the robbery and if robbers on highway, who rush upon travelers, restrain, attach, threaten to kill and actually kill them, shall be hanged.[15]

In case of defamation, Kautilya includes a false charge (calumny), contemptuous talk and intimidation. If a man, capable of doing harm to another, out of enmity, intimidates him, he shall be compelled to furnish life long security and safety to the person intimidated. Defamation of one's own nation or village was to be punished with the first amercement, that of one's caste or guild with the middle most and that of Gods and temples with the highest amercement.[16] Fines were also to be imposed according to the caste and rank. The crime of assault was committed by touching, striking and hurting. Rank also played an important part in determining the nature of and punishment for assault was in the case of defamation. A Sudra striking a Brahmin had to get his hand cut-off. Hurts

12. *Ibid.*, p. 83.
13. See, *supra* note 10, p. 32
14. See, *supra* note 5, p. 93.
15. See, *supra* note 10, p. 33.
16. See, *supra* note 5.

were distinguished as those causing bloodshed and as those not causing bloodshed. Beating a man almost to death without causing bloodshed, breaking the hands, the legs, etc. was to be punished with the first amercement.[17]

Kautilya also specify a very sound theory that each complaint must be judged by the proper consideration of the evidence available. Fines were to be imposed even for doing mischief to plants and trees. Double fines were to be imposed when any injury was done to any tree on the boundary, in places of pilgrimage or the forest of the king. Gambling and betting could be indulged in, according to Kautilya only under the supervision of the Superintendent in charge of gambling. But he was careful enough to sanction gambling under state supervision with the main objects of detecting thieves, spies and stolen properties.[18]

The administration of justice meant the determination of what is just and so it was held to be the most sacred duty of the king. He was considered to be the fountain head of justice and the highest judge in criminal and civil matters.[19] Kautilya also cited elaborate provisions regarding the conduct and character of the judges so that they might readily inspire the confidence of the litigants. Thus, if a judge unjustly drives out or shut silent any of the litigants in his court, he shall be punished with first amercement. If he defames or abuses any one of them, the punishment shall be doubled. Again if the judge does not ask what ought to be asked or leaves out what he himself has asked, he will be punished with middle-most amercement. If a judge does not inquires into necessary circumstances, enquires into unnecessary circumstances, makes unnecessary delay in discharging his duty, postpones work, help witnesses, giving them clues and causes parties to leave the court by tiring them with delay he shall be punished with highest amercement.[20]

Administration of justice was among the main functions of the State. But the rendering of justice to the people was to a great extent, depended on the truth of the oral evidence of the

---

17. *Ibid.*, p. 94.
18. *Id.*
19. See, Krishna Mohan Agrawal, Kautilya on Crime and Punishment, (1990), p. 56.
20. See, *supra* note 5, p. 100.

witnesses. So, if the witnesses gave false evidence in the case it became impossible to do justice and this led to so many evil consequences.[21] So in view of the supreme importance of justice and the role of true evidence, the law givers have laid stress on the witness's speaking the truth when giving evidence and presenting himself as witness.

The criminal justice administration during the Kautilya's time had reached a comparatively higher stage of development. The number of offences dealt with are large and indicates an advanced stage of society. Punishments prescribed to be given to the criminals, through often brutal, reveal the great anxiety of the law-giver to suppress crimes by making them correspond as far as possible with the gravity of the offence.[22] The judicial system suggested by Kautilya in Arthasastra was quite scientific and was well planned. He had laid down rules and regulations about the procedure of holding court, acquiring evidence, examination of the witnesses, appointments of judges, their conduct and punishment, etc.[23] The views of Kautilya in all these matters are very scientific and upto date.

(iii) Administration of Criminal Justice during Smrities Period

(a) Manusmriti

Smritis formed an important part as sources of knowledge of law in ancient India. Of these Smrities, Manusmriti is comprehensive treatise on the conduct of Hindu society and Hindu ways of life and Hindu polity. It has been given different names, such as Manusmriti, Manusamhita, Manudharmashastra, etc.[24]

Most of the authors have held out the view that this work was actually written between 200 B.C. to 300 B.C. during Brahmanic society and Hindu society developed according to the laws of Manusmriti. This Smriti contains 12 chapters in which the author has made an attempt to bring out a coordinated growth of society, religion and polity.

21. See, *supra* note 19, p. 59.
22. *Ibid.*, p. 5.
23. Suresh Chandra Pant, Hindu Polity State and Government in Ancient India, (1971), p. 282.
24. *Ibid.*, p. 249.

According to Manusmriti law owes its existence to God. Law is given in 'Shruti' (which is later on known as Vedas) and 'Smritis'. The king is simply to execute that law and he himself is bound by it and if he goes against law or becomes Adharmik he should be disobeyed. Puranas are full of instances where the kings were dethroned and beheaded when they went against the established principles of law. According to this theory (Divine theory), the State is created by God. The king was given the power to control and govern the people by the Divine authority or power. This theory was very popular in ancient times.[25] Manu said:

स्वेस्वे धर्मे निविष्टाना सर्वेषामनुपूर्वशः ।
वर्णानामाश्रमाणा च राजा सृष्टोऽर्भिरक्षिता ।

Brahma created the king to protect the people of all varnas and ashramas devoted to their duties.

This theory was used to serve many divergent ends. It was used to support the people with the argument that he is on the divine mission, therefore, he must do justice and is bound to follow the law given in the scriptures. They argued that the king has the authority to do anything he likes and people cannot interfere with it because the power to the king was given by God.[26]

अराजके हि लोकेऽस्मिन् सर्वतो विद्रते भयात् ।
रक्षार्थमस्य स्वस्थ राजानमसृजत् प्रभुः ।।

Manu also further said that in the original state, there was anarchy all around. People were not happy and so God created the king in order to relieve people of that deplorable state.[27]

Manu devoted the eighth chapter of his Smriti mainly to the treatment of law consisting of eighteen topics. All these eighteen topics of law was divided according to the usages and the institutes of the sacred law. When it was not possible for the

---

25. See, B.N. Mani Tripathi, Jurisprudence Legal Theory, (2003), p. 125.
26. *Ibid.*, p. 126.
27. See, *supra* note 23, p. 251.

king himself to administer justice, personally, he should appoint a learned *Brahmin*, for the purpose but by no means should he appoint a *Sudra*. The fault of an unjust decision is apportioned to the offender, the witnesses, the judge and the King.[28] The King and his officers should neither encourage litigation nor hush it up unnecessary adjournments also should not be allowed. The King should concentrate his mind to the adjudication of a case in all its aspects remembering that *"justice being violated destroys justice being preserved preserves."*

People of all castes including women may be competent witnesses specially in criminal cases. Manu describes different classes of incompetent witnesses and provides that women should be witnesses for women only and each class must have witnesses from that class alone; but at the same time, he provides that any person having personal knowledge of a particular fact may give evidence in that respect specially on failure of competent witnesses; but the evidence of women, infants and the aged must be considered with great caution.[29] In case of dispute of the witnesses, the King or the judges shall accept the evidence of majority as true. If the conflicting witnesses are equal in number, the witnesses of good qualities and meritorious witnesses will be taken into consideration. Evidence shall always be direct and he who gives false evidence is firmly bound by the fetters of varna.

Manu has also referred to oaths and ordeals, but he has not described them in details. He has also added one special mode of oath in giving evidence by touching the heads of wives and children, implying thereby that the false evidence in these cases would result in the death or injury to the wives or children.[30] Manu also advocates different degrees of punishment beginning from simple admonition and intermediate with harsh reproof and fine. In awarding punishment, the King should fully take into consideration, the time, place, motive and other facts and circumstances of the case. When a Brahmin committed an offence, he was not to be sentenced to death but his head was to be shaved. Brahmin was not to be inflicted to sentence of death but for the murder of a Brahmana he was to be branded

---

28. See, *supra* note 5, p. 104.
29. *Ibid.*, p. 105.
30. *Id.*, p. 106.

on the forehead with the sign of female organ, for drinking liquor, with the sign of wine cup and for theft of gold with the sign of the foot of a dog.[31]

The severest punishment was reserved for the shudras, specially who defamed the Brahmins. A shudra insulting a twice-born man (Brahmin) with gross invectives shall have his tongue cut-off, the reason being that he is of low caste, if he mentioned the name of twice-born classes with contempt, an iron-nail ten fingers long shall be thrust red-hot into his mouth and if he arrogantly teaches Brahmins their duties, the King shall punish him by poring hot oil into his mouth and ears. As in defamation so also in assault, nearby the whole of law is mainly determined by reference to the question of caste. Manu also provides for criminal punishment in the shape of fines for those who hurt trees, plants, animals and even inanimate goods.[32]

Adultery was regarded as one of the most heinous offences for which deterrent punishments were provided for, so that it may create awe and fear in the minds of the people are large.

न हीदृशमनायुष्यं लोके किंचन विद्यते ।
यादृशं पुरुषस्येह परदउरोपऐवनम् ।।

"There is no offence which is more ruinous to man's life than adultery."

Apart from actual sexual intercourse, any act or action with immoral sexual desire was deemed to be adultery.[33]

It is necessary to point out that according to Manu, sending valentine cards on Valentine message to any man by woman or to a woman by any man, who is not a spouse or with whom marriage is not settled, with a carnal desire amounts to an act of adultery.

---

31. See, Shraddhakar Supakar, Law of Procedure and Justice in Ancient India, (1986), p. 76.
32. See, *supra* note 5, p. 108.
33. See, M. Rama Jois, Ancient Indian Law Eternal Values in Manu Smriti, (2004), p. 86

स्त्रियं स्पृश्सेददेशे यः स्पृष्टो वामर्षयेत्तया ।
परस्परयानुमते सर्व संग्रहण स्मृतम् । ।

"A woman who tolerates being touched at her private parts by a man, and a man who tolerates being similarly touched by her all said to be guilty of adultery (strisangrahana) by mutual consent."[34]

A *Shudra* guilty of adultery with a woman of any caste specially of the twice-born class shall be sentenced to capital punishment. A wife violating her duty towards her husband was to be devoured by dogs in public place and male offender was to be burnt on a red-hot iron-bed by putting logs under it.[35]

When the parties to litigation were unable to prove their case by means of oral or documentary evidence, the courts could allow the parties concerned to prove their case through divine tests or ordeals.[36] It was the belief in ancient times that truth could be found out by applying Divya or Divine tests. Therefore, the ordeals as means of proof for finding out the truth was being resorted to.

तत्रा दिव्यं नाम तुलारोहण विषाशनं अप्सुप्रवेशो ।
लोहधारमिष्टापूर्तप्रदानमन्याश्र शापथान् कारयेत् । ।

The divine modes of proof are secured through the balance, eating poison, entering fill, holding a piece of hot iron, offering one's merit acquired through sacrifices and charity and also by 'sapatha' or special oath.

Prayaschitta was another aspect connected with offences, which has nothing to do with forensic law, but a reference to which may not be wholly irrelevant as it was made the basis of imposition of reduced penalty. Manu Smriti have laid down that every human being has to suffer the consequences of sins committed by him, either during his life in this world or after death in Hell or the other world and again, owing to remnants

---

34. *Ibid.*
35. See, *supra* note 5, p. 10.
36. See, M. Rama Jois, *Legal and Constitutional History of India*, (1990), p. 567.

of such evil deeds, to take a re-birth and suffer the consequences of offences committed in the past life and so on. This is also in conformity with the belief in punarjanma (re-birth) and karma.[37]

यथा यथा मनस्तस्य दुष्कृतं कर्म गर्हति ।
तथा तथा शरीर तत्तेनाधर्मेण मुच्यते ।।

A man becomes free from the effects of his evil deeds in proportion to the repentance in his heart provided he resolves that he shall not repeat the offence.

Great importance was attached to confession and Manu prescribes half the punishment in case of one who confessed.

(b) Yajnavalkya Smriti

Yajnavalkya's work is more systematic than Manu Smriti. This Smriti was written in between 300 B.C. to 100 B.C. He has divided his work into three parts: Achara (conduct), Vyavahara (law) and Prayashchitta (expiration). His Smriti is a great authority in the realm of Hindu law. In the first and second parts he has dealt with Rajdharma along with Achara. In the third part he dealt with Prayaschitta. The Yajnavalkya Smriti is a great authority on Vyavahara and personal rights of a man.[38] In the beginning of the chapter on Vyavahara, we get the general and special rules of procedure, dealing with court, plaint, written statement, etc. The law of oral and documentary evidence and ordeals are dealt with at a later stage.[39]

The King was primarily responsible for the administration of justice with the help of learned and virtuous assessors. In case of unavoidable pre-occupation, a learned Brahmin should replace the King. Any judge or assessor doing any deliberate injustice should be punished by the King to the extent of double the amount in dispute. The allegations of the plaintiffs should be recorded and thus recorded statement be treated as plaint. The plaint would be followed by the written statement, which also should be recorded similarly. Then it would follow the proof. The last stage would be the judgement. Thus, the four

---

37. See, *supra* note 33, p. 87.
38. See, Chakradhar Jha, History and Sources of Law in Ancient India, (1987), p. 116.
39. See, *supra* note 31, p. 47.

stages of litigation were plaint, written statement, proof and the judgement.[40]

छिग्दण्डस्तथ वाग्दण्डो धनदण्डोवधस्तथा ।
योज्याव्यस्ताः समस्ता वा ह्यपराधवशादिमे । ।
याझवल्कयः! राजधर्म प्रकरणम् ।

Yajnavalkya speaks of four classes of punishment, viz. censure, rebuke, pecuniary punishment and corporal punishment and says that these should be used either separately or jointly according to the nature of the crime. Of these, mere censure was the lightest form of punishment and rebuke came after it; pecuniary punishment included fine and forfeiture of property and corporal punishment included imprisonment, banishment, branding, cutting of offending limbs, and lastly death sentence.[41] The measure of punishment depended on the gravity of offence. If the offence be not very serious the punishment must be severe too. Thus, Yajnavalkya says that the King should inflict punishment upon those who deserve the same after ascertaining and taking note of the nature of the offence, the time and the place of the offence and the strength age, a vocation and wealth of the culprit.[42]

Abuse, assault, theft and adultery were the different types of crime, as counted by Yajnavalkya. Abuse or defamation was to be adjudicated chiefly with reference to the question of caste of the different parties. The maximum fine shall be imposed for abusing a Brahmin, the King or Gods. Yajnavalkya describes the different kinds of assaults and provides for their punishment. He also makes provisions for punishing assault, committed in respect of animals and plants as well. The fines shall be doubled, when any injury is done to a tree in a sacrificial place, boundary or a temple. A Sahasa or a heinous offence is committed when a common or another's property is taken by force. For Sahasa, the fine shall be double the value of the thing taken, but four times when the offence is denied.[43] Thieves

---

40. See, *supra* note 5, p. 114.
41. See, Priya Nath Sen, Tagore Law Lectures, General Principles of Hindu Jurisprudence, (1984), p. 343.
42. *Ibid.*
43. See, *supra* note 5, p. 121.

should be apprehended with the help of detectives. Suspicious character and previous convicts should be arrested and examined in cases of theft. In cases, where theft cannot be detected or the stolen property cannot be traced, the King's officers and villagers concerned are to blame and the latter are to compensate for the unrecovered stolen property. A woman killing her husband or child, burning a house or village should be killed by a bullock. In case of murders, investigations should be conducted on hypotheses framed according to the suspects inclinations and antecedents. Yajnavalkya used the word adultery in a wide sense and this offence was to be proved mainly by circumstantial evidence.[44] Regarding the punishment, the question of caste again was very important.

There are so many Smiritis like Parasara, Narada, Brihaspati, Katyayana, etc. which also described all about the criminal justice administration in ancient time. The views of these Smrities were less or more dominated by the views of Manu Smriti and Yajnavalkya. Regarding these Smrities it has been said by Kane that "Narada, Brihaspati and Katyayana form a triumvirate in the realm of the ancient Hindu law are composition of the legal literature." Their age may be fixed between 400 A.D. and 700 A.D. in a tentative way. All these jurists exhibited an excellent analytical insight and the most perfect acumen of elaborating any explaining the juristic principles and philosophy.

(B) Criminal Justice Administration during Medieval India

The glorious Hindu period was subjected to discontinue by the attacks of the Muslims and the beginning was made by Mohammud-bin-Quasim in 712 A.D. He came to India as invader and returned thereafter. The real penetration into India was made by Qutub-uddin Aibek who, in reality established himself firmly in India after waging series of wars and finally established his supremacy in the whole of the northern India. The Muslims, thereafter continued to rule over India for centuries till the year 1857 when the last Mughal King Bahadur

---

44. *Ibid.*

Shah Zafar was dethroned by the Britishers and the English established themselves as the next rulers of India.

(i) Criminal Justice Administration during Muslim Period

During the period when the Muslims ruled over India, many significant changes were introduced by them in the Indian legal system from time to time. The Islamic jurisprudence was imported into India by Muslims with certain modifications to suit the circumstances of the age and to satisfy the needs of the people of the time.[45] It goes to the credit of the Muslim rulers that they did not interfere with the law of the Hindus and the Hindus continued to be governed by their own laws in personal matters. Especially the Mughal rulers who ruled over India in 17th century a remarkable tolerance was shown by them to the Hindu religion.[46] They did not accept Hindu law for themselves; nor did they abolish the Hindu system of law altogether. Hindu law was allowed to be reserved for the Hindus and the Mohammedan rulers did not interfere with this system in any very appreciable way, so far as its civil aspect was concerned. The result was that in this way the Mohammedans followed their Mohammedan law and the Hindus were allowed to stick to their own system of law.[47] Thus this arose the two separate systems of personal law which practically proceeded on parallel lines and which remained to be modified later only at the time of British administration. During the Mohammedan rule, only the criminal law was largely common to the Hindus and the Muslims with the exception of the application of oaths and ordeals. The entire criminal administration of justice was based on the principles of Mohammedan criminal law and the punishments were inflicted upon criminals in accordance with the provisions of that law only.

. Crime under the Islamic law was considered to be an offence against God or the ruler or a private citizen and as such it was a private affair between the offender and his God, king or the injured person. Most of the crimes, therefore, could be compounded. Crime was not considered a social offence. Even the Emperor did not have a general power of pardon. It was

---

45. See, S.K. Puri, Indian Legal and Constitutional History, (2003), p. 18.
46. *Ibid.*
47. See, *supra* note 5, p. 200.

interesting that murder was not considered to be a crime against God or the ruler. It was a wrong done to a party and as such it could be compounded by payment of blood compensation, called *Khun Baha*.[48] The ruler was not required to take any further action. However, in case the party did not accept compensation, appropriate punishment had to be given.

The crimes were of various types. Adultery, fornication, apostasy, drinking wine, theft and highway robbery, etc. were the offences against the God. The cases of mis-rule or abuse of power or moral turpitude and other offences falling within the orbit of departmental duties were the offences against the ruler. Rebellions or effrontery against the sovereign also were such offences. Offences against citizens consisted of doing a wrong to any citizen. They could both be civil and criminal. There were minor offences, which were punished at the discretion of the *qazis*. These minor offences included counterfeiting coins, arson, stealing shrouds from tombs, poisoning, gambling and selling of wine and other intoxicants.[49]

The Emperor, the representative of God on earth was considered as 'fountain of justice'. He exercised general superintendence over all the courts created by him within his territory. Qazi was the most important person in the criminal system of judicial administration. The Muslim rulers were very much selective in their approach in appointing persons to these offices and it is said that the Mughal rulers, in particular, attached great importance to this aspect of their duty. The reason was that the entire judicial system revolved around him as he was entrusted with multifarious duties both of judicial as well as secular nature. The emperor alone have power to appoint a person as Qazi and he occupied the office during the pleasure of the Emperor. He was invested with both civil and criminal powers.[50]

The Sultans of Delhi and the Mughals sought for their judicial system models from outside India – from Arabia, Syria, Persia and Egypt and brought necessary changes to suit Indian system. The head of the state, the Sultan or the Emperor was

---

48. See, B.S. Jain, *Administration of Justice in Seventeenth Century India*, (1970), p. 57.

49. *Ibid.*, p. 58

50. See, *supra* note 45, p. 20.

regarded as the foundation of justice and final court of appeal. The emperor administered justice in person in open court and decided all types of cases. He was assisted in administration of justice by the Chief Sadar (Sadr-us-Sudur) regarding cases of religious nature and by the Chief Qazi (Qazi-ul-Quzat) in all other cases including civil and criminal.[51]

The Chief Qazi stood next to the Sultan or the emperor in the judiciary and under him were the Qazis in provincial courts (Qazi-e-Suba) in the headquarters of Districts (Sarkar) courts (Qazi-e-Sarkar) and the all big cities – town (Parganah) courts (Qazi-e-Parganah). The lowest courts were village courts known as Dehat courts and was presided over by the village headman (Chaudhary).[52] The Panchayat held it sitting in public places and administered justice to maintain peace and tranquility in the village. It had the power to inflict punishment for small offences and to decide petty disputes. The decision of the Panchayat was final and binding.

The criminal cases were decided by the Emperor, the Provincial Qazi, the Governor, the Faujdar (Faujdari Adalat) and Kotwal. Petty criminal cases relating to theft or rioting in the Pargana (town) were assigned to the local Kotwal. In course of time a whole-time Qazi was appointed to try criminal cases within the Pargana. The Faujdar also possessed some criminal jurisdiction. The Courts of the Governor (Nizam-e-suba) and provincial Qazi (Qazi-e-Suba) had also original jurisdiction in addition to hearing appeals against the decisions of the Faujdar and Kotwal.[53]

The mode of administering justice during the Muslim period was simple, speedy and without any elaborated procedure of law. People could lodge their complaints without unnecessary delay and harassment by the people of court. Justice had to be done speedily. Justice delayed was literally treated as justice denied. In case of unreasonable delay, even the judges and Qazis had to compensate the parties. The Qazis were definitely instructed to use their reason and discretion in deciding disputes without relying too rigidly on the letters of the law.[54] Sometimes extra-ordinary procedure would be

---

51. See, H.V. Sreenivasa Murthy, History of India, (Part- I, 2003), p. 266.
52. See, supra note 45, p. 30.
53. See, supra note 51, p. 267.
54. See, supra note 5, p. 213..

adopted to find out the truth most successfully. Litigation was never encouraged. Emperor did not like to vest much powers in the hands of Qazis and magistrates for fear of corruption. Generally speaking there was wonderful and essential justice. Even close friends, amiss and omarahs of the Emperor could not escape from punishment if and when found guilty.

The Islamic state and society was based on the 'Shar' or Islamic law. Shar was the legal sovereign and everyone, the ruler and the ruled were not above the law but subservient to it.[55] Muslims consider 'Shar' as divine, eternal and immutable. The Holy Prophet, God, the omnipotent being, alone had the attribute of sovereignty. The Prophet himself did not claim for himself any better position than ordinary men. Similarly, a Muslim ruler was regarded as a God's servant responsible for the observance of His law by all alike. He was thus not the people's master but only an office in trust for the supreme being.[56] The law had been divided into 'Shar' and 'Urfi'. The Shar was based on the principles enunciated by the Quran had three principle component elements, viz., Hadis, Ijma and Qiyas. The Quran was the most important source of law.[57] Most of the basic notions underlying in civilized society find such a mode of expression in the Quran. Compassion for the weaker members of the society, fairness and good faith in commercial dealings, incorruptibility in the administration of justice were all enjoined as desirable norms of behaviour without being translated into any legal structure of rights and duties. The same applies to many percepts which are more particular and more peculiarly Islamic in their terms.[58] The administration of justice was considered by them as an essential act for the fulfilment of this responsibility. The King (Emperor) as the representative of the people discharged his duties either personally or through officers appointed for this purpose. The King and his officers were to do what was 'just and right' in the eyes of the God to whom alone the King was answerable. By virtue of his office, he was the legislator, the defender of the law as well as the dispenser of justice.[59] But this holy book does not enunciate principles of law in very exact and precise terms.

---

55. See, *supra* note 51, p. 256.
56. See, U.C. Sarkar, Legal Research Essays, (1984), p. 5.
57. See, *supra* note 51, p. 256.
58. See, N.J., Coulson, A History of Islamic Law, (1997), p. 11.
59. See, *supra* note 45, pp. 18-19.

As times passed by social problems grew more intricate and complex and the governance became difficult on the basis of the revealed book, which laid down only broad principles of social life. This difficulty was overcome by incorporating Sunnah or Haddis as a source of law next to Quran. The Haddis was regarded as the best interpretations of the law and has played an important part in the development of Shar because wherever the Quran is either silent and does not contain a clear injunction, the authority of Sunnah or Haddis is sought.[60] This Haddis or Sunnah laid down the foundations of what is now called Islam.

In the course of its later development Muslim society was confronted with new problems as the existing laws were inadequate to solve them. Hence two other sources were drawn upon. These were Ijma and Qias. Ijma (universal consent) or the consensus of the opinion of the most eminent theologians of Islam was accepted as the right solution. The literal meaning of it is 'agreeing upon'. Those disputed points of law which were resolved by agreement of the persons who have a right, in nature of knowledge, to form a judgement of their own after the death of the Prophet came to be regarded as a valid source of law. As a result of agreement of the points in dispute got settled and each settled point became the essential part of the faith and disbelief in it, came to be regarded as an act of unbelief.[61] The Qiyas were the analogous inferences based on the Quran, and the Haddis were considered the most valuable and were described as the Usul-ul-Usual or the 'bases of the bases' of Islamic jurisprudence.

In the development of Islamic jurisprudence many rules and regulations issued from time to time by the rulers of different Muslim states. These regulations were based on justice and fair play and mostly related to matters like trade, property, war taxation and the like. These have come to be collectively known as the Urfi law.[62] A judge was allowed considerable discretion in the interpretation and the application of the Urfi law.

---

60. See, *supra* note 51, p. 257.
61. See, *supra* note 45, p. 19.
62. See, *supra* note 51, p. 258.

Evidence during the Muslim era was of the various types viz., statements of witnesses, oaths and written documents. The oath was taken by the Christians on the Gospel, by the Hindus on the Cow and the Muslims on the Quran. Where a witness came to give evidence, the Qazi should not direct him in any way, but quietly record his evidence.[63] A person who was blind, insane or dumb was considered as incompetent to give evidence. Slaves were also considered incompetent witnesses. When the person stood in near relationship to each other, they were considered as incompetent witnesses such as son in favour of father and grandfather, wife for husband, master for slave, but a brother was treated a competent witnesses against brother and uncle a competent witness against the nephew.[64] The evidence of a non-believer (Hindu) was not admissible against the Muslim.

The punishment in Muslim law was broadly classified as Hadd, Kisa, Dia and Tazir. Hadd literally means boundary or limit. In this case there were scheduled punishments for scheduled offences and the judges could not modify or alter them in any way.[65] In such cases the proceedings usually started at the instance of the police, though private persons could also institute them by complaints. The punishment was deterrent in nature in such cases. The usual forms of this type of punishment were stoning, scourging, amputating of limbs.[66] Kisa means retaliation. It applied in cases of killing and wounding which did not prove fatal. This was called 'blood for blood'. In case the next of kin demanded the legal punishment, it had to be awarded by the judge. However, if the next of the kin accepted the blood money, called Diya offered by the murderer and pardoned him unconditionally, the offence could be compounded and no further cognizance of it could be taken by anyone.[67] Kisa or Qisas were based on the principle of a hand for hand, a foot for foot, a nose for nose, a tooth for a tooth and a life for a life, an eye for an eye, and so forth. Such punishments were inflicted on an offender who caused a grievous injury short of death.[68]

---

63. See, *supra* note 48, p. 43.
64. See, *supra* note 45, p. 22.
65. See, *supra* note 5, p. 229.
66. See, *supra* note 45, p. 22.
67. See, *supra* note 48, pp. 60-61.
68. See, *supra* note 51, p. 263.

Diya was the 'blood money' or money compensation which could be accepted in lieu of the retaliation.[69] Tazir means censuring, prohibition, discretionary punishment and reformative punishment.[70] There was no specification of this punishment either in quality or in quantity. Sometimes even new punishments or new modes of punishments could be devised by the judges and the Kings. It was a corrective doctrine in that the punishment was awarded with a view to reform the culprit. It took cognizance of such offences as 'the use of abusive language, forger of deeds or letters, bestiality, sodomy, offences against public peace and tranquility, decency and moral, etc. not covered by Hadd (fixed).[71] The law of punishment was not uniform for all, but had to be considered according to the circumstances and the status of the accused. Men of high rank who were guilty of proved offences, were to be let-off with a warning. Merchants were sent to prison, the common people were punished with strokes of the whip. The type and quantum of punishment to be awarded was left completely at the discretion of the judge,

In addition to the above punishments, for certain offences punishments were inflicted by the Qazi and even by King on offenders which were derogatory and humiliating in character though they were not recognized by Islamic law.[72] The death sentence was imposed with great care and it was normally imposed in the case of high misdemeanor, such as treason and adultery of heinous type.

(C) Criminal Justice Administration in Modern India

(i) Pre-independence Period

Administration of criminal justice so established by the Muslim rulers was inherited by the administrators of the East India Company. The East India Company was incorporated in England on December 31, 1600 by a Charter of Queen Elizabeth which defined the constitution, powers and privileges of the

---

69. See, *supra* note 5, p. 230.
70. See, *supra* note 48, p. 62.
71. See, *supra* note 51, p. 263.
72. See, *supra* note 45, p. 23.

Company. The Company was vested in the hands of a Governor and 24 Directors and it was to enjoy an exclusive trading right into the countries lying beyond the Cape of Good Hope eastwards to the straits of Megellan. India, Asia, Africa and America fall within these geographical limits. No British subject was permitted to carry on any trade within this area without a license from the Company.[73] In the beginning, the Company was established for a period of fifteen years but the British crown was empowered to revoke the Charter even earlier on a two years notice, if Company's commercial activities were not found profitable to British trade and commerce. The Governor and 24 Directors of the Company formed the Court of Directors of the Company which was to be elected every year by the General Court.[74]

The General Court was empowered to make and issue orders for the good governance of itself, its servants and for the betterment, advancement and continuance of trade. In 1623 a Charter was issued by James I in order to strengthen the hands of the Company, in enforcing its laws and punishing the persons, subject to a jury trial in case of capital punishment.[75] It could inflict a punishment upon persons disobeying its law with a proviso that no punishment could be given which was unduly harsh or contrary to laws, statutes or customs of England.

The various Charters were issued from time to time. The Charter of 1661 which conferred wide powers on the company to administer justice in its settlement has an important bearing on the evolution of the judicial system in India. This Charter had two main features.[76] Firstly, the judicial power was granted to the Governor and Council of a factory, which meant the executive government of the place. The Charter thus drew no line of demarcation between the executive and judiciary. Secondly, justice was required to be administered according to the English law.

Now the Company no longer remained a trading association but became a territorial sovereign by a subsequent Charter of 1668 when Bombay was transferred to the Company.

73. See, M.P. Jain, Outlines of Indian Legal History, (1997), p. 5.
74. See, N.V. Paranjape, Indian Legal and Constitutional History, (1996), p. 6.
75. See, *supra* note 45, p. 32.
76. See, *supra* note 73, p. 7.

The Company was authorized to declare war and to make peace subject to the overall control of the Crown of England by yet another Charter of 1683.[77] The Charter Act of 1726 conferred the overall control of the Governor-in-Council in each of the presidency towns where the Company had established itself firmly and since then judicial system was organised on a uniform pattern in the Company's territories.

(a) Administration of Criminal Justice in India During Company's Rule

In the end of seventeenth century, the East India Company was firmly established in India at Surat, Madras, Bombay and Calcutta, though it still declared its mission purely as a trading Company. These activities of the Company made the way for the adoption of a new policy by the British Parliament in the beginning of the eighteenth century regarding its aim and relations with India. The continuous passing of various Charters for regulating the Company's acquisition of territory and administration of justice in India, from time to time, may be said to be gradual but inevitable steps on the road that led up eventually to the settling up of the British Empire in India.[78]

(1) British Settlement in Surat and Administration of Criminal Justice

Surat was an important commercial centre and enjoyed the status of an international port. It was the first place where English established their factory, in order to begin their trade. It was in the year 1612 that the East India Company at Surat was established with the permission of the local Mughal government for permanent establishment. The *firman* was issued by Jahangir the Mughal emperor in 1615 permitting the English Missionary Sir Thomas Rox to live according to their own laws, customs, religion and to remain subject to their laws, administer by their own officers.[79]

The judicial system which was created in Surat was that the President and Council constituted a court to decide all types of disputes between the Britishers *inter se* in accordance with

---

77. See, *supra* note 45, p. 33.
78. See, V.D. Kulshreshtha, Landmarks in Indian Legal and Constitutional History, (1995), p. 35.
79. See, H.V. Sreenivasa Murthy, History of India, (2003), p. 123.

their own law.[80] These privileges show that the Englishmen began to be governed by two sets of laws—the English law and the Indian law. The cases involving both Englishmen and the natives were decided by the native courts applying Indian law and those among the Englishmen themselves were settled by the English Tribunals applying English law. The President and Council of the Factory were empowered to do justice in criminal cases.[81] It was under this power that president and Council exercised criminal jurisdiction and inflicted penalties on the offenders. The death sentence could be awarded in two conditions. If there was mutiny and other felonies, and when the trial was held with the help of jury consisting of 12 or more Englishmen. There was no regular and systematic law for their guidance. The executive body of the Company happen to exercise the entire judicial functions.[82] On many occasions the English people without taking recourse to the Tribunals of the soil used to take law into their own hands. Surat lost much of its importance when the seat of the President and Council of the Company was shifted to Bombay.

(2) British Settlement at Madras and Administration of Criminal Justice

Madras was founded in 1673 on a plot of land granted to the Company by one Hindu Raja of the locality. The fort established was known as the Fort St. George. The Raja had also granted to the company full power and authority "to govern and dispose of the government of Madraspatnam" which was a small village lying near the fort. The fort came to be known as the white town and the small village of the Madraspatnam came to be known as the Black town. Black town was the name given to the village as it was inhabited by the Indians. All the white people used to live inside the fort which came to be known as the white town.

Although the ruler had authorized the Company to govern the black town but the Company did not took much interest and the old pattern of deciding the disputes continued.[83] The Agent

---

80. See, *supra* note 45, p. 34.
81. See, J.K. Mittal, India Legal History, (1985), p. 11.
82. See, *supra* note 5, p. 301.
83. See, B.S. Sinha, *Legal History of India*, (1976), p. 11

and the Council decided both civil and criminal cases in White town. The judicial powers exercised by them were vague and indefinite. The administration of justice in the Black town was decided only in a Choulltry Court in Madraspatnam being presided by Adigar, the village headman, to decide small civil and criminal cases.[84] In a certain case, the death of a native woman was alleged to be caused by an Indian and the matter was brought to the notice of the Raja by the Agent. The Raja made an order to decide the case according to the English law.

The Charter of 1661, gave very wide powers to the Company. The most important provision of this Charter was that the Company was empowered to appoint Governors and councils in their Indian settlements and that these Governors and Councils were further authorized to try all cases both civil and criminal concerning all persons belonging to the company or living under them according to the laws of England.[85] The powers given by this Charter were very much wide. No restriction was imposed regarding punishment. Even capital punishment could be inflicted by them.

The Charter of 1683 authorised the Company to establish Admiralty Courts in order to check illegal traffic and punish piracy which became so common. A Court of Admiralty was established in Madras on July 10, 1686. It consisted of three civil servants who were members of the Governor's Council.[86] The Company sent Sir John Biggs as Professional lawyer to act as a Judge-Advocate,[87] i.e. the Chief Judge of the Court of Admiralty at Madras, for smooth functioning of the Admiralty Court.[88] The Governor and the Council, with the arrival of Sir John Biggs relinquished their judicial functions and thenceforth the Admiralty Court dispensed justice in all cases including civil, criminal, mercantile and maritime. In criminal cases the court was assisted by the jury.[89]

In 1688, the Mayor's Court was started at Madras on the strength of a Charter, issued in 1687. This Charter also created

---

84. See, *supra* note 86, p. 18.
85. See, *supra* note 5, pp. 302-03.
86. See, *supra* note 73, p. 15.
87. See, *supra* note 83, p. 12.
88. See, *supra* note 78, p. 41.
89. See, *supra* note 79, p. 129.

a Corporation for Madras. The Corporation consisted of an English Mayor, twelve Aldermen and sixty or more burgesses. Out of the twelve Aldermen, three were to be English and the rest may be of any nationality. The Burgesses included the heads of various castes.[90]

The Mayor and Aldermen constituted a civil court, while the Mayor and the three senior Aldermen was justice of the peace with criminal jurisdiction. The Mayor and two Aldermen formed the quorum. The court sat once only in a fortnight and tried the criminal cases with the help of the jury. Appeals from the decisions of the Mayor's court refer to the Admiralty Court where the value exceeded three Pagodas, or in criminal case the offender was sentenced to lose life or limb. It would also punish offences by fine and imprisonment.[91]

The Choultry Court administered justice in small offences and petty civil cases amounting to two pagodas. Two of the Aldermen sat twice a week at the Choultry to decide the minor cases. Thus, the judicial system which existed in Madras was three courts, viz., the Choultry Court, The Mayor's Court and Court of Admiralty.[92] Lastly appeals from the Admiralty Court went to the High Court of Madras consisting of Governor and Council.

In Madras, the process of administration of criminal justice was very slow and tardy. Capital punishment was awarded by hanging, though natives were some times whipped to death.[93] The punishment of banishment was executed either by sending the offender out of the settlement, or deporting him to Sumatra or St. Helena to work under the Company as a slave. In a number of cases of serious offences like murder, manslaughter, misappropriation, etc. the Englishmen were sent to England. Imprisonment was quite a dreadful punishment, as the conditions in the prison were intolerable and inhuman. Forfeiture of limbs, fine, forfeiture of property, pillory, branding and whipping were some other forms of punishments which were awarded to the offenders.[94]

---

90. See, *supra* note 81, p. 20.
91. *Ibid*.
92. See, *supra* note 45, p. 36.
93. See, *supra* note 81, p. 21.
94. See, *supra* note 73, p. 20.

(3) Settlement at Bombay and Administration of Criminal Justice

The island of Bombay which was the subject of supreme sovereignty of the King of Gujarat, Sultan Bahadur, came under the control of the Portuguese in 1534. In 1661, Alfonsus VI the Portuguese King, transferred it to Charles II, the British King as dowry on the marriage of his sister Princess Catherine with Charles II. King Charles transferred the Bombay to East India Company on a nominal annual rental of £ 10 in 1688.[95] A Charter issued in the same year empowered the Company to administer Bombay by making laws and ordinances and also by enforcing them. The Company was further authorisd to establish courts of justice at Bombay for trying civil and criminal cases according to English Courts.[96]

The regular system of law and courts was brought to the Bombay by Gerald Augier. According to this system two courts were started in two divisions of Bombay. All the judges were honorary. There were some Indian judges also. A separate court of judicature was established for each of the division.[97] Above these two courts in the two divisions, there was the court of the Deputy Governor and Council. This Court had both original and appellate jurisdictions.

The administration of criminal justice was also reorganised by the judicial plan of 1672. Now the Island of Bombay was divided into four divisions, namely Bombay, Mahim, Mazagaon and Sion. In each of these divisions, a justice of peace was appointed who happen to be an English. He had power to apprehend the offender and hold inquiry and conduct preliminary investigations. He also examined witnesses. After preliminary investigation the justice of peace was to send the record to the Court of Judicature where the case was tried with the help of the jury.[98] The Court of Judicature was to sit once a month and decide criminal cases with the help of justice of peace. A court of conscience was also established which functioned under the Court of Judicature. The trials in this court were summary trials without the help of jury so that speedy

---

95. See, *supra* note 45, p. 36.
96. See, *supra* note 5, p. 305.
97. See, *supra* note 45, p. 36.
98. See, *supra* note 74, p. 16.

justice could be available to the poor litigants. This court dispensed justice without any cost payable by the litigants.[99]

In 1684 an Admiralty Court on the pattern of Madras was established. Dr. John learned in civil law, was appointed as Judge-Advocate. This Admiralty Court took cognizance of all cases of civil and criminal maters.[100] In 1688, Dr. John was dismissed by the Company as he had lost favours with the Governor.

In the year 1718, a new court of judicature was established in Bombay. This court of judicature consisted of nine judges including the Chief Justice. Three English judges constituted the quorum and the native judges played only subsidiary role of acting as assessors.[101] The bulk of the court's work was in deciding criminal cases. The concept of criminal justice during that time was that it should serve as a deterrent to others so as to prevent commission of offence in future. With this object in mind, punishments imposed were severe, barbarous and inhuman.[102] Punishments were prescribed for swearing the name of God in vain, drunkenness, adultery, theft or robbery, house breaking, assault, cheating, forgery, wounding, murder and opposing officers in the discharge of their duties. Death penalty was available for murderer. In case of theft the defaulter was asked to return back three-fold the value of the goods stolen and if he could not pay he was forced to work for the owner of the stolen property.[103]

(4) Settlement at Calcutta and Administration of Criminal Justice

English merchants got a footing in Bengal very late, as compared with Madras or Bombay. The Company constructed its factory and fort on the bank of Hoogly river. The fort came to be named a Fort Williams. In 1698 the Company secured the *zamindari* of three villages of Sultanati, Calcutta and Govindpur. Calcutta was declared to be a Presidency in 1699 to be administered by the President and Council.[104]

---

  99. See, *supra* note 81, p. 15.
100. See, M. Rama Jois, *Legal and Constitutional History of India*, (1984), p. 110.
101. See, *supra* note 45, p. 38.
102. See, *supra* note 82.
103. See, *supra* note 83, p. 15.
104. See, *supra* note 5, p. 307.

The Company never authorized to set-up any court till Mayor's Court in 1728. Accordingly one of the Council who occupied the office of "Receive of Revenues" was not only Collector but also a Magistrate. In the capacity of a magistrate he held a zamindari court which took into cognizance both civil and criminal jurisdiction.[105] All criminal cases were proceeded to sentence and punish immediately after hearing except where the crime was murder required to lash to be inflicted until death, in which case he suspends execution of the sentence until the facts and evidence were laid before the President and his confirmation of the sentence was obtained.

Governor and five senior members of the Council constituted the court of criminal jurisdiction. Indivisually each of them was to be a justice of the peace. The justice of the peace were persons appointed by the Crown, for purposes of administration of criminal justice.[106] They were responsible for the maintenance of law and order in the locality within their territorial jurisdictions. They were empowered to issue warrant for the arrest of those who were alleged or suspected to have committed offences, to grant bail to an accused to jail pending trial by quarter session.[107] Each justice of the peace could try and punish minor offences. Three justices sitting together were competent to try cases involving serious' offences also.

(5) Uniform System of Criminal Administration in Presidency Towns

The Charter of 1726 established for the first time three Mayor's Courts in the three Presidencies town on uniform basis. This Charter was rightly known as the 'Judicial Charter'. In view of the growing prosperity of the English settlements in India, the officials of the Company felt the keen necessity of better administration of the territorial units by more organized and systematic legislative and judicial organs. [108]

The Charter contained important provisions which inaugurated British system of courts and administration of justice in India. The Charter provided for the establishment of a

---

105. See, *supra* note 83, pp. 18-19.
106. See, *supra* note 100, p. 115.
107. *Ibid.*
108. See, *supra* note 5, p. 308.

Corporation in each Presidency town. Each consisted of a Mayor and nine Aldermen.[109] Mayor was required to be elected every year. He was to be elected from amongst the Aldermen and outgoing Mayor. Alderman was to hold office either or life or for the term he resided in the Presidency town. A vacancy amongst the Aldermen was to be filled by the Mayor and remaining Aldermen.[110]

The Mayor's Court had no criminal jurisdiction. It was only a civil and testamentary jurisdiction. The Governor and five senior members of the Council were appointed as justice of peace in each Presidency for the administration of criminal justice.[111] They were empowered to arrest and punish persons for petty criminal offences. Collectively three justices of peace were to form a court of record and have power to the court of Oyer and Terminer and Goal Delivery and were empowered to hold quarter sessions (four times a year) for all offences excepting high treason committed in the Presidency town and the subordinate factories.[112] The trial of criminal offences were to be held with the help of grand and petty jury. In this way, the technical forms and procedure of criminal jurisprudence of England were introduced through this Charter in India.

The Charter of 1753 which was in a modified and improved version of the Charter of 1726 placed to Mayor's Court under the Governor and Council. The Aldermen were to be appointed by the Governor and Council who also selected the Mayor from out of the panel of two names recommended by the Aldermen.[113] Now Mayor's Court could try civil suits only between European and European or natives (relating to Englishmen and other foreigners) and European. These courts continued to grant probates of will and letters of administration and were given matrimonial and admiralty jurisdictions.[114]

The court of requests to try petty cases of the value not exceeding five pagodas was also established. Under the Charter of 1753, the Courts that were functioning were the courts of

---

109. See, *supra* note 81, p. ???
110. See, Monica David, *India Legal and Constitutional History*, (1981), p. 9.
111. See, *supra* note 74, p. 22.
112. See, *supra* note 45, p. 43.
113. See, *supra* note 79, p. 138.
114. See, Harihar Prasad Dubey, *The Judicial System of India*, (1968), p. 58.

request, the Mayor's Court, the Court of the President and Council for criminal cases to hear appeals from the Mayor's Court and acted as justice of peace and held quarter sessions to decide criminal cases. The King in Council in England was empowered to hear appeals from the Court of Governor and Council in all civil cases involves a sum of 1,000 pagodas or more.[115]

The Charter also made provisions for evidence on oath by the Christians and Indians in such a manner as they according to their several casts shall esteem to be most binding on their conscience, to oblige them to speak the truth.[116] In short, the amendments introduced by the Charter of 1753, were executive oriented. So as the judicial independence is concerned the Charter of 1753 was much more inferior to that of 1726.[117] The judiciary under the Charter of 1753, was quite subservient to the executive. Thus, Ferminger rightly says, "The weakness of the judicatures of 1726 and 1753 arose from the fact that they tended to be in fact but branches of the Company's executive Government, and they, therefore, afforded imperfect means of resistance to the class interests of the Company's servants at a time when the Company's servants were bidding fair to monopolise the trade of the country."

(6) Reforms in Administration of Justice and Adoption of Adalat System

The Charter Act of 1726, introduced a uniform judicial system. But with the passage of time, the Company brought under this control the territories surrounding the Presidency towns. The necessity was felt to provide judicial system for such territories also. The Company also undertook to administer civil and revenue law and the administration of the criminal law remained with the Nawab.[118] The first Adalat system was started in 1772. In course of time, this elementary system was modified, improved and refined and introduced in Presidency towns.[119]

---

115. See, *supra* note 74, p. 29.
116. See, *supra* note 81, p. 27.
117. See, *supra* note 110, p. 12.
118. See, *supra* note 5, p. 310.
119. See, *supra* note 73, p. 55.

Warren Hastings who was the Governor of Calcutta at that time, formulated a judicial plan of 1772 for the better administration of the revenue and law for Bengal, Bihar and Orissa. According to this plan, the whole of the Diwani area was divided into several districts. In each district a Provincial Court of Diwani called the Mofussil Diwani Adalat presided over by the Collector was created for all civil cases, including real and personal property, inheritance, caste, marriage, debts, disputes accounts, contracts, partnerships and demand on rent.[120]

The system of criminal justice was also reorganised. A court of criminal judicature called the Faujdari Adalat was established in each district for the trial of murder, robbery and theft, and all other felonies, forgery, all sort of fraud, misdemeanours, assaults and fray, quarrels, adultery, etc. In it's a Qazi and a Mufti, with the assistance of two Maulvis appointed to expound the Mohammedan criminal law sat to hold trial. The function of the Qazi or Mufti was to give Fatwa in terms of this exposition.[121] The Faujdari Adalats were placed under the control of Sadar Nizamat Adalat. It was presided by a Daroga, appointed by the Nizam, representing the Nawab in his capacity of supreme criminal judge, and assisted by a Chief Qazi, a Chief Mufti and three Maulvis supervised the proceedings of the Provincial Faujdari Adalats. The proceedings of the Nizamat Sadar Adalat were supervised by the Governor and Council.[122]

The Fouzdari Adalats were not empowered to award death sentence, but they were required to transmit the evidence in capital cases with their opinion to the Sadar Nizamat Court for final decision. Fines over one hundred rupees were to be confirmed by the Sadar Court. The decoits were to be executed in their own villages and their entire village was fined. The family members of the decoits were made state-slave.

The plan of 1772 contained certain defects. Thus, new plan called the judicial plan 1774 was brought into force. Accordingly, an Indian officer called the Diwan or Amil was appointed in place of the Collector in each district and he was empowered to collect the land revenue and to act as a judge of

---

120. See, *supra* note 110, p. 15.
121. See, J.K. Mittal, Indian Legal History, (2004), p. 34.
122. See, *supra* note 110, p. 16.

the Mofussil Diwani Adalat.[123] The other changes introduced by the plan of 1774 included the division of the entire Moffusil area of Bengal, Bihar or Orisa into six divisions and setting up of a Provincial Council consisting of four or five British servants of the Provincial Council consisting of four or five British servants of the Company in each division. In 1775, Warren Hasting shifted the highest criminal court, namely, Sadar Nizamat Adalat which so far was located at Calcutta to Murshidabad.[124] Thus, the enitre criminal administration was again put under the control of Nawab.

The Regulating Act of 1773 established the Supreme Court at Calcutta with Sir Eligah Tenpey as the Chief Justice. The Supreme Court was to consist, a Chief Justice and three Puisne Judges. Section 13 of the Regulating Act empowered the Crown to establish a Supreme Court of Judicature. This provision was specially made to remove the defective state of judiciary as it existed under the Charter of 1753. It was also a Crown's Court. Chief Justice and Judges were appointed by His Majesty, being barristers of not less than five years.[125] The Supreme Court had full powers and authority to exercise all civil, criminal, administrative and ecclesiastical jurisdictions. In criminal cases it would act as a Court of Oyer and Terminer and Goel Delivery for the town of Calcutta and the factories subordinate thereto. The Supreme Court of judicature had full power and authority to hear and determine all complaints against any of His Majesty's subjects for any crime.[126] It was recognised as a Court of Record. It has jurisdiction over servants of the company also. All offences of which the Supreme Court could take cognizance were to be tried by a jury of British subjects residing in Calcutta. A mercy petition could be made to the Court by a person convicted by it for an offence which it had the competency to decide. It could refer the matter with its recommendations to the Crown of England if it so desired.[127]

In 1781, the British Parliament passed an Act of settlement to remedy the defects that became manifest by that time. As a

---

123. See, *supra* note 79, pp. 145-46.
124. See, *supra* note 45, p. 50.
125. See, *supra* note 78, p. 95.
126. See, *supra* note 114, p. 105.
127. See, *supra* note 45, p. 57.

result of the Act of settlement, provisions were made more favourable to the Governor-General and Council and many important limitations were imposed on the rights of the Supreme Court. It was provided by the Act of Settlement that the Governor-General and Council shall not be subject jointly or severally to the jurisdiction of the Supreme Court of Fort William in Calcutta for any act done in their official capacity.[128] In 1793, the British Parliament passed an Act whereby the Crown was authorized to supersede the judicial system of 1753 and establish Recorder's Courts in both Madras and Bombay. All the restrictions imposed on the Supreme Court of Judicature at Calcutta by the Act of 1781 were also imposed on the Recorder's Court at Bombay and Madras. In 1800, the British Parliament passed an Act athorising the Crown to abolish Recorder's Court at Madras and establish a Supreme Court of judicature.[129]

Lord Cornwallis, who succeeded Warren Hastings, came to India in 1786 and continued as Governor-General upto 1793. During this period he introduced several important changes in the judicial system of India. Reforms were introduced in the administration of civil and criminal justice. He introduced a judicial system based on the principle of equity and justice, set-up a gradation of civil courts, reformed criminal law, proclaimed the sovereignty of law and brought out the new Code of regulations.[130]

Criminal justice and its administration was found to be defective, so it was removed from the Indian hands. The Court of Sadar Nizamat Adalat was re-established at Calcutta under the Governor-General and Council assisted by the Chief Kazi and two Muftis. The Provincial Courts of Faujdari Courts presided over by Indians were replaced by four Circuit Courts presided over by two covenanted servants assisted by Kazis and Muftis. They were to make tour twice a year throughout the districts. Each division was to have a Court of Circuit to try, hear and determine all criminal offences. In capital offence it was the Nizamat Adalat that had to pass the final sentence. The

---

128. See, *supra* note 5, p. 317.
129. *Ibid.*
130. See, *supra* note 79, pp. 148-49.

Circuit Courts tried the cases committed to it for trial by the Magistrates. The Collector in each district was to act as the Magistrate.[131] The Magistrate and Court of Circuit had jurisdiction over all persons, Europeans as well as natives, not being British subject.

Police reforms were also carried out. In 1791 the posts of Superintendents of Police were created for Calcutta with functions of maintaining order and arresting criminals. Thus, the zamindars were deprived of police powers by the regulations of 11793 and they were replaced by Daroga who were under the control of the Company.[132] It can, therefore, be concluded that Cornwallis built the Empire on the foundations laid by his predecessors, especially by Warren Hastings. To strengthen this view one can see great truth in Smith's observation, "Taking it all in all, Cornwalli's had set the Company's ship of state on a new course, and had brought in justice and integrity to redress corruption and power politics."[133]

In 1823, Lord William Bentick became the Governor-General and remained in office till 1835. During his tenure as Governor-General, several steps were taken for reorganising and reforming the judicial system. He showed keen interest in improving the machinery of the administration of justice. With this aim in view he reorganised or consolidated the whole system of civil and criminal courts. The circuit Courts constituted at provincial headquarters were in existence for nearly forty years. But they did not play any effective role in the administration of criminal justice. Two difficulties were faced by the Circuit Courts. Firstly, large territorial jurisdiction and secondly, discharge of appellate function in civil cases as the Provincial Court of Appeal. So administration of civil and criminal justice was very much delayed at its hands.[134] Large arrears of cases under appeal had accrued in all courts to the manifest injury of the litigants and to the encouragement of litigation and crime. Lord Bentinck decided to put an end to the Circuit Courts as he felt they were not serving any useful

---

131. See, *supra* note 110, p. 31.
132. *Ibid*.
133. See, *supra* note 78, p. 143.
134. See, *supra* note 73, p. 197.

purpose.[135] According to the plan of Lord Bentick the Courts were re-modelled. The Munsiffs, the Sadar Ameens, Principal Sadar Ammens, the Zila and city Adalats and the Sadar Diwan Adalats. The Provincial Courts of appeal were abolished. The criminal administration also was strengthened by the appointment of Indians as Magistrates.

(D) Administration of Criminal Justice in India under the Crown

For the better administration of justice Government of India, 1858, transferred the administration from the East India Company to the Crown. The Indian administration was assumed directly by the Crown. To quote the statement of a well-known British statesman John Bright, made in 1862, this ended "a hundred years of crime against the docile natives of our Indian Empire".[136] Uniform Codes were passed and the next step to amalgamate the Supreme Courts and Sadar Adalats was to implement uniformity in the administration of justice.

(1) Criminal Justice Administration and Unification of Courts

Over a period of eighty years two separate and parallel systems of courts continued in Presidency towns and Moffusil area. There were the Royal Courts or Crown's Courts and the Adalats of the Company. The sources of power and authority of these courts were different. Their jurisdictions were vague and ill-defined. This confusion brought about several conflicts of the common law courts and the Chancery Courts in England during the 17th century.[137] The clash and conflicts between the two systems gradually decreased with the direct assumption of power by the Crown in 1858. It made imperative on the Crown of England to give good government to the Indians. The assumption of direct responsibility of the Government of India by the Crown made the problem of uniting the two sets of courts much easier.[138] This object was achieved by the passing of Indian High Courts Act of 1861.

---

135. See, *supra* note 100, p. 176.
136. See, *supra* note 79, pp. 156-57
137. See, *supra* note 78, p. 184.
138. See, *supra* note 45, p. 98.

The Indian High Courts Act of 1861 marks one of the most important changes of the development in the judicial system of India. The Act of 1861 empowered the crown to establish High Courts of judicature in Presidency Towns abolishing the Supreme Court and the Courts of Sadar Diwani Adalat and Sadar Nizamat (Faujdari) Adalat. The jurisdiction and powers of the High Courts were to be fixed by letters patent. The Crown was also empowered to establish a High Court in North-Western Provinces.[139] According to the Act of 1861, each High Court was to consist of one Chief Justice and not more than fifteen Puisne Judges. At least one-third of these judges including Chief Justice were to be Barristers of not less than five years standing or covenated civil servants of at least 10 years standing out of which three years of judicial experience was compulsory or pleaders of ten years standing or subordinate judge or judge of the small cause courts of at least five years service.[140] The Judges were to hold office during His Majesty's pleasure. These High Courts had both original and appellate jurisdiction in all matters including civil, criminal, admiralty, testamentary, intestate and matrimonial.[141]

Criminal jurisdiction was made available over the native criminal and crimes committed within the local limits of the Presidency towns and jurisdiction was to be exercised by hearing appeal as well as by acting as a Court of Reference and Revision from the decision given by the other subordinate criminal courts.[142] The Courts were also given the powers to transfer any criminal case or appeal from one court to another court in the interest of justice. The High Court was to be a Court of Record. The Court was also empowered to admit and enroll the Advocates and *Vakils*. It could also take disciplinary action against them. The qualifications necessary for Advocates,[143] Pleaders and Attorneys were to be laid down by the High Court. The decision of the High Court was final in appeals for criminal cases and no further appeal lay to any other court. However, in civil cases appeal from the decision of the High Court lay to the Privy Council.

---

139. See, *supra* note 79, p. 165
140. See, *supra* note 45, p. 98
141. See, *supra* note 5, p. 342.
142. See, *supra* note 121, p. 134.
143. See, *supra* note 74, p. 117.

Changes in the earlier High Court Acts were made by the passing of the Indian High Court Act, 1911. The number of Judges in each High Court was raised from sixteen to twenty. The Act also empowered His Majesty to establish additional High Courts and gave powers to the Governor-in-General to appoint additional judge for a period of two years. Subsequently, Government of India Act, 1915 was passed by the British Parliament, contained provisions regarding the composition, constitution and working of the High Court. The Act declares the High Courts to be the Courts of Record.[144] It removed the limitation on the number of judges and vested power in the King-in-Council to determine the number of judges in each High Court. First time the age of retirement of judges of High Court was fixed sixty years to give security of tenure.

In 1935, the British Parliament enacted the Government of India Act which sought to remodel the constitution of the country on federal lines.[145] This Act also conferred a dignified position to the High Courts. It ensured security of the tenure of the Judges and secured independence of High Courts. Since appointment of High Court judges was in the hands of the Crown, power to confer jurisdiction on the High Courts was divided between the Centre and the Provinces. The administrative control over a High Court was vested in the Provincial Government concerned.

The Government of India Act, 1935 changed the structure of the Indian Government from 'unitary' to that of the 'federal'. It established the foundation for a federal framework in India.[146] This necessitated the creation of Federal Court, as an independent court to decide future disputes between the units. A Federal Court was set-up at Delhi in 1937. It consisted of a Chief Justice and six other judges, though only a Chief Justice and two other Judges were appointed. They were to hold office until the age of sixty-five years.[147]

The Federal Court is at once the interpreter and the guardian of Constitution. In order to administer justice Federal

---

144. See, *supra* note 79, p. 158.
145. See, *supra* note 73, p. 293.
146. See, M. Romaswamy, The Law of the Indian Constitution, (1938), p. 85.
147. See, *supra* note 79, p. 158.

Court must be independent of Federal, Provincial and State Government. It had original jurisdiction in mattes involving the interpretation of the Act of 1935 or of federal laws or the determination of rights and obligations arising thereunder where the parties to the dispute were any two or more, namely the Federation, any of the Province, or any of the Federal State.[148] This dispute must involve any question whether of law and fact on which the existence of a legal right depends. The Federal Court gives special leave to appeal. The Federal Court was not a Court of criminal appeal, except in those cases where the validity of a law is challenged.[149] The appeal can be brought only if the court concerned gives a certificate. Otherwise, the Privy Council remained the highest Court to which appeals from High Courts in criminal cases can be taken.

The seat of the Privy Council was outside India. It was the highest court of appeal for Indians and played an important role in the administration of justice of this country for a period of about two and a quarter centuries.[150] Appeals against the decisions of the High Courts and the Federal Courts laid to the Privy Council. It possessed right to grant special leave to appeal, in cases where regular appeal did not lie or the Court below refused permission for appeal. The Privy Council as a Court of Justice occupied a unique position in view of the great expansion of the British Empire. The Privy Council proved equal to the challenge and the onerous responsibility which it was called to discharge. Persons of integrity and who by virtue of legal learning and professional efficiency, were highly qualified used to be appointed as the members of the Council.[151] The jurisdiction of the Privy Council over India had to end along with the end of the British sovereignty and emergence of free India. But its contribution and model is of eternal value, and a source of inspiration to all those concerned with the administration of justice in India. Regarding the unique role of Privy Council the observation of Sri K.M. Munshi (an eminent member of the legal profession, the Constitutional Assembly of

---

148. Government of India Act, 1935, Sec. 208.
149. *Ibid.*, Sec. 205.
150. See, *supra* note 114, p. 367.
151. See, *supra* note 100, p. 197.

India) speaking on the occasion of the abolition of the Privy Council's jurisdiction over India said:

> The British Parliament and the Privy Council are the two great institutions which the Anglo-Saxon race has given to mankind. The Privy Council during the law few centuries has not only laid down law, but coordinated the concept of right and obligations throughout all the dominions and colonies of the British Common Wealth. So far as India is concerned, the role of the Privy Council has been one of the most important one. It has been a great unifying force and for us Indians it became the instrument and embodiment of the rule of law, a concept on which alone we have based the democratic institution which we have set-up in our Constitution.

(2) Criminal Justice Administration and Codification

The Charter Act of 1833 played an important role in shaping and moulding the future of law-making in India. It was considered compulsory to prepare a Code for criminal law, evidence, limitation and also Code to regulate the civil and criminal procedures in the whole of India by the same legislation.[152] The laws passed by the All India Legislature were called as 'Acts' and not Regulations. The laws made by the legislature were required to be placed before the British Parliament through the Board of Control for approval.[153]

Lord Macaulay was appointed as the Law Member of the Council under the Charter Act, 1833. He emphasized the urgency of codification of Indian laws by arranging them in a systematically written Code. Section 53 of the Act made provisions for the appointment of Law Commission in India for the purpose of codification and consolidation of the Indian Laws. The first Law Commission was appointed in 1834 with Lord Macaulay as the Chairman.

As the system of administration of criminal justice was most unsatisfactory and chaotic eondition, the local government directed the Commission to take its first step to tackle this

---

152. See, *supra* note 78, p. 246.
153. See, *supra* note 74, p. 193.

branch of law. The Commission was specially instructed to draft an Indian Penal Code. Though the Draft was submitted in 1837, it did not become law until 1860. The First Law Commission made a very comprehensive proposal that an Act should be passed making the substantive law of England as the law of the Land (*Lex Loci*) subject to certain conditions and restrictions. [154]

In view of the extensive modifications suggested by the First Law Commission in the administration of law and justice in India, it became necessary to enhance the law-making powers of the Legislative Council. In this regard the Charter Act of 1853 made some improvements in the status of the law members and the Second Law Commission was appointed in 1853. The most important recommendation of the Second Law Commission was the amalgamation of the Supreme Courts and the Sadar Courts and the passing of uniform Codes of civil procedure and criminal procedure for all the courts of India.[155] As a result, the Civil Procedure Code was passed in 1859, The Indian Penal Code in 1860 and the Code of Criminal Procedure Code in 1861.

After the policy of codification was enunciated by the Second Law Commission, the Third Law Commission was appointed in 1861 for the purpose of preparing a body of Substantive Law of India. It was a great achievement of the Third Law Commission that it submitted drafts of six major Acts of legislations, namely, Indian Succession Act, 1885, Law of Contract, 1872, Law of Negotiable Instruments, Law of Specific Performances, Law of Evidence, 1872, Law of Transfer of Property and the Law of Criminal Procedure (Revised), 1872 within a short span of nine years.[156]

(3) Post-Independence Period

After the Independence of the country in 1947, and with the inaguration of the Republic in 1950 under the new Constitution, the problem of law revision arose in a new form. When India became independent, the old laws prevailing in the country were not abrogated they were continued lock, stock and barrel of independent India. It was declared in Indian Constitution that "all the laws in force in the territory of India

---

154. See, *supra* note 5, p. 351.
155. *Ibid.*, p. 352.
156. See, *supra* note 45, p. 124.

immediately before the commencement of the Constitution are to continue in force until altered, repealed of amended."[157] In this way all statutes, which were in force in the pre-constitution era remained in operation in India as well, after 1950. This was done to maintain legal continuity and to avoid creation of a vacuum in the area of law and justice.[158] In India, several laws have remained unrevised for long.

After India attained the independence, many reforms were felt necessary in the system of law inherited from the colonial days. Many Codes needed through revision, amendment and reconsideration. Keeping in view all these facts the Lok Sabha on the 19th November, 1954 discussed a non-official resolution,[159] "This House resolved that a Law Commission be appointed to recommend revision and modernization of laws criminal, civil and revenue, substantive, procedural or otherwise and particular, the civil and criminal and procedure codes and the Indian Penal Code, to reduce the quantum of case-law and to resolve the conflicts in the decisions of the High Courts on many points with a view to realize that justice is simple, speedy, cheap, effective and substantial." On 5th August, 1956, Shri C. C. Biswas, the Law Minister, announced in the Lok Sabha the appointment of a Law Commission. It was the Fifth Law Commission after 1833 but after independence of India it was the First Law Commission. It consisted of eleven members including Shri M.C. Setalvad, the Attorney-General of India, who was appointed its chairman. Other members were selected from both the Bar and the Bench. In the first instance the Commission was appointed for a short-term, upto the end of 1956.[160] The Fourteenth report which was submitted by the Law Commission was related to the reforms of judicial administration in India. It was the most important piece of work undertaken by the Commission. The Commission suggested that clean, speedy and less expensive administration of justice, which is of great importance.[161] It was not concerned with detailed scrutiny of the provisions of the Code of Criminal

---

157. The Constitution of India, 1950, Article 372.
158. See, *supra* note 73, pp. 560-61.
159. See, *supra* note 121, p. 264.
160. See, *supra* note 78, p. 255.
161. See, *supra* note 81, p. 268.

Procedure, but it referred some recommendations with regard to the law of criminal procedure. A systematic examination of the code was subsequently undertaken by the Law Commission not only for giving concrete form to the recommendations made in fourteenth report but also with the object of attempting a general revision.[162] The main task of the Commission was to suggest measures to remove ambiguities. A comprehensive report for the revision of the Code, namely, the Forty-first Report was presented by the Law Commission in September, 1969. This report was related to Criminal Procedure Code, 1898. The Commission in its attempt of wholesale revision of the present Code of Criminal Procedure enacted during the colonial regime submitted a draft of the new Code of Criminal Procedure consisting of about 484 Sections for the consideration of the Government.[163] The report running into two volumes deals comprehensive with the existing law and the necessity for change in modern context. Broadly the main recommendations related to the simplification of law of prosecution and separation between judiciary and executive wings. For this purpose the magistracy was to be divided into Judicial Magistrates and Executive Magistrates. Judicial Magistrates should be put under control of the High Court and Executive Magistrates should be put under the control of State Government.[164] Summons on the witness be served by post. Changes were recommended in the provisions of Section 161 and 167 of the Code. For petty offences the personal appearances of the offender in the court be dispensed with and he be allowed to plead guilty and pay the fine. The appellate jurisdiction of the Supreme Court under Art. 134 be enlarged. The Judges should be required to state reasons for awarding a particular punishment, in case of capital offences.[165] Anticipatory bail be obtained by a person from High Court or Court of Sessions in certain cases. Lastly, the Commission recommended that the District Public prosecutors should be given greater powers and their status should be raised.

---

162. See, N.D. Basu, Code of Criminal Procedure, (2001), p. 1.
163. New Code of Criminal Procedure has been enacted, namely, Code of Criminal Procedure, 1973.
164. Forty-fifth Report of Fifth Law Commission in 1968-69.
165. *Ibid.*

The recommendations of the Commission were examined carefully by Government and the Code of Criminal bill drafted in 1970. Embodying the recommendations of the Joint Committee lastly, new Code of Criminal Procedure came into force on April 1, 1974.[166] Known as the Code of Criminal Procedure, 1973, it was further amended in 1978, 1980 and again in 2004.

The present Indian Penal Code which was enacted in 1860, is about 145 years old, hence it needs to be thoroughly revised or rather re-stated keeping in view the socio-economic changes in the India society particularly the post-independence era. The existing Penal Code is essentially based on the English law of crimes which no longer suits our needs and traditions.[167] The Indian Evidence Act, 1872 which is also more than 130 years old, need to be re-drafted to met the recent Indian requirements.

III. SUM-UP

The administration of criminal justice is reaching its present form passed through various stages. In the primitive society when a wrong was done against an individual he had to resort to self-help and it was based on private vengeance. Later on, when individual organised themselves in the form of society, certain rights were recognized by the society as belonging to every individual. If a wrong was done against an individual it was counted wrong against the society. In the earliest *Dharamsastras* there is a reference that administration of justice as an important function of the King. The King was looked upon social and moral order for the purpose of Dharma. He was endowed with the powers of *danda*, i.e. the punishment. In some ancient societies the natural elements of ordeals (fire, water, wind, etc.) are considered as Gods and as such was approached to criminal justice. The Kautilya's Arthashastra, Manusmriti, Yajnavalkya, etc. also referred to different type of ancient criminal justice in India. The Hindu rulers followed more or less similar law and procedure for distributing of criminal justice with little modifications. This system prevailed

---

166. See, *supra* note 162, p. 2.
167. See, *supra* note 74, p. 191.

all over India for centuries. It was badly affected after inception of Islam and Muslim invasions. They imposed their own laws on a large part of this country. During this period criminal justice was administered according to the Mohammedan law of crimes. The Mohammedan criminal law was based on the Quran, a holy book of Muslims. The provisions of Quran were found inadequate to meet the requirements of a large community. The Western colonialism overpowered the whole territory and come to influence all the aspects of social life of Indians. The English, when they took over administration of Bengal, Bihar or Orissa, did not disturb for sometime the Mohammedan law of crime which was well established but in defective form. When the East India Company came to India there was influence of Mohammedan laws but later on the English Government modified and reshaped the criminal laws in India for the good and welfare of the society. Some positive steps were taken to remove the defects in the criminal law. The Charter of 1833 was the first step in this regard which ultimately resulted in the unification and codification of criminal law of India. The passing of Indian Penal Code and Criminal Procedure Code based on English law, superseded to a great extent by the British regulations. They made extensive use of the principle of equity, justice and good conscience for this purpose.

3

Criminal Justice Administration in India : At Work

I. INTRODUCTION

Crime is not only a recent experience. Every generation has been threatened by crime and violence. The concept of crime, however, has varied from society to society and from age to age and thus the criminal law reflects the prevalent norms and values of that society. The crime is a normal phenomenon in every society. According to sociologists, Prins and Durkhain, *"criminality proceeds from the very nature of humanity itself, it is not transcendent but immanent."* He emphasis the point further and said that, *"crime is normal in human societies, because the fundamental conditions of social organisation logically imply it. A society exempt from crime would require a standardisation of the moral concepts of all individual, which is neither possible nor desirable."*[1]

---

1. See, K.D. Gaur, *Criminal Law and Criminology*, (2002), p. 52.

In modern societies, it is extremely difficult to name any specific act universally regarded person as criminal. If the crime is viewed only as violation of criminal codes promulgated and enforced by the State and its agencies, however, it can hardly said to be existed in primitive societies in which political and legal institutions were undeveloped. In such societies conduct was largely controlled by customs and standards shared by virtually all members of the society.[2] The concept of crime is essentially concerned with the conduct of individuals in society. It is well said that the man by nature is social and his interests are best protected as a member of society. Everyone owns certain duties towards his fellowmen and at the same time has certain rights and privileges which he expects others to endure for him. Although most people prefer to follow a 'live and let-live' policy, there are a few who for some reason of the other deviate from the normal path and associate themselves with anti-social activities. This obviously imposes an obligation on the State to maintain normalcy in society.

In most countries the criminal law is continued in a single statute known as the Criminal Code or Penal Code. Although the criminal codes of the most English-speaking countries are derived from English criminal law but England itself has never had a criminal code. English criminal law still consists of a collection of statutes of varying age. Interest in codification was not limited to England. A similar process ensured in India under British rule, and a Criminal Code was written during the 1830 and eventually enacted in 1860.[3] More than any other branch of law, criminal law is the mirror of public opinion and the concept of crime has always been dependent on public opinion.[4]

The general purpose of criminal law is to provide a mechanism for the administration of criminal justice. Its main object is 'to ensure the accused a full and fair trial in accordance with the established principles of natural justice.'

---

2. A New Survey of Universal Knowledge, *Encyclopaedia Britannica*, Vol. 6, (1966), p. 754.
3. *The New Encyclopaedia Britannica*, Vol. 16, (2002), p. 797.
4. See, S.N. Misra, *Indian Penal Code*, (2004), p. 1.

II. CONCEPT OF CRIME

In modern civilized societies only violations of rules promulgated and enforced by agencies of Government are technically treated as crimes. Although crime is sometimes viewed in a very broad way as the violation of any important group standard or as the equivalent of anti-social, immoral and sinful behaviour. Therefore, crime involves the idea of a public as opposed to a private wrong with the consequent intervention between the criminal and injured party by an agency representing the community or public as a whole.[5] In this view, crime is the intentional commission of an act deemed socially harmful or dangerous and usually specifically, defined, prohibited and punishable under the criminal law.

The dictionary meaning of the term crime is that it is an act punishable by law as being forbidden by statute. The Indian Penal Code does not define crime *per se*, but contents itself with defining an 'offence' as a thing made punishable by the code.[6] It is, however, difficult to offer a clear and precise definition of crime. The concept of crime involves the idea of a public as opposed to a private wrong with the consequent intervention between the criminal and the injured party by an agency representing the community as a whole. Crime is thus the intentional commission of an act, deemed socially harmful or dangerous and the reason for making any given act a crime is the public injury that would result from its frequent perpetration. The society, therefore takes steps for its prevention by prescribing specific punishments for each such crime.[7]

The concept of crime is a relative one. It is changing and has changed with the socio-economic background of the society. It has always depended on the force, movement of public and social opinion from country to country, and in some country from century to century. Most civilized members of the society obey authority and compliance may vary in tolerance. It is when people deviate beyond the level of social tolerance, that their organs of justice in the society.[8] Criminal behaviour is an

---

5. See, *supra* note 2.
6. See, *supra* note 1.
7. See, Sankar Sen, *Crimes in Modern Society*, (1983), p. 3.
8. See, Mehraj Uddin, *Crime and Correction*, (1981), p. 23.

integral part of social behaviour, that can be understood only in relation to the personal social situation and the sequence of which it is a part. The personality of the offender, the social world in which he lives and previous experience growing out of interaction between the individual and the environmental situation play a vital role in the social process leading to criminal behaviour.[9]

The fundamental dimensions of crime as deviant behaviour and crime as a social problem, if viewed in their wider perspective may take us to dangerous and delicate area like criminogenic components in the administrative system. The infiltration of illegitimate, para criminal elements into public life through subterranean stream is perhaps a social reality but criminologists are students of society and are interested not in power but in the assessment of the extent of criminalization our system suffer from.[10]

III. CONCEPT OF ADMINISTRATION OF CRIMINAL JUSTICE

With the march of time, crimes are becoming more and more sophisticated. It is, therefore, essential that if the forces which have to meet the challenges of crime are to prove equal to the task, they must keep abreast of and acquire the technique of handling and controlling such crimes.[11] The administration of criminal justice all over the world seems to be guided by one cherished principle, i.e. the protection of rights of the accused and it is to be secured at all costs while a criminal system determining liabilities. This is the reason for which the entire criminal jurisprudence has been dedicated thereon and plethora of criminal laws has been enacted with the changing social attitudes towards crimes and criminals. When any crime has been committed the offender is apprehended, tried, punished or acquitted or even in some situations he is released on probation when the reformative slogan dominates floor of the court, even

---

9. *Ibid.*
10. See, Justice V.R. Krishna Iyer, *Crime and Correction Process—Key Issues in Contemporary Criminology*, CMLJ, Vol. 28, Oct.-Dec. 1992, p. 269.
11. See, H.R. Khanna, *Some Reflections on Criminal Justice*, JILI, Vol. 17, No. 4, Oct.-Nov., 1975, p. 508.

if, he is found guilty. The entire criminal justice system is concerning more in defending rights of the accused than inflicting punishment.[12] The quality of justice determines the quality of society and of governance. Just as pollution poisons the physical atmosphere, the poor justice system poison the social atmosphere. Equal and fair justice is the hallmark of any civilized society. The quality of justice in any civilized society depends in large measure on the quality of judges and lawyers.[13]

The administration of justice is a device adopted by the modern civilized community by replacing the primitive practice of weakening private vengeance and violent self-help. Salmond observes, in his inimitable style, that one of the most important elements in the transition from the natural to the civil state is the substitution of the force of the organised community for the force of individuals, as the instrument of the redress and punishment of injuries. Private vengeance is transmuted into the administration of criminal justice, while civil justice takes the place of violent self-help.[14]

The expression 'administration of justice' can be interpreted in a narrow as well as wider sense. The narrow meaning flows from the dictionary meaning of the expression. Justice is administered in a case after its institution till the pronouncement of judgement and execution of the decree, judgement or order.[15] In the wider sense, the expression shall include all the aspects connected with the administration of justice. In this sense it means the application of the state of the sanction of physical force to the rule of justice. It is the forcible defence of rights and suppression of wrongs. The administration of justice properly so called therefore, involves in every case two parties, the plaintiff and the defendant, a right-claimed or a wrong complained of by the former as against the latter, a judgement in favour of the one or the other

---

12. See, H.D. Mondal, *Crime Victims and Their Treatment in the Administration of Criminal Justice*, Central Indian Law Quarterly, Jan-March, 2001, p. 32.
13. See, Subhash Chandra Singh, *Criminal Justice : An Overview*, CrLJ, March 1999, p. 44.
14. See. K. Madhavan, *The Criminal Justice System*, CBI Bulletin, July 1992, pp. 4-5.
15. *Ibid.*

and execution of this judgement by the power of the State. It includes all the functions of court of justice, whether they conform to the forgoing type or not. It is to administer justice in the strict sense that the tribunals of the State are established and is by reference to this essential purpose that they must be defined.[16] But when once established, they are found to be useful instrument, by virtue of their constitution, procedure, authority or special knowledge for the fulfilment of other more or less analogous functions. To these secondary and non-essential activities of the courts, no less than to their primary and essential functions, the term administration of justice has been extended. They are miscellaneous and indeterminate in character and number and tend to increase with the advancing complexity of modern civilization.

Every government whatever is its form, must uphold the law and maintain order in the society which it governs. There are the basic functions, which any government out to perform. This is essentially done through what is called as 'criminal justice system'. The system as the very term suggests consists of all the functionaries, who are concerned with the basis functions of the State, i.e. maintenance of law and order. As per the Oxford Dictionary, the term 'system' means *"set of connected things or parts"*, *"set of organs in body with common structure or function."* The various functionaries involved in the process of maintenance of law and order are governmental functionaries, such a police, prosecution, judiciary and prison.[17] All these functionaries though perform its functions independently are interdependent and interrelate to one unit when issue is seen in its totality. The issue is to achieve the goal of the system, which is to ensure justice, punishment to the criminal and compensation to innocent involved in the process.

The criminal justice system may be considered of at least three perspectives. First, it can be considered a normative system that is a body of legal rules expressing social values through prohibitions backed by penal sanctions against conduct viewed as seriously wrong or harmful. Secondly, criminal justice system can be regarded as an administrative system. This view

---

16. See, P.J. Fitzgerald, *Salmond on Jurisprudence*, (2002), pp. 104-05.
17. See, Nikhil Jaiparkash Gupta, *Criminal Justice System in India—Whither Commentment?* CBI Bulletin, Jan. 2004, p. 14.

comprehends the official apparatus for enforcing the criminal law, including the police and other frontline enforcement agencies, prosecutorial authorities, the judiciary, and penal and correctional facilities and services.[18] A third view of criminal justice is that of a social system. In this perspective, defining and responding to criminal conduct involves all elements of society. This definition of criminal conduct includes not only the penal law enacted by the legislature but also the way in which these provisions are interpreted by the citizens at all level. These three aspects of the criminal justice system may be integrated in examining particular phases of criminal justice and in interpreting the system as a whole.[19] Criminal justice as a whole results from the interaction between legal rules, administrative practice, and social attitudes and behaviour.

The criminal justice process in its broader sense begins in social disorganization and ends in rehabilitation of criminals in society. The law as an instrument of social solidarity and cohesion initiates the process by defining and identifying anti-social behavior which approximates to the notion of criminal conduct. All governments in civilized societies of the world owe it to their people to defend them against these criminal advances of the socially undesirable and mentally diseased persons.[20] Because law breaking by such people is a normal and highly dangerous phenomenon, the Government or the law-makers create law enforcement agencies to identify and wean out those who indulge in law-breaking and need to be punished by way of removal from social intercourse.

Suppression of crime essentially requires certain agencies to detect and apprehend the criminals, to adjudicate upon their guilt or innocence and if convicted, subject them to punishment through various penal institutions. These multiple functions of detection, trial and administration of punishment are discharged by different agencies of justice, viz. the police, the criminal law courts and correctional institutions like prisons where the offender is kept after his conviction.[21] The police is

---

18. See, Sanford H. Kadish, *Encyclopedia of Crime and Justice*, (1983), p. 450.
19. *Ibid.*
20. See. P.D. Sharma, *Police and Criminal Justice Administration in India*, (1985), p. 33.
21. See, N.V. Paranjape, *Criminology and Administration of Criminal Justice*, (1985), p. 110.

primarily concerned with the detection of crimes, apprehension of the criminals and to bring them to a criminal court for trial. On the other hand, the criminal courts conduct the trial of the accused on the basis of evidence available and decide whether he is guilty or innocent under the existing law. It also awards different punishments to the convicted persons for the offences committed by them. After conviction the offender is sent to institutions like the prison, jail, reformatory institutions, etc. to undergo his term of sentence. Therefore, it is evident that the police, the criminal courts and the prison are the main agencies of criminal justice administration. Besides these, the system of parole and probation are yet two other agencies of justice which seek to reform the corrigible and young offenders during the term of their sentence and return them to normal society as a law abiding citizen.

IV. CRIMINAL JUSTICE ADMINISTRATION IN ENGLAND

The modern criminal law of England derives from the English common law of crime. This body of law had its origins in judicial decisions which by the middle of the 13th century were applied throughout the realm and thus 'common' to it. Even in the medieval period, however, legislation played an important role in the development of the English law of crimes. In some instances legislation was confined to matters of procedure or the stipulation of penalties, leaving definition of the elements of the offences of judicial precedents.[22] English criminal law still consists of a collection of statutes of varying age, the oldest still in force being the Treason Act (1315), and a set of general principles that are chiefly expressed in the decisions of the courts. England's lack of a criminal code is not due to a lack of effort. In the early 19th century there have been several attempts to create a code. The first effort (1833-53) was by two panels of criminal law commissioners, who systematically surveyed the prevailing state of the criminal.

The conception of the crime is very old, though the actual wrongs which were classified as crimes were drastically redefined at the conquest. According to Pollock and Maitland,

---

22. See, *supra* note 2, p. 763.

on thieve of the conquest the law of wrongs had four essential elements, i.e. the punishment of out lawry, the recognition of blood feud, tariffs of war and bot and wite (that is the punishment of life and limb) and the existence of pleas of the crown.[23]

At the time of the conquest, however, the King's peace remained local and personal; it died with King and it was confined to certain places, the seasons of the ear. The King's peace was destined to grow and flourish till it had covered the face of England at all times and in all seasons. When this had come to pass no man committed violence without being liable to a fine at the suit of the King. Yet the fact that the wrong was a breach of the peace did not prevent the injured party from recovering compensation from wrong doer.[24]

In the twelfth century Henry II was able to substitute a simple notion of liability. He set apart certain wrongs as matters for the interference of the Crown. In this century three salient features in the law of wrong emerged. These were a few crimes of wide definition, such as robbery with violence (punishable at the discretion with death of maiming), wite became a discretionary (amercement) and out-lawry had grown into a matter of process rather than punishment.[25]

The criminal courts in England are the Magistrates Courts and the Crown Courts. Those offences considered least serious are summary offences, triable only in the Magistrate's Courts. Those offences considered most serious and triable only in the Crown Court. A large number of offences such as theft and most burglaries are triable either way in a Magistrate Court or the Crown Court.[26] The Magistrates may decide that the case is so serious that it should be committed to the Crown Court for trial. If they decide not to commit it to the Crown Court, the defendant still has an absolute right to elect trial by jury. In practice a majority of either way offences are dealt with in Magistrate's Courts, since neither the defendant not the

---

23. See, A.K.R. Kiralfy, *Potter's Historical Introduction to English Law*, (1958), pp. 346-47.
24. *Ibid.*, p. 351.
25. Se, Sir Jamesh Fitzjames Stephen, *A History of the Criminal Law of England*, (1883), p. 81.
26. See, Andrew Asworth, *Principles of Criminal Law*, (1999), p. 4.

Magistrates think Crown Court trial necessary. Finally, it should be added that virtually all prosecutions of persons under eighteen years are brought in youth courts, where hearing are less formal and take place before especial trained Magistrates.[27]

V. CRIMINAL JUSTICE ADMINISTRATION IN AMERICA

In the colonization of British North America, the common law of crime was received and applied in America. With the rupture of sovereignty in the colonies at the time of the American Revolution, however a strong movement arose to establish all law, including the criminal law, on the foundation of legislative enactments. Initially, this took the form of legislative enactments that simply declared. Initially, this took the form of legislative enactments that simply declared the common law, including the common law of crime to be in effect except as displayed by particular statutory provisions.[28]

Today the paradigm of penal legislation, both in substance and format in the Model Penal Code, promulgated by the American Law Institute in 1962. The Code is a comprehensive reformation of the principles of criminal liability that is drawn from previous codes, decisional codes, decisional law and scholarly commentary. It has been substantially adopted in many States and is the prominent source of guidance in revision and reform of substantive law in the United States.[29] The Model Penal Code establishes a hierarchy of substantive criminal proscriptions and a corresponding hierarchy of social values. It can be considered as having two dimensions. The first consists of the principle of criminal liability and the second of the definition of various specific crimes.

Under the legal system in the United States, there is a definite series of steps that are taken in the handling of any person who is believed to have violated the law. This procedure has been set-up by the courts and the legislatures of all the States, as well as by the federal courts and the United States Congress. In this process, a number of rights and safeguards are

---

27. See, R.M. Jackson, *The Machinery of Justice in England*, (1967), pp. 138-39.
28. See, *supra* note 18, p. 451.
29. *Ibid.*

guaranteed to every accused person, in both the State and the federal courts. The process is started by the commission of the crime.[30] It proceeds through the investigation by the appropriate police agency, to a decision to prosecute, to an arrest, to detention in jail or freedom to await trial while out on bail, to the criminal trial, to the sentencing, to the serving of the sentence or release on probation, to a return to freedom on the street.

American society is primarily regulated by two legal systems—State and federal. Most of laws regulating the conduct are State laws i.e. laws that are promulgated by the State and local governments or State Court decisions. The federal legal system is headed by the United States Supreme Court, which has original jurisdiction and appellate jurisdiction.[31] A Court's jurisdiction refers to matters that it is legally authorized to hear and jurisdiction obviously cannot be invoked unless there is a legal dispute. A more particular aspect of the court concept is the distinction between trial courts, of which there are many and bulk of judicial work and the appellate courts, of which there are relatively few. Trial Courts stated legal purpose is to resolve disputes by applying legal principles to facts presented in a case.[32]

The criminal justice system in America proceeds from the crime take place within a city and the police department is called for. The police conduct an investigation and make a report. Evidence is gathered and they talk to the suspect and secure a search warrant for arrest from the Municipal Court. The suspect of arrested is informed of his constitutional rights. The defendant is booked if he does not release on bail, he is placed in a cell. The defendant is then indicated at the preliminary hearing held by the inferior court. The next step is a superior court hearing where he makes his plea of guilty.[33] A probation officer makes recommendations based on several factors,

30. See, Charles, F. Hempwill, *Criminal Procedure : The Administration of Justice*, (1978), pp. 3-4.
31. George T. Felkenes, *Criminal Law and Procedure*, (1976), p. 8.
32. Russel R. Wheclar and Howard R. Whitcomb, *Judicial Administration : Text and Readings*, pp. 12-13.
33. Neil C. Chamelin, Vernon B. Fox, M. Wisenand, *Introduction to Criminal Justice*, (1975), pp. 4-5.

including the fact that the defendant has been involved in similar incidents in the past. The judge then sentences the defendant, in this instance, to a stay in a State prison.

VI. CRIMINAL JUSTICE ADMINISTRATION IN INDIA

The criminal justice system exists because the society has deemed it appropriate to enforce the standards of human conduct so necessary to protect individuals and the community. It seeks to fulfill its goal of protection through enforcement of reducing the risk of crime and apprehending, prosecuting, convicting and sentencing those individuals who violates the rules and laws promulgated by society. The offender finds that the criminal justice system will punish him for his violation by removing him from society and simultaneously will try to dissuade him from repeating such anti-social acts through rehabilitation. The criminal justice system consists of three major components – law enforcement, agencies, i.e. police courts and corrections. Each one of the components of the criminal justice system shares certain common goals. They collectively exist to protect society, maintain order and prevent crime.[34] But they also individually contribute to these goals in their own special way.

The police as law enforceable agency are responsible for controlling crime and maintaining order. The courts are responsible for judging the suspected offender by determining innocence or guilt. The prosecution and defence are an integral part of this sub-system. Finally, the goal of the correction sub-system is institutionalizing or monitoring the activities of the offender and rehabilitating him to full and useful participation in society. Two integral parts of the corrections sub-system are probation and parole.[35]

(A) Police as a Law Enforcement Agency

The police as law enforcement agency is a component of the criminal justice system. The police are the first line of

---

34. See, Roberty D. Pursley, *Introduction to Criminal Justice*, (1977), p. 7.
35. See, *supra* note 33, pp. 7-8.

defence against social disorder and criminality. According to the Police Act, 1861, the policing body is an 'instrument for the prevention and detection of crime.' Prevention, as an objective precedes detection. Prevention involves all the efforts directed towards eliminating the causes of crimes. The police have been given various powers by the Criminal Procedure Code, 1973 and the Police Act, 1861. These can be used effectively to prevent crimes being perpetrated in their presence or within their knowledge and as an adjunctive to the investigation of crimes by keeping known criminals under control. It is in this view that the role of the police in the prevention of crime is to be appreciated.[36] The most obvious function of the police is to locate the persons who have committed crimes, by proper investigation, collect the evidence available against them, to arrest such persons and to bring them to the courts to be dealt with according to law. The powers of arrest, search, etc. granted to the police are for this purpose only and are regulated by law.[37]

(i) Powers of Police under Criminal Procedure Code, 1973

The law of criminal procedure is meant to be complementary of criminal law and has been designed to look after the process of its administration. In view of this objective, the Criminal Procedure Code creates the necessary machinery for the detection of crime, arrest and suspected criminals, collection of evidences, determination of guilt or innocence of the suspected person, and imposition of proper punishment on the guilty person. The criminal procedure also aims at providing due safeguards against possible harassment to the innocent persons in its process of shifting of burden of proof from criminals to non-criminals. It further attempts to strike a just balance between the need to give wide powers to the functionaries under the Criminal Procedure Code to make the investigative and adjudicatory processes strong and effective, and the need to control the probable misuse or abuse of these powers.[38]

---

36. See, P.S. Bawa, *K. Krishnamuthi's Police Dairies*, (2002), p. 2.
37. See, Mitter, *Police Diaries Statements, Reports*, Vol. I, (1981), p. 1.
38. See, R.V. Kelkar, *Lectures on Criminal Procedure*, (1990), p. 1.

(a) Role of Police in the Prevention of Crimes

There are certain provisions in Criminal Procedure Code, 1973 to prevent crime, when there are apprehensions of it. Certain persons can be arrested by police under the condition when a Executive Magistrate receives information that any person is likely to commit a breach of peace or disturb the public tranquility.[39] Two things are necessary for this purpose, i.e. that information must be received by Magistrate and to his satisfaction that there are sufficient grounds for proceedings the main condition for initiating an application is the imminence of breach of peace. The person, against whom such an application is taken out, is almost certain to perform a wrongful act. The object of the proceedings is preventive and not penal. Proceedings taken with a view to ensure good behaviour in future and not to punish for offences committed in the past. Sections 107 to 111 of the Criminal Procedure code under which the police may apply to the Magistrate for taking security from habitual offenders or persons likely to commit breach of peace or distributive of public tranquility or commit offence.[40]

One of the main purpose of administration of criminal justice is prevention of crime. The Code with a view to prevent commission of crimes enables those who are responsible for maintenance of law and order to take preventive measures so that crime may not be committed. For this purpose every police officer may interpose (active intervention) to prevent cognizable offence.[41] Every police officer receiving information of a design to commit any cognizable offence, shall communicate such information to the police officer to whom he is subordinate and to any other officer whose duty is to prevent to take cognizance of the commission of any such offence.[42] A police officer may arrest after knowing of a design to commit an offence and it must appear to him that the commission of the cognizable offence could not be prevented otherwise than by arrest.[43] Further a police office may of his own authority interpose to prevent any injury attempted to be committed in his view to any

---

39. The Criminal Procedure Code, 1973, Sec. 107.
40. *Ibid.*, Ss. 107 to 111.
41. *Ibid*, Sec. 149.
42. *Ibid.*, Sec. 150.
43. *Ibid.*, Sec. 151.

public property, moveable or immovable.[44] Section 153 of the Criminal Procedure Code specifically authorizes an officer-in-charge of Police Station to enter any place without a warrant enter any place within the limits of such for the purpose of inspection or searching for nay weights or measures which he may have reason to believe is false.

(b) Information to the Police and their Powers to Investigate

The First Information report (FIR) is the information recoded under Section 154 of the Criminal Procedure Code. It is an information given to a police officer relating to the commission of an offence. It is also an information given by an informant on which the investigation is commenced. It must be distinguished from information received after the commencement of the investigation which is covered under Section 161 to 162 of the Criminal Procedure Code.[45] It is well settled that the First Information Report is not substantive evidence but can only be used to corroborate or contradict the evidence of the informant given in court or to impeach his credit.[46]

First Information Report (FIR) is the first report based on which starts the police investigation. It is a very important document in a criminal case. The information about the offence committed is to be given to the Police Station having territorial jurisdiction where the offence has been committed. But this does not mean that it cannot be lodged elsewhere. Every information relating to the commission of cognizable offence, if given orally to the officer-in-charge of a Police Station, shall be reduced to writing by him or under his direction and be read over to the informant. Every such information shall be signed by the person giving it and shall be entered in a book to be kept by such officer in such form as the State Government may prescribe in this behalf.[47] The information recorded under Section 154 of Criminal Procedure Code is usually known as the First Information Report.[48] It is an information which is given to the

---

44. *Ibid.*, Sec. 152.
45. See, *supra* note 37, p. 15.
46. State of Bombay vs. Rusy Mistry, AIR 1960 SC 391.
47. The Criminal Procedure Code, 1973, Sec. 154(1).
48. *Ibid.*, Sec. 154

police officer of a cognizable offence. It is an information first in point of time and on the basis of this information that investigation into the offence commences. Sometimes it may happen that more than one person go at or about the same time and make statements to the police about the same cognizable offence. In such a situation the police officer has to use common sense and record one of the statements as First Information Report.[49]

First Information Report is a very valuable document and the accused is entitled to know the contents of that report to connect him with the offence so that he may be in a position to protect his interests by cross-examining the prosecution witnesses in respect to any addition or alterations in the story of the prosecution which may subsequently be made in evidence.[50] In nearly every trial, it is important for the judicial officer, to know as to what were the facts given out immediately after the occurrence and reported to the police.

When the aggrieved approaches the police and prays for registration of First Information Report the police has no option but to register it and thereafter start investigation.[51] Refusal to record a First Information Report on the ground that the place of crime does not fall within the territorial jurisdiction of the Police Station amounts to dereliction of duty. Information about cognizable offence would have to be recorded and forwarded to the Police Station having jurisdiction. A message sent by telephone to the Police officer and recorded by him in his station diary which disclosed an information regarding a cognizable offence is the information within Sec. 154 of Criminal Procedure Code which is popularly known as the First Information Report. A cryptic and anonymous telephone message which did not clearly specify a cognizable offence cannot be treated as the First Information Report.[52]

Section 154 deals with information relating to a cognizable offence whereas Section 155 deals with information relating to a non-cognizable offence. If any person gives an information of a non-cognizable offence to an officer-in-charge of a Police Station

49. See, *supra* note 38, p. 53.
50. Deviya *vs*. State of Coorg, AIR 1956 Mys. 51.
51. Munna Lal *vs*. State of HP, 1992 CrLJ 1558.
52. See, Ratanlal and Dhirajlal, *The Code of Criminal Procedure*, (2002), p. 25.

then he shall enter or have cause to enter the substance of the information in books to be kept by such officer in form of prescribed by the State Government.[53] The officer shall then refer the information to the Magistrate. The Code, therefore, enjoins that the police shall not investigate a non-cognizable case without the order of a competent Magistrate.[54] Once such an order is given by the Magistrate, the police officer receiving the order may exercise the same power in respect of the investigation as an officer-in-charge of a Police Station may exercise in a cognizable case.[55] Where a case relates to two or more offences of which at least, one is cognizable, the case shall be deemed to be a cognizable case even though the other offences are non-cognizable.[56]

In the case of a cognizable offence the police may hold an investigation irrespective of any order of the court. Courts have no control in such cases over the investigation or over the action of the police holding such investigation.[57] No proceeding of a police officer in any such case shall, at any stage be called in question on the ground that the case was one which such officer was not empowered.[58] Under section 156(3) a Magistrate may order investigation into an offence by the police when no complaint has been made to him but he has information about a cognizable case. Section 156(3) enables a Magistrate to order the investigation of an offence of which he may have taken cognizance under Section 190 of Criminal Procedure Code.[59] Once the learned Magistrate gives such a direction the police take cognizance of the offence and starts investigation. The investigation of a cognizable offence begins when a police officer-in-charge of a Police Station has reason to suspect the commission of a cognizable offence. Though the basis for the suspicion is essentially the First Information Report as recorded under Sec. 154, yet it is legally possible that the suspicion may be based on any other information of the police.[60] This provision

---

53. The Criminal Procedure Code, 1973, Sec. 155(1).
54. *Ibid.*, Sec. 155(2)
55. *Ibid.*, Sec. 155(3)
56. *Ibid.*, Sec. 155(4)
57. *Ibid.*, Sec. 165(1).
58. *Ibid.*, Sec. 156(2)
59. *Ibid.*, Sec. 190.
60. *Ibid.*, Sec. 157(1).

is really designed to keep the Magistrate informed of the investigation of such a cognizance offence so as to be able to control the investigation and if necessary to give appropriate direction under Sec. 159. Every such report sent to a Magistrate, if the State Government so direct, the report shall be submitted through such a superior officer of police as may be appointed by the State Government for this purpose.[61] On receiving the report, the superior officer may give such directions to the officer-in-charge of the Police Station as he thinks fit, and shall, after recording such instructions on such report, transmit the same without delay to the Magistrate.[62]

While investigating into an offence, the police will ordinarily go to the persons who are acquainted with the facts and circumstances of the case without sending for them. But in certain cases the police may by a written order require the attendance of any person who appears to be acquainted with the facts and circumstances of the case. It may be noted that male person below fifteen years. of age or woman shall be required to attend at any place other that the place in which such male person or woman resides.[63] A police officer has given special order to examine orally any person supposed to be acquainted with the facts and circumstances of the case.[64] Such person shall be bound to answer truly all questions relating to such questions the answers to which would have a tendency to expose him to a criminal charge or to a penalty or forfeiture.[65] The police officer may reduce into writing any statement made to him in the course of an examination and if he does so, he shall make a separate and true record of the statement of each such person whose statement he records.[66]

Section 162(1) clearly says that "no statement made by any person to a police officer in the course of an investigation shall, if reduced to writing be signed by the person making it." The provision is intended as a statutory safeguard against improper police practices; and a contravention of the provision will be

---

61. See, *supra* note 38, pp. 54-55.
62. The Criminal Procedure Code, 1973, Sec. 158.
63. *Ibid.*, Sec. 160(1).
64. *Ibid.*
65. *Ibid.*
66. *Ibid.*, Sec. 161(3).

considered as impairing the value of the evidence given by the person making and signing a statement before the police during the investigation of a crime.[67]

Any confession made to a police officer is totally inadmissible in evidence.[68] The statements recorded by the police in the course of the investigation cannot be used for any purpose other that those mentioned in Section 162 of the Code. Therefore, the Code provide a special provision for the recoding of confessions and statements made to Magistrate in the course of investigation.[69] Magistrate shall before recoding any such confession explain to the person making it that he is not bound to make a confession that is against him and the magistrate shall not record such confession statement which he believes is not made voluntarily.[70] If at any time before the confession is recorded the person appearing before the Magistrate state that he is not willing to make the confession, the Magistrate shall not authorize the detention of such person in police custody.[71]

Whenever an officer-in-charge of police station or a police officer making an investigation has reasonable grounds for believing that anything necessary for the purposes of an investigation into any offence which he is authorised to investigate may be found in any place within the limits of the police station of which he is in charge, or to which he is attached, and that such thing cannot in his opinion be otherwise obtained without undue delay, such officer may, after recording in writing the grounds of his belief and specifying in such writing, so far as possible the thing for which search is to be made, search, or cause search to be made, for such thing in any place within the limits of such station.[72] If he is unable to conduct the search in person, and there is no other person competent to make the search present at the time, he may, after recording in writing his reasons for so doing, require any officer subordinate to him to make the search, and he shall deliver to such subordinate officer an order in writing, specifying the place

---

67. See, *supra* note 38, p. 59.
68. The Evidence Act, 1872, Sec. 25.
69. The Criminal Procedure Code, 1973, Sec. 164(1).
70. *Ibid.*, Sec. 164(2).
71. *Ibid.*, Sec. 164(3).
72. *Ibid.*, Sec. 165(1).

to be searched, and so far as possible, the thing for which search is to be made; and such subordinate officer may thereupon search for such thing in such place.[73]

Copies of any record made under sub-section (1) or sub-section (3) shall forthwith be sent to the nearest Magistrate empowered to take cognizance to the offence, and the owner or occupier of the place searched shall, on application, be furnished, free of cost, with a copy of the same by the Magistrate.[74]

Whenever there is reason to believe that the delay occasioned by requiring an officer-in-charge of another police station to cause a search to be made under sub-section (1) might result in evidence of the commission of an offence being concealed or destroyed, it shall be lawful for an officer-in-charge of a police station or a police officer making any investigation under this Chapter to search, or cause to be searched, any place in the limits of another police station in accordance with the provisions of section 165, as if such place were within the limits of his own police station.[75]

A person arrested without a warrant cannot be detained by the police for more than 24 hours. If the police officer considers it necessary to detain such a person for a longer period for the purpose of investigation, he can do so only after obtaining a special order of a Magistrate.

(c) Power to Seek Police Custody

Whenever any person is arrested and detained in custody, and it appears that the investigation cannot be completed within the period of twenty-four hours, and there are grounds for believing that the accusation or information is well-founded, the officer-in-charge of the police station or the police officer making the investigation, if he is not below the rank of sub-inspector, shall forthwith transmit to the nearest Judicial Magistrate a copy of the entries in the diary hereinafter prescribed relating to the case, and shall at the same time forward the accused to such Magistrate.[76]

---

73. *Ibid.*, Sec. 165(3).
74. *Ibid.*, Sec. 165(5).
75. *Ibid.*, Sec. 166(3).
76. *Ibid.*, Sec. 167(i).

The Magistrate to whom all accused person is forwarded, whether he has or not jurisdiction to try the case, from time to time, authorise the detention of the accused in such custody as such Magistrate thinks fit, a term not exceeding fifteen days in the whole; and if he has no jurisdiction to try the case or commit it for trial, and considers further detention unnecessary, he may order the accused to be forwarded to a Magistrate having such jurisdiction.

Provided that the Magistrate may authorize the detention of the accused person, otherwise than in the custody of the police, beyond the period of fifteen days, if he is satisfied that adequate grounds exist for doing so, but no Magistrate shall authorise the detention of the accused person in custody for a total period exceeding:

(i) Ninety days, where the investigation relates to an offence punishable with death, imprisonment for life or imprisonment for a term of not less than ten years; and

(ii) Sixty days, where the investigation relates to any other offence.

And, on the expiry of the said period of ninety days, or sixty days, as the case may be, the accused person shall be released on bail if he is prepared to and does furnish bail, and every person released on bail.

No Magistrate shall authorize detention in any custody unless the accused is produced before him and No Magistrate of the second class, not specially empowered in this behalf by the High Court, shall authorize detention in the custody of the police.

For the avoidance of doubts, it is hereby declared that, notwithstanding the expiry of the period the accused shall be detained in Custody so long as he does not furnish bail and the production of the accused person may be proved by his signature on the order authorizing detention.[77]

The officer-in-charge of the police station or the police officer making the investigation, if he is not below the rank of a sub-inspector, may, where a Judicial Magistrate is not

---

77. *Ibid.*, Sec. 167(2).

available, transmit to the nearest Executive Magistrate, on whom the powers of a Judicial Magistrate or Metropolitan Magistrate have been conferred, a copy of the entry in the diary hereinafter prescribed relating to the case, and shall, at the same time, forward the accused to such Executive Magistrate, and thereupon such Executive Magistrate, may, lot reasons to be recorded in writing, authorises the detention of the accused person in such custody as he may think fit for a term not exceeding seven days in the aggregate; and on the expiry of the period of detention so authorized, the accused person shall be released on bail except where an order for further detention of the accused person has been made by a Magistrate competent to make such order; and, where an order for such further detention is made, the period during which the accused person was detained in custody under the orders made by an Executive Magistrate shall be taken into account in computing the period.[78]

Provided that before the expiry of the period aforesaid, the Executive Magistrate shall transmit to the nearest Judicial Magistrate the records of the case together was a copy of the entries in the diary relating to the case which was transmitted to him by the officer-in-charge of the police station or the police officer making the investigation, as the case may be.

A Magistrate authorizing detention in the custody of the police shall record his reasons for so doing and any Magistrate other than the Chief Judicial Magistrate making such order shall forward a copy of his order, with his reasons for making it, to the Chief Judicial Magistrate.[79]

If any case triable by a Magistrate as a summons-case, the investigation is not concluded within a period of six months from the date on which the accused was arrested, the Magistrate shall make an order stopping further investigation into the offence unless the officer making the investigation satisfies the Magistrate that for special reasons and in the interests of justice the continuation of the investigation beyond the period of six months is necessary.

---

78. *Ibid.*, Sec. 167(2A)
79. *Ibid.*, Sec. (167(5).

Where any order stopping further investigation into an offence has been made, the Sessions Judge may, if he is satisfied, on an application made to him or otherwise, that further investigation into the offence ought to be made and direct further investigation to be made into the offence subject to such directions with regard to bail and other matters as he may specify. [80]

(d) Power to release of accused when evidence is deficient

If, upon an investigation, it appears to the officer-in-charge of the police station that there is not sufficient, evidence or reasonable ground of suspicion to justify the forwarding of the accused to a Magistrate, such officer shall, of such person is in custody, release him on his executing a bond, with or without sureties, as such officer may direct, to appear, if and when so required, before a Magistrate empowered to take cognizable of the offence on a police report, and to try the accused or commit him for trial.[81]

(e) Power to sent cases to Magistrate when evidence is sufficient

If, upon an investigation, it appears to the officer-in-charge of the police station that there is sufficient evidence or reasonable ground, such officer shall forward the accused under custody to a Magistrate empowered to take cognizance of the offence upon a police report and to try the accused or commit him for trial, or, if the offence is bailable and the accused is able to give security from him for his appearance before such Magistrate on a day fixed and for his attendance from day to day before such Magistrate until otherwise directed.

When the officer-in-charge of a police station forwards an accused person to a Magistrate or takes security for his appearance before such Magistrate, he shall send to such Magistrate any weapon or other article which it may be necessary, to produce before him, and shall require the complainant (if any) and so many of the persons who appear to such officer to be acquainted with the facts and circumstances of the case as he may think necessary, to execute a bond to appear

---

80. *Ibid.*, Sec. 167(6).
81. *Ibid.*, Sec. 169.

before the Magistrate as thereby directed and prosecute or give evidence (as the case may be) in the matter of the charge against the accused.

If the court of the Chief Judicial Magistrate is mentioned in the bond, such court shall be held to include any court to which such Magistrate may refer the case for inquiry or trial, provided reasonable notice of such reference is given to such complainant or persons.

The officer in whose presence the bond is executed shall deliver a copy thereof to one of the persons who executed it, and shall then send to the Magistrate the original with his report.[82]

(f) Power to maintain Diary of Proceedings in Investigation

Every police officer making an investigation shall day by day enter his proceeding in the investigation in a diary, setting forth the time at which the information reached him, the time at which he began and closed his investigation, the place or places visited by him, and a statement of the circumstances ascertained through his investigation. [83]

Any Criminal Court may send for the police diaries of a case under inquiry or trial in such court, and may use such diaries, not as evidence in the case, but to aid it in such inquiry or trial.

Neither the accused nor his agents shall be entitled to call for such diaries, nor shall he or they be entitled to see them merely because they are referred to by the court; but, if they are used by the police officer who made them to refresh his memory, or if the court uses them for the purpose of contradicting such police officer, the provisions of section 161 or section 145, as the case may be, of the Indian Evidence Act, 1872, shall apply. [84]

(g) Power to submit charge sheet to Magistrate

Every investigation shall be completed without unnecessary delay. As soon as it is completed, the officer-in-

---

82. *Ibid.,* Sec. 170.
83. *Ibid.,* Sec. 172(1).
84. *Ibid.,* Sec. 172(3).

charge of the police station shall forward to a Magistrate empowered to take cognizance of the offence on a police report, a report in the form prescribed by the State Government, stating:[85]

(a) The names of the parties;

(b) The nature of the information;

(c) The names of the persons who appear to be acquainted with the circumstances of the case;

(d) Whether any offence appears to have been committed and, if so, by whom;

(e) Whether the accused has been arrested;

(f) Whether he has been released on his bond and, if so, whether with or without sureties; and

(g) Whether he has been forwarded in custody under section 170.

The officer shall also communicate, in such manner as may be prescribed by the State Government, the action taken by him, to the person, if any whom the information relating to the commission of the offence was first given.

Whenever it appears from a report forwarded under this section that the accused has been released on his bond, the Magistrate shall make such order for the discharge of such bond or otherwise as he thinks fit.

When such report is in respect of a case where evidence is sufficient, the police officer shall forward to the Magistrate along with the report:

(a) All documents or relevant extracts thereof on which the prosecution proposes to rely other than those already sent to the Magistrate during investigation; and

(b) The statements recorded under section 161 of all the persons whom the prosecution proposes to examine as its witness.

If the police officer is of opinion that any part of any such statement is not relevant to the sub-matter of the proceeding or

---

85. *Ibid.*, Sec. 173.

that its disclosure to the accused is not essential in the interests of justice and is inexpedient in the public interest, he shall indicate that part of the statement and append a note requesting the Magistrate exclude that part from the copies to be granted to the accused and stating his reasons for making such request.

Where the police officer investigating the case finds it convenient so to do, he may furnish to the accused copies of all or any of the documents.

Notwithstanding in it shall be deemed to preclude further investigation in respect of an offence after a report has been forwarded to the Magistrate and, whereupon such investigation, the officer-in-charge of the police station obtains further evidence, oral or documentary, he shall forward to the Magistrate a further report or reports regarding such evidence in the form prescribed.

Where the police officer investigating the case finds convenient, he may furnish to the accused all copies and documents.[86]

Report submitted under Section 173 of Criminal Procedure Code is called 'completion report' or 'charge-sheet'. The police charge-sheet corresponds to a complaint made by a private person on which criminal proceedings are initiated. Submission of charge-sheet means that the preliminary investigation and preparation of the case is over and the Magistrate can then take cognizance of the offence. After the filing of the charge-sheet and the posting of the case for further cross-examination there can be no further investigation into the case by the police.

(h) Power to Arrest a Person

Arrest is a process of taking into custody of a person by another, where such latter person is an officer of the State or a private person empowered to do so, under the authority of the law. The purposes of arrest are to ensure its presence of the accused in a court of law in case a charge is leveled against him in a court of law; and to prevent him from continuing his unlawful activities in special cases. The fixing of the identity of the offender and arresting him is the aim of police investigation. Arrest is the outward and obvious signal for the completion of

---

86. *Ibid.*, Sec. 173(7).

investigation in the vast majority of cases.[87] During the course of investigation of a cognizable case to police officer can at any time fell the necessity of arresting the culprit. There may be only a suspicion against him.[88] Arrest of the offender, especially of the dangerous and violent type, does have a highly beneficial effect on the morale of the society. Timely arrest of the accused person in serious cases is an essential step in investigation and failure in this regard considerably weakens the position of the prosecution.[89]

Arrest means apprehension of a person by legal authority resulting in deprivation of his liberty. The arrested person is entitled to know of the grounds of his arrest as soon as possible. Every police officer or other person arresting any person without warrant shall forthwith communicate to him full particular of the offence for which he is arrested or other grounds for such arrest. If the arrest is not for a non-bailable offence, the police officer must also inform the arrested person that he is entitled to be admitted to bail and must also give him an opportunity to furnish bail.[90] A police officer making an arrest without warrant shall without unnecessary delay sent the person arrested before a Magistrate having jurisdiction in the case or before the office-in-charge of a Police Station.[91] No police officer shall detain a person arrested without warrant for more than 24 hours exclusive the time necessary for the journey from the place of arrest to the Magistrate's Court.[92] This right has also been incorporated in the Constitution as one of the fundamental right.[93] The fundamental right of protection against arrest is set forth in Article 22 of our Constitution. According to Article 22 (1), "No person who is arrested shall be detained in custody without being informed as he be denied the right of consult, and to be defended by a legal practitioner of his choice. (2) Every person who is arrested and detained in custody shall be produced before the nearest Magistrate within

---

87. *Ibid.*, Sec. 41.
88. See, *Mitter's Police Diaries, Statements, Reports,* (1981), pp. 592-93.
89. Rambal Singh *vs.* State, 1958 CrLJ 1402.
90. The Criminal Procedure Code, 1973, Sec. 50.
91. *Ibid.*, Sec. 56.
92. *Ibid.*, Sec. 57.
93. See, The Constitution of India, Article 22(2).

a period of 24 hours of such arrest including the time necessary for the journey from the place of arrest to the court of the Magistrate and no such person shall be detained in custody beyond the said period without the authority of a Magistrate."

Powers to arrest without a warrant are mainly and widely conferred on the police. A police officer may arrest without a warrant any person actually concerned or reasonably suspected to be concerned in a cognizable offence;[94] or any person found in possession of any implement of house breaking without any lawful excuse;[95] who has been proclaimed as an offender by State Government[96] in whose possession anything is found which may reasonably be suspected to be stolen property, and who may be reasonably suspected of having committed an offence with reference to such property[97] and obstructing a police officer in the discharge of his duties who have escaped from lawful custody,[98] suspected of being deserted from any armed forces.[99] Any person concerned or reasonably suspected to be concerned in any act committed at a place outside India which if committed in India would be punishable as an offence for which he would be liable to be apprehended or detained in custody in India[100] and being a released convict commit a breach of any rule made under Section 365(5) of Criminal Procedure Code.[101]

Any officer-in-charge of a Police Station may arrest without warrant any person belonging to one or more of the categories of persons specified in Sections 109 and 110, e.g. persons taking precautions to conceal their presence with a view of committing a cognizable offence; habitual robbers, house breakers, thieves, etc., persons habitually indulging in the commission of certain social and economic offences.[102]

---

94. The Code of Criminal Procedure, 1973, Sec. 41(1)(a).
95. *Ibid.*, Sec. 41(1)(b).
96. *Ibid.*, Sec. 41(1)(c).
97. *Ibid.*, Sec. 41(1)(d).
98. *Ibid.*, Sec. 41(1)(e).
99. *Ibid.*, Sec. 41(1)(f).
100. *Ibid.*, Sec. 41(1)(g).
101. *Ibid.*, Sec. 356(5)—The State Government may by notification make rules to carry on the provisions relating to the notification of residence or change of, or absence from, residence by released convicts.
102. See, *supra* note 38, p. 26.

When any person in the presence of a police officer has committed a non-cognizable offence gives false name or address on demand of such officer he may be arrested by such officer.[103] Officer-in-charge of Police Station shall report to the District Magistrate of all persons arrested without warrant[104] and no person shall be discharged except on his own bond, or on bail, or under the special order of a Magistrate.[105] If a person in lawful custody escapes or is rescued, the person whose custody he escaped or was rescued may immediately pursue and arrest him in any place in India.[106]

(i) Power of Search and Seizure

If any person acting under a warrant of arrest, or any police officer having authority to arrest, has reason to believe that the person to be arrested has entered into, or is within, any place, any person residing in, or being in-charge of, such place shall, on demand of such person acting as aforesaid or such police officer, allow him such free ingress thereto, and afford all reasonable facilities for a search therein. [107]

If ingress to such place cannot be obtained it shall be lawful in any case for a person acting under a warrant and in any case in which a warrant may issue, but cannot be obtained without affording the person to be arrested an opportunity of escape, for a police officer to enter such place and search therein, and in order to effect an entrance into such place, to break open any outer or inner door or window of any house or place, whether that of the person to be arrested or of any other person, if after notification of his authority and purposes, and demand of admittance duly made, he cannot otherwise obtain admittance

Provided that, if any such place is an apartment in the actual occupancy of a female (not being the person to be arrested) who, according to custom, does not appear in public, such person or police officer shall, before entering such apartment, give notice to such female that she is at liberty to withdraw and shall afford her every reasonable facility for

---

103. The Code of Criminal Procedure, Sec. 42(1).
104. *Ibid.*, Sec. 58.
105. *Ibid.*, Sec. 59.
106. *Ibid.*, Sec. 60(1).
107. *Ibid.*, Sec. 47(1).

withdrawing, and may then break open the apartment and enter it.[108]

Any police officer or other person authorised to make an arrest may break open any outer or inner door or window of any house or place in order to liberate himself or any other person who, having lawfully entered for the purpose of making an arrest, is detained therein. [109]

Whenever a person is arrested by a police officer under a warrant which does not provide for the taking of bail, or under a warrant which provides for the taking of bail but the person arrested cannot furnish bail, and whenever a person is arrested without warrant, or by a private person under a warrant, and cannot legally be admitted to bail, or is unable to, furnish bail.

The officer making the arrests or, when the arrest is made by a private person, the police officer to whom he makes over the person arrested, may search such person, and place in safe custody all articles, other than necessary wearing-apparel, found upon him and where any article is seized from the arrested person, a receipt showing the articles taken in possession by the police officer shall be given to such person.

Whenever it is necessary to cause a female to be searched, the search shall be made by another female with strict regard to decency. [110] The officer or other person making any arrest under this Code may taken from the person arrested any offensive weapons which he has about his person, and shall deliver all weapons so taken to the court or officer before which or whom the officer or person making the arrest is required by this Code to produce the person arrested.[111]

(j) Powers of the Police to Maintain Law and Order under the Police Act, 1861

One of the most important functions of the police is to maintain law and order and this is also one of the most difficult functions for the police in a democracy. In a democratic country like India, such as the right of assembly, right to speech, right to movement, etc. are guaranteed by the Constitution, and to

108. *Ibid.*, Sec. 47(2).
109. *Ibid.*, Sec. 47(3).
110. *Ibid.*, Sec. 51.
111. *Ibid.*, Sec. 52.

control such rights when their existence threatens the normal existence of the State.[112] The police administration remains responsible to the society for the maintenance of peace and law and order. Though modern civilization has advanced man in many ways, it does not seem to have weakened him further from crime. New threats to the peace, comfort, security and welfare of citizens, rapidly increasing urban criminals and ostensibly law abiding citizens, some of the office holders and political bosses, the use of modern science by criminals and increasing traffic congestion present grave problems to the police administration.[113]

The policeman indeed is a guardian of the law. He is no guardian of the moral conduct of the individual except when these moral principles are endorsed by law of the land by being embodied in a statute. It is the duty of every police officer to prevent the commission of offence and public nuisance to apprehend all persons whom he is legally authorised to apprehend upon existing sufficient grounds.[114]

Assembly of persons is not generally harmful. But if its purpose if unlawful then police is liable to give general direction and control if its purpose is a show or exercise of violence. The District Superintendent of Police Assistant (DSP) may direct the conduct of assemblies and processions on the public roads and streets.[115] He may also issue a licence on such an application specifying the names of the licences and defining conditions on which such assembly or procession is to be permitted. He may also regulate the extent to which music may be used in streets on the occasion of festivals and ceremonies.[116]

Any Magistrate or District Superintendent of Police or Assistant District Superintendent of Police or any police officer-in-charge of a Station may stop any procession which violates the conditions of a licence and may order to disperse the assembly and any assembly neglects or refused to obey any order shall be deemed to be an unlawful assembly.[117]

112. See, *supra* note 36, p. 47.
113. See, Ram Lal Gupta, *Guide to Police Laws in India*, (1961), p. 4.
114. The Police Act, 1861, Sc. 23.
115. *Ibid.*, Sec. 30(1).
116. *Ibid.*, Sec. 30(4).
117. *Ibid.*, Sec. 30(A).

It is the duty of the police to keep assemblies and processions only on public roads and public streets, through fares, other places of public resorts, etc.; and prevent obstructions on the occasion of assemblies and processions on public roads and streets, in the neighbourhood of places of worship, or when such public place may be thronged or liable to be obstructed.[118] Every person opposing or not obeying the orders shall be liable on conviction before a Magistrate, to fine not exceeding two hundred rupees.[119]

Any person who commits on any road, street, or throughfare any of offences namely; slaughtering cattle, furious riding, etc. cruelty to animal, obstructing passengers, exposing goods sale, throwing dirt into street, being found drunk or riotous, indecent exposure of person or neglect to protect dangerous places to the obstruction, inconvenience, annoyance, risk, danger or damage shall on conviction be liable to a fine not exceeding Rs. 50 or the imprisonment not exceeding eight days.[120]

The adequate powers have been vested in the police under Section 34 of the Police Act, to deal with acts of commission or omission which cause obstruction, inconvenience, annoyance, risk, danger or damage to any person in public. All these are courtesies pertaining to matters of care, comfort, convenience and the safety of others.

Policing in democratic societies governed by rule of law is indeed a difficult and challenging assignment. Police in India as a component of criminal justice system works entirely as a law enforcement agency. All sections of society can help improve the status of the police force. At least, they can afford not to disparage the police without rhyme or reason. If they can extend cooperation in law enforcement, there is bound to be a welcome response from the other side which eventually will result in greater social defence and a better law and order situation.

(B) The Criminal Courts in India

With the development of society men learned that they

---

118. *Ibid.,* Sec. 31.
119. *Ibid.,* Sec. 30.
120. *Ibid.,* Sec. 34.

could survive individually only by living under the structure of an organized society. The courts have long been a part of governmental framework. We can define a court as an agency set-up by government to define and apply the law, to order its enforcement, and to settle disputed points on which individuals or groups do not agree.

All of the procedures in the administration of justice revolve around the court system. If an individual is believed to have violated the law, the concern is to bring the person before the courts in a proper manner, to provide him a trial in court, and to follow through with the disposition or judgement made by the court.[121] Courts are charged with monitoring procedures and with coordinating the activities of those criminal justice practitioner engaged in the prosecutorial and trial processes to insure that justice is carried out in a fair and impartial manner within a constitutional framework, in order to sustain innocence or probe the guilt of the accused.[122] The court is also responsible for sentencing, based on the protection of society and the rehabilitation of the offender of the convicted criminal.

In the criminal justice system the court is the final arbiter, the front-line defender of democracy, personal freedom, human dignity and public protection. It is only institution capable of identifying and maintaining the proper balance between the competing rights of individual and those of the State and society. It has the responsibility of enforcing the criminal law against defendants who commit crimes and the same time protecting the same defendants from the violation of their rights by criminal agents. It is to the courts that everyone turns to see that justice is done.[123] The purpose of criminal law is two-fold. Firstly, it attempts to control the behaviour of human being. Failing in this the secondly criminal law seeks to sanction uncontrolled behaviour by punishing the law violator. "Laws are made to be broken," is not philosophically or legally accepted even though laws are broken. Laws are made to protect individual and society. Sanctions, in the form of

---

121. See, Dean Roscue Pound, *Justice According to Law*, (1952), pp. 89-91.
122. See, Harry W. More, *Principles and Procedure in the Administration of Justice*, (1975), p. 19.
123. Gerald D. Robin, *Introduction to the Criminal Justice System*, (1990), p. 168.

punishment, all designed to prevent conduct that violates these rules of society.[124] Human beings respond to a system of rewards and punishment. Freedom and liberty are the rewards; fine, imprisonment and death have been the traditional modes of punishment meant for the violation of the criminal law.

The courts include those judicial agencies at all levels of the Government that perform administration of criminal justice. The courts are responsible for reviewing the actions of law enforcement agencies to ensure that the police have not violated the legal rights of the accused, the courts are given the authority and responsibility to review the actions of other agencies of criminal justice to ensure that their actions do not violate the rigid of the convicted offender.[125] After the accused has been found guilty and after a consideration of all factors, the court must determine whether the offender should be removed from society in order to protect the safety of life and property. Thus, the function of the court is responsible supervision. The court has a high duty and a solemn responsibility to overview the work of the police, the prosecutor and defence or opposing counsel.[126] To preserve the due process of law throughout the arrest to release procedure in the administration of criminal justice.

(i) Hierarchy of Criminal Courts in India

Trial courts throughout the world have long been bifurcated into lower and upper courts. Exodus (1813-26) records that moses assistants to handle lesser cases and reserved large issues and appeals for himself. Imperial administration before and since the Roman Empire have permitted indigenous courts to deal with many petty criminal matters according to indigenous law.[127]

In India, on January 26, 1950, the Federal Court gave way to Supreme Court under the new Constitution and thus began an exciting new era in Indian legal history. The court was inaugurated on Jan. 28, 1950, with very broad jurisdiction. Referring to the extensive jurisdiction conferred on the Supreme

---

124. See, *supra* note 33, pp. 180-81.
125. See, *supra* note 34, p. 9.
126. See, *supra* note 122, p. 19.
127. See, Sanford H. Kadish, *Encyclopedia of Crime and Justice*, (1983), p. 41.

Court by the Constitution, the first Attorney-General, M.C. Setalvad observed at the time of the inauguration of the courts,[128] under Article 131 of the Indian Constitution, the Supreme Court has an exclusive original jurisdiction in cases arising between the Centre and the Constituent State of between the State. The Supreme Court has been empowered to issue directions, orders or writs like the *habeas corpus, mandamus, certiorari,* prohibition and *quo warranto* for the enforcement of the fundamental rights which have been guaranteed by the Constitution to the people of India.[129] The Supreme Court has thus been made the guardian of the freedom and liberties of the Indian people. The Supreme Court has also jurisdiction to decide disputes arising out of the election of the President and the Vice-President.[130] The Supreme Court has jurisdiction to report to the President that a member of the Public Service Commission may be removed from office on the ground of misbehaviour.[131]

The Supreme Court is primarily a court of appeal and an extensive appellate jurisdiction has been conferred on the court. Articles 132 and 136 of the Constitution deal with the appellate jurisdiction of the Supreme Court in constitutional, civil and criminal matters. In criminal matters the Indian Constitution for the first time set-up a court of criminal appeal over the High Courts and creates a right of second appeal.[132] Article 134 of the Constitution for the first time, provide for an appeal to the Supreme Court from any judgement, final order or sentence in a criminal proceeding of a High Court as of right where the High Court has on an appeal reversed an order of acquittal of an accused and sentenced him to death;[133] and where the High Court has withdrawn for trial before itself any case from any court subordinate to its authority and has in such trial convicted the accused and sentenced him to death.[134]

---

128. See, M.P. Jain, *Outlines of Indian Legal History,* (1997), pp. 348-49.
129. The Constitution of India, 1950, Article 32.
130. *Ibid.,* Art. 71.
131. *Ibid.,* Art. 317.
132. See, V.S. Kulshreshtha, *Landmarks in Indian Legal and Constitutional History,* (1995), p. 204.
133. The Constitution of India, 1950, Article 134(a).
134. *Ibid.,* Art. 134(b).

An appeal may lie to the Supreme Court in any criminal case if the High Court certifies that the case is a fit one for appeal to the Supreme Court. The certificate of the High Court would, of course, be granted only where some substantial question of law or some matter of great public importance or the infringement of some essential principles of justice are involved. Appeal may also lie to the Supreme Court from a criminal proceeding if the High Court certifies that the case involves a substantial question of law as to interpretation of the Constitution.[135] Except it, no appeal lies from a criminal proceeding of the High Court to the Supreme Court under the Constitution but Parliament has been empowered to make any law conferring on the Supreme Court further powers to hear appeals in criminal matters.[136]

The Constitution does not make detailed provisions for defining the jurisdiction of the High Courts. Article 225 continues in force the jurisdiction of the High Courts, and the law administered by them, as they have been doing immediately before the commencement of the Constitution, subject to the provisions of the Constitution and any law made by the appropriate legislature. The jurisdiction of the High Courts is varied and diverse. The High Courts enjoys original as well as appellate jurisdiction; civil as well as criminal; ordinary as well as extraordinary; general as well as special jurisdiction.[137]

The original criminal jurisdiction of the High Courts has been completely taken away by the Criminal Procedure Code, 1973[138] and the appellate jurisdiction of the High Court, similarly, is both civil and criminal.[139] The High Court has got superintendence over all courts throughout the concerned State.[140] The Criminal Procedure Code, 1973 also provides that the superintendence over the courts of Judicial Magistrates is to be so exercised as to ensure an expeditious and proper disposal of cases in such courts.[141] The Criminal Procedure Code gives to

---

135. *Ibid.*, Art. 132.
136. See, Durga Das Basu, *Introduction to the Constitution of India*, (2001), p. 301.
137. See, *supra* note 128, p. 301.
138. See, The Constitution of India, 1950, Art. 225.
139. *Ibid.*, Art. 125(b).
140. *Ibid.*, Art. 217.
141. The Criminal Procedure Code, 173, Sec. 483.

the High Court various powers including those relating to reference, appeal, revision, and transfer of cases. It also recognizes specifically the inherent power of the High Court to prevent the abuse of the process of any court, or to secure the ends of justice.[142]

Besides the High Courts in every State there are classes of Criminal Courts, Courts of Session, Judicial Magistrate of the first class, Metropolitan Magistrate in Metropolitan area, Judicial Magistrate of second class and Executive Magistrate.

The State Government can establish a Court of Session for every session division. The court is to be presided over by a judge appointed by the High Court. The High Court may also appoint Additional Session Judges and Assistant Session Judges to exercise jurisdiction in the Court of Session. An Assistant Sessions Judge is subordinate to the Sessions Judge.[143]

In every district there shall be established as many courts of Judicial Magistrate of the first class and of the second class and at such places, the State Government may after consultation with the High Court.[144] The High Court is also required to appoint a Judicial Magistrate of the first class to be the Chief Judicial Magistrate of the District[145] and Judicial Magistrate of the first class to be an Additional Chief Judicial Magistrate and such a Magistrate shall have all the powers of a Chief Judicial Magistrate as the High Court may direct.[146]

The High Court may designate any Judicial Magistrate of the first class in any sub-division as the Sub-divisional Magistrate and relieve him of the responsibilities specified as occasion requires.[147]

In every metropolitan area, there shall be established as many courts of Metropolitan Magistrate and at such places as the State Government may after consultation with the High Court. The presiding officers of such courts shall be appointed by the High Court. The jurisdiction and powers of every such Magistrate extend throughout the metropolitan area.[148] It may

142. *Ibid.*, Sec. 6.
143. *Ibid.*, Sec. 9.
144. *Ibid.*, Sec. 11(1).
145. *Ibid.*, Sec. 12(1)
146. *Ibid.*, Sec. 12(2).
147. *Ibid.*, Sec. 12(3).
148. *Ibid.*, Sec. 16.

also appoint Additional Chief Metropolitan Magistrates and such Magistrates shall have generally all the powers of a Chief Metropolitan Magistrate.[149] The Chief Metropolitan Magistrate and every Additional Chief Metropolitan Magistrate shall be subordinate to the Sessions Judge, and every other metropolitan Magistrate shall subject to the general control of the Session Judge, be subordinate to the Chief Metropolitan Magistrate.[150]

The Criminal Procedure Code has adopted the policy of separation of the judiciary from the executive. Therefore, it has created the separate category of courts which are distinct from the Courts of Judicial Magistrate. The object of the policy of separation is to ensure the independent functioning of the judiciary freed of all suspicion of executive influence and control.[151]

In every district and in every Metropolitan area, the State Government may appoint as many persons as it thinks fit to be Exective Magistrate; it may also appoint an Additional District Magistrate and for a sub-division a Sub-division Magistrate.[152]

(ii) Powers of Courts under Criminal Procedure Code, 1973

One important purpose of arrest is to secure the presence of the accused person at the time of his enquiry or trial and to ensure that he is available to receive sentence on conviction. If this purpose is achieved without forcing detention on the accused during inquiry or trial, it would be an ideal blending of two apparently conflicting claims namely freedom of the individual and the interests of justice.[153]

(a) Grant of Bail

Bail is a generic term used to mean judicial release from custody. The right to bail, the right to be released from jail in a criminal case, after furnishing sufficient security and bond has been recognized in every civilized society as a fundamental aspect of human rights. This is based upon the principle that the object of a criminal proceeding is to secure the presence of the

149. *Ibid.*, Sec. 17.
150. *Ibid.*, Sec. 19
151. See, *supra* note 38; p. 16.
152. The Criminal Procedure Code, 1973, Sec. 20.
153. See, *supra* note 38, p. 117.

accused charged of a crime at the time of the inquiry, trial and investigation before the court and to ensure the availability of the accused to serve the sentence, if convicted. It would be unjust and unfair to deprive a Epson of his freedom and liberty and keep him in confinement, if his presence in the court, whenever required for trial is assured.

The Code of Criminal Procedure, 1973 under Sections 436 to 450 has laid down in detail the norms for grant of bail and bonds in criminal cases. There is no definition of bail in the Code, although the term 'bailable offence' and 'non-bailable' has been defined in the Code of Criminal Procedure.[154] A person who is unable to meet the conditions of release imposed or who is released on condition that he return to custody after specified hours is entitled to a prompt reconsideration of such conditions and, if they are not removed, to have the judge set forth in writing the reasons for them. Subject to the same limitations, the judicial officer may at any time amend his order to impose additional or different conditions of release. One who has been unable be obtain his release at all, or except upon the condition that he return to custody after specified hours, is entitled to a prompt appeal.

(1) In what cases bail to be taken

When any person other than a person accused of a non-bailable offence is arrested or detained without warrant by an officer-in-charge of a police station, or appears or is brought before a court, and is prepared at any time, whilein the custody of such officer or at any stage of the proceeding before such court to give bail, such person shall be released on bail.[155]

Provided that such officer or court, if he or it thinks fit, may, instead of taking bail from such person, discharge him on his executing a bond without sureties for his appearance.

Where a person has failed to comply with the conditions of the bail-bond as regards the time and place of attendance, the court may refuse to release him on bail, when on a subsequent occasion in the same case he appears before the court or is brought in custody and any such refusal shall be without

---

154. The Criminal Procedure Code, 1973, Sec. 2(a).
155. *Ibid.*, Sec. 436.

prejudice to the powers of the court to call upon any person bound by such bond to pay the penalty.[156]

(2) When bail may be taken in case of non-bailable offence

When any person accused of, or suspected of, the commission of any non-bailable offence is arrested or detained without warrant by an officer-in-charge of a police station or appears or is brought before a court other than the High Court or Court of Session, he may be released on bail, but such person shall not be so released if there appear reasonable grounds for believing that he has been guilty of an offence punishable with death or imprisonment for life and such person shall not be so released if such offence is a cognizable offence and he had been previously convicted of an offence punishable with death, imprisonment for life or imprisonment for seven years or more, or he had been previously convicted on two or more occasions of a non-bailable and cognizable offence.[157]

If it appears to such officer or court at any stage of the investigation, inquiry or trial as the case may be, that there are not reasonable grounds for believing that the accused has committed a non-bailable offence, but that there are sufficient grounds for further inquiry into his guilt, the accused shall, subject to the provisions of section 446A and pending such inquiry, be released on bail], or, at the discretion of such officer or court on the execution by him of a bond without sureties for his appearance.[158]

(3) Direction for grant of bail to person apprehending arrest

When any person has reason to believe that he may be arrested on an accusation of having committed a non-bailable offence, he may apply to the High Court or the Court of Session for direction under this section; and that court may, if it thinks fit, direct that in the even of such arrest, he shall be released on bail.[159]

When the High Court or the Court of Session makes a direction it may include such conditions in such directions in the

---

156. *Ibid.*, Sec. 437(2).
157. *Ibid.*, Sec. 437(1).
158. *Ibid.*, Sec. 437(2).
159. *Ibid.*, Sec. 438(1).

light of the facts of the particular case, as it may thinks fit, including :

(i)   A condition that the person shall make himself available for interrogation by a police officer and when required;

(ii) A condition that the person shall not, directly or indirectly, make any inducement, threat or promise to any person acquainted with the facts of the case so as to dissuade him from disclosing such facts to the court or to any police officer;

(iii) A condition that the person shall not leave India without the previous permission of the court; and

(iv) Such other condition as may be imposed under sub-section (3) of section 437, as if the bail were granted under that section.[160]

If such person is thereafter arrested without warrant by an officer-in-charge of a police station on such accusation, and is prepared either at the time of arrest or at any time while in the custody of such officer to give bail, he shall be released on bail, and if a Magistrate taking cognizance of such offence decides that a warrant should issue in the first instance against that person, he shall issue a bailable warrant in conformity with the direction of the court. [161]

(4) Special powers of High Court or Court of Session regarding bail

A High Court or Court of Session may direct:

(a) That any person accused of an offence and in custody be released on bail, and if the offence is of the nature specified in sub-section (3) of section 437, may impose any condition, which it considers necessary for the purposes mentioned in that sub-section;

(b) That any condition imposed by a Magistrate when releasing any person on bail be set aside or modified:

---

160. *Ibid.*, Sec. 438(2).
161. *Ibid.*, Sec. 438(3).

Provided that the High Court or the Court of Session shall, before granting bail to a person who is accused of an offence which is triable exclusively by the Court of Session or which, though not so triable is punishable with imprisonment for life, give notice of the application for bail to the Public Prosecutor unless it is, for reasons to he recorded in writing, of opinion that it is not practicable to give such notice.[162]

A High Court or Court of Session may direct that any person who has been released on bail under this Chapter be arrested and commit him to custody.

If an accused person who has been released on bail attempts to obstruct the smooth progress of a fair trial either by suborning or by intimidating prosecution witnesses or tries to jump bail and to abscond or to run away to a foreign country, it would be just and reasonable that his bail is cancelled and he is arrested and committed to custody.[163]

Provisions have also been made in the Criminal Procedure Code regarding the form of bond, amount of bond and reduction (Sec. 440), bond of accused and sureties (Sec. 441), discharge from custody (Sec. 442), power to order sufficient bail when that first taken in insufficient (Sec. 443), discharge of sureties (Sec. 444), deposit instead of recognizance (Sec. 445), procedure in case of bond has been forfeited (Sec. 446), in case of insolvency or death of surety (Sec. 447) and power to direct levy of amount due on certain recognizance (Sec. 450), etc.[164]

(b) Trial by Criminal Court

Criminal court in India have recognised that the primary object of Criminal Procedure Code is to ensure a fair trial to the accused person. This view has also been accepted by the Law Commission of India that the requirement of a fair trial, relate to the character of the court, the venue, the mode of conducting the trial, rights of the accused in relation to defence and other rights.[165]

---

162. *Ibid.*, Sec. Sec. 439(1)(b).
163. *Ibid.*, Sec. 439(2).
164. *Ibid.*, Sec. 40.
165. 37th Law Commission Report, p. 2.

(1) Framing of Charge

The basic requirement of a fair trial in criminal cases is to give precise information to the accused as to the accusation against him. In all trials under the Code of Criminal Procedure the accused is informed to the accusation in the beginning itself. In case of serious offences the code required that the accusations are to be formulated and reduced to writing with great clarity and precision. This 'charge' is then to be read and explained to the accused person.[166]

The provisions regarding charge are contained in Sections 211-224 and 464. Every charge shall state the offence with which the accused is charged. If the law which creates the offence gives it any specific name, the offence may be described in the charge by that name only and if the law does not give any specific name so much of the definition of the offence must be stated as to give the accused notice of the matter with he is charged. If the accused, having been previously convicted of any offence, is liable, by reason of such previous conviction, to enhanced punishment, or to punishment of a different kind, for a subsequent offence, and it is intended to prove such previous conviction for the purpose of affecting the punishment which the court may think fit to award for the subsequent offence, the fact date and place of the previous conviction shall be stated in the charge; and if such statement has been omitted, the court may add it at any time before sentence is passed. [167]

The charge shall contain such particulars as to the time and place of the alleged offence, and the person (if any) against whom, or the thing (if any) in respect of which, it was committed, as are reasonably sufficient to give the accused notice of the matter with which he is charged.

When the accused is charged with criminal breach of trust or dishonest misappropriation of money or other moveable property, it shall be sufficient to specify the gross sum or, as the case may be, described the movable property in respect of which the offence is alleged to have been committed, and the dates between which the offence is alleged to have been committed, without specifying particular items or exact dates.[168]

---

166. See, *supra* note 38, p. 162.
167. The Criminal Procedure Code, 1973, Sec. 211(7).
168. *Ibid.*, Sec. 212 (2).

When the nature of the case do not accused sufficient notice of the matter with which he is charged, the charge shall also contain such particulars of the manner in which the alleged offence was committed as will be sufficient for that purpose. In every charge words used in describing an offence shall be deemed to have been used in the sense attached to them respectively by the law under which such offence is punishable.[169]

No error in stating either the offence or the particulars required to be stated in the charge, and no omission to state the offence shall be regarded at any stage of the case as material, unless the accused was in fact misled by such error or omission, and it has occasioned a failure of justice.[170]

Any court may alter or add to any charge at any time before judgment is pronounced and every such alteration or addition shall be read and explained to the accused.

For every distinct offence of which any person is accused there shall be a separate charge and every such charge shall be tried separately and if the accused committed three offences of same kind within a year, he may be charged and tried at one trial.[171]

If a single act or series of acts is of such a nature that it is doubtful which of several offences the facts which can be proved will constitute, the accused may be charged with having committed all or any of such offences, and any number of such charges may be tried at once: or he may be charged in the alternative with having committed some one of the said offences.[172]

If in such a case the accused is charged with one offence, and it appears in evidence that he committed a different offence for which he might have been charged under the provisions of sub-section (1), he may be convicted of the offence which he is shown to have committed, although he was not charged with it.[173]

---

169. *Ibid.*, Sec. 214.
170. *Ibid.*, Sec. 215.
171. *Ibid.*, Sec. 219(1).
172. *Ibid.*, Sec. 221(1).
173. *Ibid.*, Sec. 222(2).

When a person is charged with an offence consisting of several particulars, a combination of some only of which constitutes a complete minor offence, and such combination is proved, but the remaining particulars are not proved, he may be convicted of the minor offence, though he was not charged with it.[174] The following persons may be charged and tried together, namely—

(a) Persons accused of the same offence committed in the course of the same transaction;[175]

(b) Persons accused of an offence and persons accused of abetment of, or abetment to commit, such offence;

(c) Persons accused of more than one offence of the same kind, within the meaning of section 219 committed by them jointly within the period of twelve months;

(d) Persons accused of different offences committed in the course of the same transaction;

(e) Persons accused of an offence which includes theft, extortion, cheating, or criminal misappropriation, and persons accused of receiving or retaining, or assisting in the disposal or concealment of, property possession of which is alleged to have been transferred by any such offence committed by the first-named persons, or of abetment of or attempting to commit any such last-named offence;

(f) Persons accused of offences in respect of stolen property the possession of which has been transferred by one offence; and

(g) Persons accused of any offence relating to counterfeit coin and persons accused of any other offence under the said Chapter relating to the same coin, or of abetment of or attempting to commit any such offence. Provided that where a number of persons are charged with separate offences and such persons do not fall within any of the categories specified in this section, the Magistrate may, if such persons by an application in writing, so desire, and, if he is satisfied that such

---

174. *Ibid.*, Sec. 222.
175. *Ibid.*, Sec. 223.

persons would not be prejudicially affected thereby, and it is expedient so to do, try all such persons together.[176]

When a charge containing more heads than one is framed against the same person, and when a conviction has been had on one or more of them, the complainant, or the officer conducting the prosecution, may, with the consent, of the court, withdraw the remaining charge or charges, or the court of its own accord may stay the inquiry into, or trial of, such charge or charges and such withdrawal shall have the effect of an acquittal on such charge or charges, unless the conviction be set aside, in which case the said court (subject to the order of the court setting aside the conviction) may proceed with the inquiry into, or trial of, the charge or charges so withdrawn.

No finding sentence or order by a court of competent jurisdiction shall be deemed invalid merely on the ground that no charge was framed or on the ground of any error, omission or irregularity in the charge including any misjoinder of charge, unless, in the opinion of the court of appeal, confirmation or revision, a failure of justice has in fact been occasioned thereby.[177]

(2) Trial Before a Court of Session

In every trial before a Court of Session, the prosecution shall be conducted by a public prosecutor. When the accused appears or in brought before the court in pursuance of an offence, the prosecutor shall open his case by describing the charge brought against the accused and stating by what evidence he proposed to prove the guilt of the accused.[178]

If, upon consideration of the record of the case and the documents submitted herewith, and after hearing the submissions of the accused and the prosecution in this behalf, the Judge considers that there is not sufficient ground for proceeding against the accused, he shall discharge the accused and record his reasons for so doing.[179]

---

176. *Ibid.,* Sec. 223
177. *Ibid.,* Sec. 464(1).
178. *Ibid.,* Sec. 226.
179. *Ibid.,* Sec. 227.

If the accused pleads guilty; the Judge shall record the plea and may, in his discretion, convict him and if the accused refuses to plead, or does not plead, or claims to be tried the Judge shall fix a date for the examination of witnesses, and may, on the application of the prosecution, issue any process for compelling the attendance of any witness or the production of any document or other thing.[180]

On the date so fixed, the Judge shall proceed to take all such evidence as may be produced in support of the prosecution.

The Judge may, in this discretion, permit the cross-examination of any witness to be deferred until any other witness or witnesses have been examined or recall any witness for further cross-examination.

If after taking the evidence for the prosecution, examining the accused and hearing the prosecution and the defence on the point, the Judge considers that there is no evidence that the accused committed the offence, the judge shall record an order of acquittal.[181]

Where the accused is not acquitted he shall be called upon to enter on his defence and adduce any evidence he may have in support thereof.

If the accused puts in any written statement, the Judge shall file it with the record. If the accused applies for the issue of any process for compelling the attendance of any witness or the production of any document or thing, the Judge shall issue such process unless he considers, for reasons to be recorded, that such application should be refused on the ground that it is made for the purpose of vexation or delay or for defeating the ends of justice.

When the examination of the witnesses for the defence is complete, the prosecutor shall sum up his case and the accused or his pleader shall be entitled to reply: Provided that where any point of law is raised by the accused or his pleader, the prosecution may, with the permission of the Judge, make his submissions with regard to such point of law.

---

180. *Ibid.*, Sec. 230.
181. *Ibid.*, Ss. 231-32.

After hearing arguments and points of law, the Judge shall give a judgment in the case. If the accused is convicted, the Judge shall hear the accused on the question of sentence, and then pass sentence on him according to law.[182]

(3) Trial of Cases by Magistrates

Warrant case means a case relating to an offence punishable with death, imprisonment for life or imprisonment for a term exceeding two years. Warrant cases are more serious than summon cases[183] and the trial of more serious amongst the warrant cases are triable by a court of session, while the not so serious warrant cases are triable by Magistrates.

When in any warrant-case instituted on a police report, the accused appears or is brought before a Magistrate at the commencement of the trial.

If, upon considering the police report making examination, if any, of the accused as the Magistrate thinks necessary and after giving the prosecution and the accused an opportunity of being heard, the Magistrate considers the charge against the accused to be groundless, he shall discharge the accused, and record his reasons for so doing.

If, upon such consideration examination, if any, and hearing, the Magistrate is of opinion that there is ground for presuming that the accused has committed an offence triable which such Magistrate is competent to try and which, in opinion could be adequately punished by him, he shall frame in writing a charge against the accused.

The charge shall then be read and explained to the accused, and he shall be asked whether he pleads guilty of the offence charged or claims to be tried. If the accused pleads guilty, the Magistrate shall record the plea and may, in his discretion, convict him.

If the accused refused to plead or claim to be tried or the Magistrate does not convict the accused then the Magistrate shall fix a date for the examination of witnesses. The Magistrate may on the application of the prosecution, issue a summons to any of its witnesses directing him to attend or to produce any

---

182. *Ibid.*, Ss. 233-35.
183. *Ibid.*, Sec. 2(x).

document or other thing. On the date so fixed, the Magistrate shall proceed to take all such evidence as may be produced in support of the prosecution.[184]

The accused shall then be called upon to enter upon his defence and produce his evidence; and if the accused puts in any written statement, the Magistrate shall file it with the record.

If the accused, after he had entered upon his defence, applies to the Magistrate to issue any process for compelling the attendance of any witness for the purpose of examination or cross-examination, or the production of any document or other thing, the Magistrate shall issue such process unless he considers that such application should be refused on the ground that it is made for the purpose of vexation or delay or for defeating the ends of justice.

When, in any warrant-case instituted otherwise than on a police report the accused appears or is brought before a Magistrate, the Magistrate shall proceed to hear the prosecution and take all such evidence as may be produced in support of the prosecution.

The Magistrate may, on the application of the prosecution, issue a summon to any of its witnesses directing him to attend or to produce any document or other thing.

If, upon taking all evidence the Magistrate considers, for reasons to be recorded that the case against the accused has been made out which, if unrebutted, would warrant his conviction, the Magistrate shall discharge him.

Nothing, shall be deemed to prevent a Magistrate from discharging the accused at any previous stage of the case if, for reasons to be recorded Magistrate, he considers the charge to be groundless.[185]

If, when such evidence has been taken, or at any previous stage of the case, the Magistrate is of opinion that there is ground for presuming that the accused has committed an offence, which such Magistrate is competent to try and which, in his opinion, could be adequately punished by him, he shall

184. *Ibid.*, Ss. 238-41.
185. *Ibid.*, Ss. 243-45.

frame in writing a charge against the accused.

The charge shall then be read and explained to the accused, and he shall be asked whether he pleads guilty or has any defence to make.

If the accused pleads guilty, the Magistrate shall record the plea, and may, in his discretion convict him and if the accused refuses to plead, or does not plead or claims to be tried or if the accused is not convicted he shall be required to state, at the commencement of the next hearing of the case or, if the Magistrate for reasons to be recorded in writing so thinks fit, forthwith whether he wishes to cross-examine any, and if so which of the witnesses for the prosecution whose evidence has been taken.

If he says he does so wish, the witnesses named by him shall be recalled and, after cross-examination and re-examination they shall be discharged. The evidence of any remaining witnesses for the prosecution shall next be taken and after cross-examination and re-examination (if any), they shall also be discharged. The accused shall then be called upon to enter upon his defence and produce his evidence.[186]

(4) Trial of Summon Cases and Summary Trial

A summons case means a case relating to an offence, and not being a warrant case.[187] Thus, it means that it is a case relating to offence not punishable with death, imprisonment for life or imprisonment for a term exceeding two years.

When in a summons-case the accused appears or is brought before the Magistrate, the particulars of the offence of which he is accused shall be stated to him, and he shall be asked whether he pleads guilty or has any defence to make, but it shall not be necessary to frame a formal charge.

If the accused pleads guilty, the Magistrate shall record the plea as nearly as possible in the words used by the accused and may, in his discretion convict him.

Where a summons has been issued and the accused desires to plead guilty to the charge without appearing before the

---

186. *Ibid.*, Ss. 246-47.
187. *Ibid.*, Sec. 2(w).

Magistrate, he shall transmit to the Magistrate, by post or by messenger, a letter containing his plea and also the amount of fine specified in the summons.

The Magistrate may, in his discretion, convict the accused in his absence, on his plea of guilty and sentence him to pay the fine specified in the summons, and the amount transmitted by the accused shall be adjusted towards that fine, or where a pleader authorised by the accused in this behalf pleads guilty on behalf of the accused, the Magistrate shall record the plea as nearly as possible in the words used by the pleader and may, in his discretion, convict the accused on such plea and sentence him as aforesaid.[188]

If the Magistrate does not convict the accused the Magistrate shall proceed to hear the prosecution and take all such evidence as may be produced in support of the prosecution, and also to hear the accused and take all such evidence as he produces in his defence.

The Magistrate may, if he thinks fit, on the application of the prosecution or the accused, issue a summons to any witness directing him to attend or to produce any document or other thing.

A Magistrate may, before summoning any witness on such application, require that the reasonable expenses of the witness incurred in attending for the purposes of the trial be deposited in court.

If the Magistrate, upon taking the evidence he may, of his own motion, cause to be produced, finds the accused not guilt, he shall record an order of acquittal.

A Magistrate may, convict the accused of any offence which form the facts admitted or proved he appears to have committed, whatever may be the nature of the complaint or summons if the Magistrate is satisfied that the accused would not be prejudiced.

If the summons has been issued on complaint and on the day appointed for the appearance of the accused, or any day subsequent thereto to which the hearing may be adjourned, the complainant does not appear, the Magistrate shall

---

188. *Ibid.*, Ss. 251-53.

notwithstanding anything hereinbefore contained, acquit the accused unless for some reason he thinks it proper to adjourn the hearing of the case to some other day.

Provided that where the complainant is represented by a pleader or by the officer conducting the prosecution or where the Magistrate is of opinion that the personal attendance of the complainant is not necessary, the Magistrate may dispense with his attendance and proceed with the case.[189]

If a complainant, at any time before a final order is passed in any case, satisfies the Magistrate that there are sufficient grounds for permitting him to withdraw his complaint against the accused, or if there be more than one accused, against all or any of them, the Magistrate may permit him to withdraw the same, and shall thereupon acquit the accused against whom the complaint is so withdrawn.

In any summons that case instituted otherwise than upon complaint, a Magistrate of the first class or, with the previous sanction of the Chief Judicial Magistrate, any other Judicial Magistrate, may, for reasons to be recorded by him, stop the proceedings at any stage without pronouncing any judgment and where such stoppage of proceedings is made after the evidence of the principal witnesses has been recorded, pronounce a judgment of acquittal, and in any other case release the accused, and such release shall have the effect of discharge.

When in the course of the trial of summon-case relating to an offence it appears to the magistrate punishable with imprisonment for a term exceeding six months, it appears to the Magistrate that in the interests of Justice, the offence should be tried in accordance with the procedure for the trial of warrant-cases, such Magistrate may proceed to re-hear the case and may recall any witness who may have been examined.[190]

(5) Power to Try Summarily

Any Chief Judicial Magistrate; any Metropolitan Magistrate; any Magistrate of the first class specially empowered in this behalf by the High Court, may any of he thinks fit, try in a summary way all or any of the following offences.

---

189. *Ibid.*, Ss. 254-56.
190. *Ibid.*, Ss. 257-59.

(i) Offences not punishable with death, imprisonment for life or imprisonment for a term exceeding two years;

(ii) Theft, under section 379, section 380 or section 381 of the Indian Penal Code, where the value of the property stolen does not exceed two hundred rupees;

(iii) Receiving or retaining stolen property, under section 411 of the Indian Penal Code, where the value of the property does not exceed two hundred rupees;

(iv) Assisting in the concealment or disposal of stolen property, under section 414 of the Indian Penal Code where the value of such property does not exceed two hundred rupees;

(v) Offences under sections 454 and 456 of the Indian Penal Code;

(vi) Insult with intent to provoke a breach of the peace, under section 504 and criminal intimidation, under section 506 of the Indian Penal Code;

(vii) Abetment of any of the foregoing offences;

(viii) An attempt to commit any of the foregoing offences, when such attempt is an offence; and

(ix) Any offence constituted by an act in respect of which a complaint may be made under section 20 of the Cattle-Trespass Act, 1871.

When, in the Course of a summary trial it appears to the Magistrate that the nature of the case is such that it is undesirable to try it summarily, the Magistrate shall recall any witnesses who may have been examined and proceed to re-hear, the case in the manner provided by this Code.

The High Court may confer on any Magistrate invested with the powers of a Magistrate of the second class power, to try summarily any offence which is punishable only with fine or with imprisonment for a term not exceeding six months with or without fine, and any abetment of or attempt to commit any such offence.

In every case tried summarily, the Magistrate shall enter, in such form as the State Government may direct, the following particulars, namely:

(a) The serial number of the case;

(b) The date of the commission of the offence;

(c) The date of the report of complaint;

(d) The name of the complainant (if any);

(e) The name, parentage and residence of the accused;

(f) The offence complained of and the offence (if any) proved, and in cases coming under clause (ii), clause (iii) or clause (iv) of sub-section (1) of section 260, the value of the property in respect of which the offence has been committed;

(g) The plea of the accused and his examination (if any);

(h) The finding;

(i) The sentence or other final order;

(j) The date on which proceedings terminated.

In every case tried summarily in which the accused does not plead guilty, the Magistrate shall record the substance of the evidence and a Judgment containing a brief statement of the reasons for the finding.

Every such record and judgment shall be written in the language of the court. The High Court may authorize any Magistrate empowered to try offences summarily to prepare the aforesaid record or judgment or both by means of an officer appointed in this behalf by the Chief Judicial Magistrate, and the record or judgment so prepared shall be signed by such Magistrate.[191]

(6) Special Procedure of Evidence

Whenever, in the course of any inquiry, trial or other proceeding, it appears to a Court of Magistrate that the examination of a witness is necessary for the ends of justice, and that the attendance of such witness cannot be procured without an amount of delay, expense or inconvenience which, under the circumstances of the case, would be unreasonable, the Court or Magistrate may dispense with such attendance and may issue a commission for the examination of the witness.

Provided that where the examination of the President or the Vice-President of India or the Governor of a State or the Administrator of a Union Territory as a witness is necessary for

---

191. *Ibid.*, Ss. 260-265.

the ends of justice, a commission shall be issued for the examination of such a witness.

The court may, when issuing a commission for the examination of a witness for the prosecution direct that such amount as the court considers reasonable to meet the expenses of the accused including the pleader's fees, be paid by the prosecution.

If the witness is within the territories to which this Code extends, the commission shall be directed to the Chief Metropolitan Magistrate or Chief Judicial Magistrate, as the case may be, within whose local jurisdiction the witness is to be found.

If the witness is in India, but in a State or an area to which this Code does not extend the commission shall be directed to such court or officer as the Central Government may, by notification specify in this behalf.

If the witness is in a country or place outside India and arrangements have been made by the Central Government with the Government of such country or place for taking the evidence of witnesses in relation to criminal matters, the commission shall be issued in such form, directed to such court or officer, and sent to such authority for transmission as the Central Government may, by notification prescribe in this behalf.

Upon receipt of the commission, the Chief Metropolitan Magistrate of Chief Judicial Magistrate, or such Metropolitan or Judicial Magistrate as he may appoint in this behalf, shall summon the witness before him or proceed to the place where the witness is, and shall take down his evidence in the same manner, and may for this purpose exercise the same powers, as in trials of warrant cases.

The parties to any proceeding in which a commission is issued may respectively forward any interrogatories to the issue, and it shall be lawful for the Magistrate, court or officer to whom the Commission is directed, or to whom the duty of executing it is delegated, to examine the witness upon such interrogatories.

Any such party may appear before such Magistrate, court or officer by pleader, or if not in custody, in person, and may examine, cross-examine and re-examine (as the case may be) the said witness.

After any commission has been duly, executed, it shall be returned, together with the deposition of the witness examined thereunder, to the court or Magistrate issuing the commission; and the commission, the return thereto and the deposition shall be open at all reasonable times to inspection of the parties, and may, subject to all just exceptions, be read in evidence in the case by either party, and shall form part of the record.

In every case in which a commission is issued, the inquiry, trial or other proceeding may be adjourned for a specified time reasonably sufficient for the execution and return of the commission.

Any court, Judge or Magistrate exercising jurisdiction in any foreign country or place outside India, as the Central Government may, by notification, specify in this behalf, and having authority under the law in force in that country of place, to issue commissions for the examination of witnesses in relation to criminal matters.

The deposition of a civil surgeon or other medical witness, taken and attested by a Magistrate in the presence of the accused or taken on commission, may be given in evidence in any injury or other proceeding, although the deponent is not called as a witness.

If the court may thinks fit, and shall, on the application of the prosecution or the accused, summon and examine any such deponent as to the subject matter of his deposition.

Any document purporting to be a report under the hand of any such gazetted officer of the Mint or of the India Security Press (including the office of the Controller of Stamps and Stationery) as the Central Government may, by notification, specify in this behalf, upon any matter or thing duly submitted to him for examination and report in the course of any proceeding, may be used as evidence in any inquiry, trial or other proceeding, although such officer is not called as a witness.

Any document purporting to be a report under the hand of a Government scientific expert, upon any matter or thing duly submitted to him for examination or analysis and report in the course of any proceeding, may be used as evidence in any inquiry, trial or other proceeding. The court may, if it thinks fit, summon and examine any such expert as to the subject matter of his report.

Where any such expert is summoned by a court and he is unable to attend personally, he may, unless the court has expressly directed him to appear personally, depute any responsible officer working with him to attend the court, if such officer is conversant with the facts of the case and can satisfactorily depose in court on his behalf

This provision applies to the following Government scientific experts, namely:

(a) Any Chemical Examiner or Assistant Chemical Examiner to Government;

(b) The Chief Inspector of Explosives;

(c) The Director of the Finger Print Bureau;

(d) The Director, Haffkeine Institute, Bombay;

(e) The Director [Deputy Director or Assistant Director of a Central Forensic Science Laboratory or a State Forensic Science Laboratory]; and

(f) The Serologist to the Government.

Where any document is filed before any court by the prosecution or the accused, the particulars of every such document shall be included in a list and the prosecution or the accused, as the case may be, or the pleader for the prosecution or the accused, if any, shall be called upon to admit or deny the genuineness of each such document.

Where the genuineness of any document is not disputed, such document may be read in evidence in any inquiry trial or other proceeding without proof of the signature of the person to whom it purports to be signed, provided that the court may, in its discretion, require such signature to be proved.

When any application is made to any court in the course of any inquiry, trial or other proceeding, and allegations are made therein respecting any public servant, the applicant may give evidence of the facts alleged in the application by affidavit, and the court may, if it thinks fit, order that evidence relating to such facts be so given.

The evidence of any person whose evidence is of a formal character may be given by affidavit and may, subject to all just exceptions, be read in evidence in any inquiry, trial or other proceeding and the court may, if it thinks fit, and shall, on the application of the prosecution or the accused, summon and examine any such person as to the facts contained in his affidavit.

Affidavits shall be confined to, and shall state separately, such facts as the deponent is able to prove from his own knowledge and such facts as he has reasonable ground to believe to be true, and in the latter case, the deponent shall clearly state the ground of such belief and the court may order any scandalous and irrelevant matter in the affidavit to be struck out or amended.

In any inquiry, trial or other proceeding, a previous conviction or acquittal may be proved, in addition to any other mode provided by any law for the time being in force. (a) By an extract certified under the hand of the officer having the custody of the records of the court in which such conviction or acquittal was held, to be a copy of the sentence or order, or (b) In case of a conviction, either by a certificate signed by the officer-in-charge of the jail in which the punishment or any part thereof was undergone, or by production of the warrant of commitment under which the punishment was suffered together with, in each of such cases evidence as to the identity of the accused person with the person so convicted or acquitted.

If it is proved that an accused person has absconded and that there is no immediate prospect of arresting him, the court competent to try [or commit for trial] such person for the offence complained of, may, in his absence, examine the witnesses (if any) produced on behalf of the prosecution, and record their depositions and any such deposition may, on the arrest of such person, be given in evidence against him on the inquiry into, or trial for, the offence with which he is charged, if the deponent is dead or incapable of giving evidence or cannot be found or his presence cannot be procured without an amount of delay, expense inconvenience which, under the circumstances of the case, would be unreasonable and if it appears that an offence punishable with death or imprisonment for life has been committed by some person or persons unknown, the High

Court or the Sessions Judge may direct that any Magistrate of the first class shall hold an inquiry and examine any witnesses who can give evidence concerning the offence and any depositions so taken may be given in evidence against any person who is subsequently accused of the offence, if the deponent is dead or incapable of giving evidence or beyond the limits of India.[192]

(7) Judgement in Criminal Trial

The main functions of the criminal courts are to decide as to the guilt or innocence of the accused person tried before it and if such person is found guilty of any offence, to determine as to the appropriate punishment or other method of dealing with him. In every trial, irrespective of its nature, the court will have to give a judgement in the case at the conclusion of the trial. The judgement is the final decision of the court, given with reasons, on the question of guilt or innocence of the accused person.

The judgment in every trial in any Criminal Court of original jurisdiction shall be pronounced in open court by the presiding officer immediately after the termination of the trial or at some subsequent time of which notice shall be given to the parties or their pleaders. By delivering the whole of the judgment or reading out the whole of the judgment and explaining the substance of the judgment in a language, which is understood by the accused or his pleader.

Where the judgment is delivered, the presiding officer shall cause it to be taken down in short hand, sign the transcript and every page thereof as soon as it is made ready, and write on it the date of the delivery of the judgment in open Court.[193]

Every judgment shall be written in the language of the court contain the point or points for determination, the decision thereon and the reasons for the decision, specify the offence (if any) of which, and the section of the Indian Penal Code or other law under which, the accused is convicted and the punishment to which he is sentenced. If it be a judgment of acquittal, shall

---

192. *Ibid.*, Ss. 284-299.
193. *Ibid.*, Sec. 353.

state the offence of which the accused is acquitted and direct that he be set at liberty.

When the conviction is for an offence punishable with death or, in the alternative, with imprisonment for life or imprisonment for a term of years, the judgment shall state the reasons for the sentence awarded, and, in the case of sentence of death, the special reasons for such sentence.[194]

When a court imposes a sentence of fine or a sentence (including a sentence of death) of which fine forms a part, the court may, when passing judgment order the whole or any part of the fine recovered to be applied in defraying the expenses properly incurred in the prosecution, and the payment to any person of compensation for any loss or injury caused by the offence, when compensation is, in the opinion, of the court, recoverable by such person in a Civil Court.[195]

When the accused is sentenced to imprisonment, a copy of the judgment shall, immediately after the pronouncement of the judgment, be given to him free of cost.[196]

The original judgment shall be filed with the record of the proceedings and where the original is recorded in a language different from that of the court and the accused so requires, a translation thereof into the language of the court shall be added to such record.[197]

In cases tried by the Court of Session or a Chief Judicial Magistrate, the court or such Magistrate as the case may be, shall forward a copy of its or his finding and sentence (if any) to the District Magistrate within whose local jurisdiction the trial was held.[198]

VII. SUM-UP

In our system of criminal justice, the right of the defendant to be represented by counsel is fundamental right. An individual forced to answer a criminal charge needs the assistance of a lawyer to protect his legal rights and to help him

---

194. *Ibid.,* Sec. 354.
195. *Ibid.,* Sec. 357.
196. *Ibid.,* Sec. 363.
197. *Ibid.,* Sec. 364.
198. *Ibid.,* Sec. 365.

understand the nature and consequences of the proceedings against him. Counsel is needed to maintain effective and efficient criminal justice. The key to understand the court system is jurisdiction, which differentiates the lower courts, the trial courts and the appellate courts. In all the courts the accused is entitled to a fair trial. The trial must be conducted in a calm and dispassionate atmosphere. The Government, or prosecution always has the burden of proving guilt, and innocence must be assumed until the contrary is proved. Guilt must be established solely on the basis of evidence produced in court under circumstances assuring the accused a reasonable opportunity to disprove or explain away the evidence.

There can be no civilized life without a legal order and there can be no stable legal order unless it secures justice to the people. There can be no justice through law unless there is commitment of the court and the judge to advance people's interest.

CHAPTER

4

Correctional Institutions and Criminal Justice Administration in India

I. INTRODUCTION

Correction is the third and final phase of the criminal justice process. Beginning with law enforcement as the case-finding phase, the courts determine by trial under due process of law and corrections attempts to rehabilitate the neutralized and deviant behaviour of adult criminals and juvenile delinquents. The successes and failures of the criminal justice system are measured in the field of corrections. The productivity of the entire criminal justice system is judged by the productivity of corrections.[1]

The basic purpose of the criminal justice system is to eliminate, or at least to reduce, crime and delinquency. It is to the benefit of the society as a whole to remove those conditions

---

1. See Neil C. Chamelin, Vernon B. Fox, M. Wisenand, *Introduction to Criminal Justice*, (1975), pp. 4-5.

that spawn crime. The factors that contribute to the making of delinquents and criminals are many and complex.[2]

Over the centuries, corrections and punishment have been synonymous. Even today, this attitude is held by a sizable segment in society particularly in cases that involves serious crimes. Although basic attitudes towards punishment have not significantly changed. Today, through more 'humane' techniques, society acts as the agent of punishment on behalf of the victim rather than permitting the private settling of feuds. In some views, punishment has been defended as permitting the offender the feeling of having atoned for his or her anti-social action while reaffirming the appropriateness of non-criminal behaviour among the law abiding members of society.[3]

The reformative view of penology suggests that punishment is only justifiable if it looks to the future and not to the past. "It should not be regarded as settling an old account but rather as opening a new one." Thus, the supporters of this view justify prisonisation not solely for the purpose of isolating criminals and eliminating them from society but to bring about a change in their mental outlook through effective measures of reformation during the term of their sentence.

The modern systems of probation, parole and juvenile justice reformatories and open institutions have provide potentially helpful in elimination of isolationism from which preventive and corrections scheme have suffered for long. The working of prison institutions have been remodeled to suit the modern corrective methods of treatment of offenders. The correctional process is charged with carrying out two fundamental responsibilities of government, i.e. the protection of society and the rehabilitation of the convicted offenders. The correctional function is apportioned primarily among prison, probation, parole and juvenile justice system.

II. PRISON ADMINISTRATION AND CRIMINAL JUSTICE SYSTEM

Crimes and criminals are the by-product of a social system.

---

2. See, Charles, F. Hempwill, *Criminal Procedure : The Administration of Justice,* (1978), pp. 3-4.
3. See, Roberty D. Pursley, *Introduction to Criminal Justice,* (1977), p. 7.

In other words, roots of crimes lie deep in society of which the individual is an integral part. When a crime is committed, the guilty is subjected to punishment according to the law of the land. The modes of punishment may vary keeping in view the offence committed. When a person is adjudged guilty of having committed a crime and sentence to imprisonment, prison is usually the place where he is to be kept while undergoing sentence.[4]

The history of prisons in India and elsewhere clearly reflects upon the changes in the society's outlook for reaction to crimes from time to time. The system of imprisonment represents a curious admixture of different objectives of punishment. Thus, it may be intended to deter the offender or used as a method of retribution or vengeance by making the life of the offender unfavourable and unpleasant in the prison.

The fact that the criminals undergoing imprisonment in prison are leading an isolated life thus incapacitating them from committing the crime again fulfils the preventive purpose of punishment. This also helps to keep the crimes under control.

As early as in 1597, jails were established. The jails of old times were miserable places, which afforded opportunities for graduation to a life of crime. Recidivism was rampant. Men, women and children, first offenders and habituals were all hurled together like "rats in a hamper and pigs in asty".[5] Prisons in the modern sense of the term were unknown in the medieval times; a person could be incarcerated while trial was pending. It was in the 18th century that cellular prisons were built.

The prisons in India were in a terrible condition when the East India Company took over some of the provinces of India. During the period preceding the British rule, the prisoners were ill-treated, tortured and subjected to barbarous treatment. However, with the advent of the British rule, some serious efforts to improve the conditions of prison and prisoners were initiated. Many Committees were appointed from time to time to look into the system of prison management and suggest

---

4. See, B.R. Sharma and Vandana Kashyap, *Prison System in India : A Historical Retrospection*, CMLJ, No. 2, Vol. 30, April-June, 1994, p. 136.
5. See, M.J. Sethna, *Society and Criminal*, (1971), p. 303.

measures to eradicate evils which were existing there. It was the result of these recommendations by the Committees that better amenities to the various kinds of jail inmates were extended and the number of prisoners which could be accommodated in each of the existing jails was also prescribed.[6] The Committee for jail reforms headed by Justice A.N. Mulla which gave suggestions on various aspects of jail administration including those relating to modernization of jails and segregation of young prisoners from the hardened criminals.

The real purpose of sending criminals to prison is to transform them into honest and law abiding citizens by inculcating in them distaste for crime and criminality. But in actual practice, the prison authorities try to bring out reformation of inmates by use of force and compulsive methods. Consequently, the change in inmates is temporary and lasts only till the period they are in prison and as soon as they are released, they quite often return to the criminal world. It is for this reason that modern trend is to lay greater emphasis of psychiatric conditions of the prisoners so that they can be rehabilitated to normal life in the community. This objective can be successfully achieved through the techniques of probation and parole.

(A) Administration of Prison under Prison Act, 1894

The State Government shall provide, for the prisoners in the territories under such Government, accommodation in prisons constructed and regulated in such manner as to comply with the requisitions in respect of the separation of prisoners.[7]

An Inspector-General shall be appointed for the territories subject to each State Government, and shall exercise, subject to the orders of the State Government, the general control and superintendent of all prisons situated in the territories under such Government.[8]

For every prison there shall be a Superintendent, a Medical Officer (who may also be the Superintendent), a Medical

---

6. See, Vijay K. Jindal, *Punjab Jail Manual*, (1996), p. 1.
7. See, The Prison Act, 1894, Sec. 5.
8. *Ibid.*, Sec. 5.

Subordinate, a Jailer and such other officers as the State Government thinks necessary.

Whenever it appears to the Inspector General that the number of prisoners in any prison is greater than can conveniently or safely be kept therein, and it is not convenient to transfer the excess number to some other prison or whenever from the outbreak of epidemic disease within any prison, or for any other reason, it is desirable to provide for the temporary shelter and safe custody of any prisoners, provision shall be made, by such officer and in such manner as the State Government may direct, for the shelter and safe custody in temporary prisons of so many of the prisoners as cannot be conveniently or safely kept in the prison.[9]

All officers of a prison shall obey the directions of the Superintendent; all officers subordinate to the Jailer shall perform such duties as may be imposed on them by the Jailer with the sanction of the Superintendent or be prescribed by rules.[10]

Subject to the control of the Superintendent, the Medical Officer shall have charge of the sanitary administration of the prison, and shall perform such duties as may be prescribed by rules made by the State Government.

Whenever the Medical Officer has reason to believe that the mind of a prisoner is, or is likely to be, injuriously affected by the discipline or treatment to which he is subjected, the Medical Officer shall report the case in writing to the Superintendent, together with such observations as he may think proper. This report, with the orders of the Superintendent, shall forthwith be sent to the Inspector General for information.[11]

On the death of any prisoner, the Medical Officer shall forthwith record in a register the particulars, so far as they can be ascertained, namely: (1) The day on which the deceased first complained of illness or was observed to be ill, (2) The labour, if any, on which he was engaged on that day, (3) The scale of his diet on that day, (4) The day on which he was admitted to

---

9. *Ibid.*, Sec. 7.
10. *Ibid.*, Sec. 8.
11. *Ibid.*, Sec. 17.

hospital, (5) The day on which the Medical Officer was first informed of the illness, (6) The nature of the disease, (7) When the deceased was last seen before his death by the Medical Officer or Medical Subordinate, (8) When the prisoner died, and (9) (In cases where a post-mortem examination is made) an account of the appearances after death, together with any special remarks that appear to the Medical Officer to be required.[12]

The Jailer shall reside in the prison, unless the Superintendent permits him in writing to reside elsewhere.

The Jailer shall not, without the Inspector General's sanction in writing, be concerned in any other employment.

Upon the death of a prisoner, the Jailer shall give immediate notice thereof to the Superintendent and the Medical Subordinate.

The Jailer shall be responsible for the safe custody of the records to be kept, for the commitment warrants and all other documents confided to his care, and for the money and other articles taken from prisoners.[13]

Every criminal prisoner shall also, as soon as possible after admission, be examined under the general or special orders of the Medical Office, who shall enter or cause to be entered in a book, to be kept by the Jailer, a record of the state of the prisoner's health, and of any wounds or marks on his person, the class of labour he is fit for it sentenced to rigorous imprisonment, and any observation which the Medical Officer thinks fit to add.[14]

In the case of female prisoners the search and examination shall be carried out by the matron under the general or special orders of the Medical Officer.

All money or other articles in respect whereof no order of a competent Court has been made, and which may with proper authority be brought into the prison by any criminal prisoner or sent to the prison for his use, shall be placed in the custody of the Jailer.[15]

---

12. *Ibid.*, Sec. 15 .
13. *Ibid.*, Sec. 16-18.
14. *Ibid.*, Sec. 24(2).
15. *Ibid.*, Sec. 25.

No prisoner shall be removed from one prison to another unless Medical Officer certifies that the prisoner is free from any illness rendering him unfit for removal and no prisoner shall be discharged against his will from prison, if labouring under any acute or dangerous distemper, nor until, in the opinion of the Medical Officer, such discharge is safe.[16]

In a prison containing female as well as male prisoners, the females shall be imprisoned in separate buildings, or separate parts of the same building, in such manner as to prevent their seeing, or conversing or holding any intercourse with the male prisoners.[17]

In a prison where male prisoners under the age of twenty-one are confined, means shall be provided for separation them altogether from the other prisoners and for spearing those of them who have arrived at the age of puberty from those who have not unconverted criminal prisoners shall be kept apart from convicted criminal prisoners; and civil prisoners shall be kept apart from criminal prisoners.[18]

No cell shall be used for solitary confinement unless it is furnished with the means of enabling the prisoner to communicate at any time with an officer of the prison, and every prisoner so confined in a cell for more than twenty-four hours, whether as a punishment or otherwise, shall be visited at least once a day by the Medical Officer or Medical Subordinate.[19]

Every prisoner under sentence of death shall, immediately on his arrival in the prison after sentence, be searched by, or by order of, the Jailer and all articles shall be taken from him which the Jailer deems it dangerous or inexpedient to leave in his possession.

Every such prisoner shall be confined in a cell apart from all other prisoners, and shall be placed by day and by night under the charge of a guard.[20]

A civil prisoner or an unconvicted criminal prisoner shall be permitted to maintain himself, and to purchase, or receive

---

16. *Ibid.,* Sec. 26.
17. *Ibid.,* Sec. 27(1).
18. *Ibid.,* Sec. 27(2-4).
19. *Ibid.,* Sec. 20.
20. *Ibid.,* Sec. 30.

from private source at proper hours, food, clothing, bedding or other necessaries, but subject to examination and to such rules as may be approved by the Inspector General.[21]

Civil prisoners may, with the Superintendent's permission, work and follow any trade or profession.

Civil prisoners finding their own implements, and not maintained at the expense of the prison, shall be allowed to receive the whole of their earnings; but the earnings of such as are furnished with implements or are maintained at the expense of the prison shall be subject to a deduction, to be determined by the Superintendent, for the use of implements and the cost of maintenance. [22]

Provisions shall be made by the Superintendent for the employment (as long as they so desire) of all Criminal prisoners sentenced to simple imprisonment; but no prisoner not sentenced to rigorous imprisonment shall be punished for neglect of work excepting by such alteration in the scale of diet as may be established by the rules of the prison in the case of neglect of work by such a prisoner.[23]

Whoever, introduces or removes or attempts by any means whatever to introduce or remove into or from any prison, or supplies or attempts to supply to any prisoner outside the limits of a prison, any prohibited article and every officer of a prison who, contrary to any such rule, knowingly suffers any such article to be introduce into or removed from any prison, to be possessed by any prisoner, or to be supplied to any prisoner outside the limits of a prison and whoever, contrary to any such rule, communicates or attempts to communicate with any prisoner and whoever abets any offence made punishable, shall, on conviction before a Magistrate, be liable to imprisonment for a term not exceeding six months, or to fine not exceeding two hundred rupees, or to both.[24]

When any person in the presence of any officer of a prison, commits any offence specified in the last foregoing section and refuses on demand of such officer to state his name and residence, or gives a name or residence which such officer

---

21. *Ibid.*, Sec. 31.
22. *Ibid.*, Sec. 34(2).
23. *Ibid.*, Sec. 36.
24. *Ibid.*, Sec. 42.

knows, or has reason to believe, to be false, such officer may arrest him, and shall without unnecessary delay make him over to a Police-officer, and thereupon such Police-officer shall proceed as if the offence has been committed in his presence.[25]

Wilful disobedience to any regulation of the prison shall have been declared a prison-offence; any assault or use of criminal force; the use of insulting or threatening language; immoral or indecent or disorderly behaviour; wilfully disabling himself from labour; contumaciously refusing to work; filing cutting altering or removing handcuffs, fetters or bars without due authority; wilful idleness or negligence at work by any prisoner sentenced to rigorous imprisonment; wilful mismanagement of work by any prisoner sentenced to rigorous imprisonment; wilful damage to prison-property; tampering with or defacing history-tickets, records or documents; receiving possessing or transferring any prohibited article; feigning illness; wilfully bringing a false accusation against any officer or prisoner; omitting or refusing to report, as soon as it comes to his knowledge, the occurrence of any fire, any plot or conspiracy, any escape, attempt or preparation to escape, and any attack or preparation for attack upon any prisoner or prison-official; and conspiring to escape, or to assist in escaping, to commit any other of the offences aforesaid.[26]

The Superintendent may examine any person touching any such offence, and determine thereupon, and punish such offence by a formal warning; change of labour to some more irksome or serve form for such period as may be prescribed by rules made by the State Government; hard labour for a period not exceeding seven days in the case of convicted criminal prisoners not sentenced to rigorous imprisonment; such loss of privileges admissible under the remission system for the time being in force as may be prescribed by rules made by the State Government; the substitution of gunny or other coarse fabric for clothing of other material, not being woollen, for a period which shall not exceed three months; imposition of handcuffs of such pattern and weight in such manner and for such period, as may be prescribed by rules made by the State Government;

---

25. *Ibid.*, Sec. 43.
26. *Ibid.*, Sec. 45.

imposition of fetters of such pattern and weight, in such manner and for such period, as may be prescribed by rules made by the State Government; separate confinement for any period not exceeding three months; penal diet, that is, restriction of diet in such manner and subject to such conditions regarding labour as may be prescribed by the State Government. Provided that such restriction of diet shall in no case been applied to a prisoner for more than ninety-six consecutive hours, and shall not be repeated except for a fresh offence nor until after an interval of one week; cellular confinement for any period not exceeding fourteen days. "Cellar confinement means such confinement with or without labour as entirely means such from communication with, but not from sight of, other prisoners".

Whipping provided that the number of stripes shall not exceed thirty. Provided that no female or civil prisoner liable to the imposition of any form of handcuffs fetes or to whipping.[27]

No punishment of penal diet, either singly or in combination, or of whipping, or of change of labour, shall be executed until the prisoner to whom such punishment has been awarded has been examined by the Medical Officer, who, if he considers the prisoner fit to undergo the punishment, shall certify accordingly in the appropriate column of the punishment-book.

If he considers the prisoner unfit to undergo the punishment, he shall like manner record his opinion in writing and shall state whether the prisoner is absolutely unfit for punishment of the kind warded, or whether he considers any modification necessary.[28]

If any prisoner is guilty of any offence against prison-discipline which, be reason of his having frequently committed such offences or otherwise, in the opinion of the Superintendent, is not adequately punishable by the infliction of any punishment which he has power, the Superintendent may for ward such prisoner to the Court of the District Magistrate or of any Magistrate of the first class or Presidency Magistrate having jurisdiction, together with a statement of the circumstances, and such Magistrate shall thereupon inquire into and try the charge

---

27. *Ibid.*, Sec. 46.
28. *Ibid.*, Sec. 50(2).

so brought against the prisoner, and, upon conviction, may sentence him to imprisonment which may extend to one year, such term to be in addition to any term for which such prisoner was undergoing imprisonment when he committed such offence or may sentence him to any of the punishments provided also that no person shall be punished twice for the same offence.[29]

The State Government may make rules in consistent with the Act for regulating the transmission of appeals and petitions from prisoners and their communications with their friends; for the appointment and guidance of visitors of prisons and in regard to the admission, custody, employment, dieting, treatment and release of prisoners.[30]

(B) Parole and Criminal Justice System

Parole is known as a pre-mature release of offenders after a strict scrutiny of long-term prisoners, under the rules laid down by various governments. Premature release from prison is conditional subject to his behaviour in society and accepting to live under the guidance and supervision of Parole Officer. The world 'parole' means "a term to designate conditional release granted in a penal institution."[31] So in the parole, part of the sentence is served and it is then that convict is released on parole on condition of good behaviour and if he is found to have improved and abstained from criminal conduct, he gets remission of the rest of the sentence and for sometime at least a part of the sentence.[32]

Thus, what is now called parole was from its start tied to the concepts of offender reformation and indeterminacy in sentencing. Walter Clofton in 1870, (in-charge of Irish Prison) advocated reform of the individual as a purpose of imprisonment and moreover, urged that "tickets of leave" be given to those who showed a change in attitude. Those released by a ticket for leave were supervised either by police or by an Inspector of released prisoners. Finally, the paroling function may be important as 'safety valve' to help control the levels of

---

29. *Ibid.*, Sec. 52.
30. *Ibid.*, Sec. 59(24-27).
31. See, J.P.S. Sirohi, *Criminology and Criminal Administration*, (1992), p. 264.
32. *Ibid.*

prison populations in relation to capacities, and thus to avert the dangers and costs of overcrowding. In some jurisdictions, boards have been directed by courts to speed up parole for some offenders so as to relieve prison crowding. In others, programmes of early parole for selected offender have been designed with the explicit aim of avoiding additional prison construction.[33]

Parole is the procedure through which prisoners are selected for release and the service through which they are furnished guidance, control and assistance in serving the last part of their sentence within the free community. Society has a real interest in the release of prisoners, since these individuals have been committed for definite terms by the criminal justice system, and release on parole sometimes seems to fly in the face of the sentence that was meted out.[34] It is, therefore, important that the parole system include both a careful selection process for those to be released, as well as a workable system for supervision after the selection is made.

In India prison life did not emerge out of the social movements but they were the outcomes of the worst conditions of treatment in prisons which our political sufferers faced during the prison life. They repeatedly launched protests with the prison authorities and made all possible efforts to see that the rigours of prison life are mitigated and the prisoners are humanly treated. In the meantime the reformatory movement which was gaining strength in the field of penology all over the world also gave impetus to the cause of corrective methods of treatment of the offenders rather than keeping them confined into the small prison cells.

Parole involves supervision, as compared with other types of releases from prison, such as discharge, conditional release, expiration of sentence and mandatory release. Release by court order, pardon, or escape, of course do not involve parole supervision.[35] It is a function of the executive branch of Government. It is based on the Chief Executive's right to commute or suspend sentences imposed by courts. The

---

33. See, Sanford H. Kadish, *Encyclopedia of Crime and Justice*, (1983), pp. 1249-51.
34. See, *supra* note 2 p. 257.
35. See, *supra* note 1, p. 416.

authority to release offenders for cause and good conduct is usually delegated to a Parole Board. Release on Parole is generally based on inmate readiness, past conduct and a prognosis for success. The prisoner signs a parole agreement. If the agreement is violated or a new crime committed, the parolee may be returned to prison following a revocation hearing.[36]

The Parole Board consists of parole administrators, who are from among the respectable members of society. The members of the Parole Board are assigned the function of discharging convicted prisoners on parole after careful scrutiny. The Parole board takes administrative decision on paroling out prisoners and while acting as such they are performing a quasi-judicial function.[37] Another important function assigned to the parole personnel is to prepare a case history of parolees and help and advise them in the process of their rehabilitation. There is also a set of field workers functioning outside the prisons. These field personnel keep a close supervision over parolees and report the cases of parole violations to the parole authorities. Thus the parole organisation consists of three agencies, viz. the Parole board, the case investigation and the parole supervisors; all of them work in close liaison with each other.[38]

The system of parole serve to met the ends of justice in two ways. Firstly, it serves as an effective punishment by itself in as much as a parolee is deterred from repeating crimes due to the threat of his return to prison or a similar institution if they violated parole conditions. Secondly, it serves as an efficient measure of safety and treatment reaction to crime by affording a series of opportunities for the parolee to prepare himself for the normal life in society.[39]

The parole system as a corrective measure and rehabilitative process has now, been expanded in the form of open jails and open air camps in recent years. Open air-institutions are essentially a twentieth century device for

---

36. See, Harry W. More, *Principles and Procedure in the Administration of Justice*, (1975), p. 19.

37. See, N.V. Paranjape, *Criminology and Penology*, (2001), p. 332.

38. *Ibid.*

39. See, N.V. Paranjape, *Criminology and Administration of Criminal Justice*, (1970), p. 185.

rehabilitating offenders to normal life in the society through an intensive after-care programme.

(C) Probation and Criminal Justice System

In criminal justice system 'probation' means the conditional suspension of imposition of a sentence by the court, in selected cases, especially of young offenders, who are not sent to prison but are released on probation, on agreeing to abide by certain conditions. Word 'probation' is derived from the Latin word, *'Probera'*, which means 'to test' or 'to prove'. Homer S. Cunings has observed that probation is a matter of discipline and treatment. If the probationers are carefully chosen and supervision work is performed with intelligence and understanding one can work miracles in rehabilitation of the offenders.[40]

Probation is a form of criminal sanction imposed by a court upon an offender, nearly always after a verdict or a plea of guilty but without the prior imposition of a term of imprisonment. Probation may be linked to a jail term, known as a split sentence, whereby the judge sentences the offender to a specified jail term to be followed by a specified period on release on probation.[41]

An international definition of probation is that it consists of "the conditional suspension of punishment while the offender is placed under personal supervision and is given individual guidance or treatment."[42] The object of probation is the protection of society by preventing the crime through rehabilitation of the offender in the society as its useful member without curbing his freedom, subjecting him to unsavory prison life and depriving him of his social and economic obligations.[43]

Probation system is not the outcome of any deliberate legislative or judicial action but grew gradually as a result of some kind of hearted ordinary citizen's concern for young

---

40. See, Harudaya Ballav Das, *A Study on the Prospect of Reformative Criminal Justice with Special Reference to Probation of Offender Act and Law Relating to Victimology*, CrLJ, June, 1991, p. 66.
41. See, *supra* note 33, p. 1240.
42. See, J.C. Mcclean, *Criminal Justice and Treatment of Offenders*, (1960), p. 158.
43. See, K.D. Gaur, *Criminal Law and Criminology*, (2002), p. 52.

offender in custody.[44] The history of probation can be traced back to the medieval concept of 'benefit of clergy' permitted clergy and other literates to escape the severity of the criminal law. It meant suspension of the execution of sentence for an indefinite period as long as the delinquent behaved well.

In Indian probation is used as an institutional method of treatment which is a necessary appendage of the concept of crime. Probation developed as an alternative to imprisonment especially of short-term, has now taken within its wings all the offences except those punishable with death or imprisonment for life. The current compelling constraints of Section 361 of the Code of Criminal Procedure, 1973, have made probation as a more viable method of dealing with offenders than imprisonment, because judge is required to record special reasons for not granting probation to all the eligible offenders irrespective of their age.[45]

The first legislative effort appears in India when probation received statutory recognition for the first time in 1898 through Section 562 of the Code of Criminal Procedure, 1898.[46] Under the provision of this section, the first offender convicted of theft, dishonest, mis-appropriation or any other offence under the Indian Penal Code punishable with not more than two years' imprisonment could be released on probation of good conduct at the discretion of the court. Later, the Children Act, 1908 also empowered the court to release certain offenders on probation of good conduct.

The scope of probation law was extended further by the legislation in 1923. Consequent upon the Indian Jail Reforms Committee's Report (1919-20), the first offenders were to be treated more liberally and could ever be released unconditionally after admonition. Then the Government of India in 1931, prepared a draft of Probation of Offender Bill and circulate it to the provincial governments for their views. The Bill could not, however, be proceeded further due to pre-occupation of the provincial Governments.[47] In 1934,

---

44. See, *supra* note 31, p. 231.
45. See, *supra* note 43, p. 898.
46. The Code of Criminal Procedure, 1973, Sec. 360.
47. See, V.N. Paranjape, *Criminology and Penology*, (2005), pp. 447-48.

Government of India, informed the local governments that there were no prospects of the central legislation being enacted on probation and they were free to enact suitable laws on the lines of the draft Bill.

After independence, a Probation Conference was held in Bombay in 1952. This conference was milestone in progress of probation law in India. Consequently, All India Jail Manual Committee was formed to review the working of Indian Jail and suggest measures for reform in the system.[48] The Committee also highlighted the need for a central law on probation with greater emphasis on release of offenders on probation of good conduct so that they are reclaimed as self-reliant members of society.[49] Thus, with a reformative bias and to insure this concept in the arena of administration of criminal justice, the Probation of Offenders' Act was enacted in 1958 in India to provide correctional services to the offenders. In other words, it is a curative jurisprudence in dealing with the offenders and more particularly it relates to first offenders, where no previous conviction is proved against them. The whole object of the Act is to prevent conversion of youthful offenders into obdurate criminals of matured age, in case they are sentenced to undergo substantive imprisonment in jail.[50] The provisions of Probation of Offenders' Act, which brings about reform of the offenders and for their disciplined conduct and rehabilitation and normal life in society.

When any person is found guilty of having committed an offence punishable under Section 379 or Section 380 or Section 381 or Section 404 or Section 420 of the Indian Penal Code (45 of 1860) or any offence punishable with imprisonment for not more than two years, or with fine, or with both, under the Indian Penal Code or any other law, and no previous conviction is proved against him and the court, by which the person is found guilty is of opinion that, having regard to the circumstances of the case including the nature of the offence and the character of the offender, it is expedient so to do, then, notwithstanding anything contained in any other law for the

---

48. *Ibid.*
49. All India Jail Manual Committee Report (1957), para 135.
50. See, *supra* note 40, p. 66.

time being in force, the court may, instead of sentencing him to any punishment or releasing him on probation of good conduct.[51]

When any person is found guilty of having committed an offence not punishable with death or imprisonment for life and the court by which the person is found guilty is of opinion that, having regard to the circumstances of the case including the nature of the offence and the character of the offender, it is expedient to release him on probation of good conduct, then, notwithstanding any thing contained in any other law for the time being in force, the court may, instead of sentencing him at once to any punishment, direct that he be released on his entering into a bond, with or without sureties, to appear and receive sentence when called upon during such period, not exceeding three years, as the court may direct, and in the meantime to keep the peace and be of good behavior:

Provided that the court shall not direct such release of an offender unless it is satisfied that the offender or his surety, if any, has a fixed place of abode or regular occupation in the place over which the court exercises jurisdiction or in which the offender is likely to live during the period for which he enters into the bond.[52]

Before making any order, the court shall take into consideration the report, if any, of the probation officer concerned in relation to the case.

When an order is made, the court may, if it is of opinion that in the interests of the offender and of the public it is expedient so to do, in addition pass a supervision order directing that the offender shall remain under the supervision of a probation officer named in the order during such period, not being less than one year, as may be specified therein, and may in such supervision order impose such conditions as it deems necessary for the due supervision of the offender.

The court making a supervision order shall require the offender, before he is released, to enter into a bond, with or without sureties, to observe the conditions specified in such order and such additional conditions with respect to residence,

---

51. The Probation of Offenders' Act, 1958, Sec. 3.
52. *Ibid.*, Sec. 4(1).

abstention from intoxicants or any other matter as the court may, having regard to the particular circumstances, consider fit to impose for preventing a repetition of the same offence or a commission of other offences by the offender.[53]

The court making a supervision order shall explain to the offender the terms and conditions of the order and shall forthwith furnish one copy of the supervision order to each of the offenders, the sureties, if any, and the probation officer concerned.

The Court directing the release of an offender may, if it thinks fit, make at the same time a further order directing him to pay such compensation as the court thinks reasonable for loss or injury caused to 'any person by the commission of the offence; and such costs of the proceedings as the court thinks reasonable'.[54]

When any person under twenty-one years of age is found guilty of having committed an offence punishable with imprisonment (but not with imprisonment for life), the court by which the person is found guilty shall not sentence him to imprisonment unless it, is satisfied that, having regard, to the circumstances of the case including the nature of the offence and the character of the offender.

For the purpose of satisfying itself whether it would not be desirable to deal with an offender the court shall call for a report from the probation officer and consider the report, if any, and any other information available to it relating to the character and physical and mental condition of the offender.[55]

The report of a probation officer shall be treated as confidential; provided that the court may, if it so thinks fit, communicate the substance thereof to the offender and may give him an opportunity of Producing such evidence as may be relevant to the matter stated in the report.[56]

If, on the application of probation officer, any court which passes an order in respect of an offender is of opinion that in the interests of the offender and the public it is expedient or necessary to vary the conditions of any bond entered into by the

---

53. *Ibid.*, Sec. Sec. 4(4).
54. *Ibid.*, Sec. 5.
55. *Ibid.*, Sec. 6.
56. *Ibid.*, Sec. 7.

offender, it may, at any time during the period when the bond is effective, vary the bond by extending or diminishing the duration thereof, so, however, that it shall not exceed three years from the date of the original order or by altering the conditions thereof or by inserting additional conditions therein. Provided that no such variation shall be made without giving the offender and the surety or sureties mentioned in the bond an opportunity of being heard.[57]

If any surety refuses to consent to any variation proposed to be made, the court may require the offender to enter into a fresh bond and if the offender refuses or fails to do so, the court may sentence him for the offence.

Notwithstanding anything hereinbefore contained, the court which passes an order in respect of an offender may, if it is satisfied on an application made by the probation officer that the conduct of the offender has been such as to make it unnecessary that he should be kept any longer under supervision, discharge the bond or bonds entered into by him.[58]

If the court which passes an order in respect of an offender or any court which could have dealt with the offender in respect of his original offence has reason to believe on the report of a probation officer or otherwise, that the offender has failed to observe any of the conditions of the bond or bonds entered into by him, it may issue a warrant for his arrest or may, if it thinks fit, issue a summon to him and his sureties, if any, requiring him or them to attend before it at such time as may be specified in the summons.

The court before which an offender is so brought or appears may either remand him to custody until the case is concluded or it may grant him bail, with or without surety, to appear on the date, which it may fix for hearing.[59]

If the court, after hearing the case, is satisfied that the offender has failed to observe any of the conditions of the bond or bonds entered into by him, it may forthwith sentence him for the original offence; or where the failure is for the first time,

57. *Ibid.*, Sec. 8(1).
58. *Ibid.*, Sec. 8(3).
59. *Ibid.*, Sec. 9(2).

then without prejudice to the continuance in force of the bond, impose upon him a penalty not exceeding fifty rupees.[60]

In any case where any person under twenty-one years of age is found guilty of having committed an offence and the court by which he is found guilty declines to deal with him, and passes against him any sentence of imprisonment with or without fine from which no appeal lies or is preferred, then, notwithstanding anything contained in the Code or any other law, the court to which appeals ordinarily lie from the sentences of the former court may, either of its own motion or on an application made to it by the convicted person or the probation officer, call for and examine the record of the case and pass such order thereon as it thinks fit. When an order has been made in respect of an offender, the Appellate Court or the High Court in the exercise of its power of revision may set aside such order and in lieu thereof pass sentence on such offender according to law. Provided that the Appellate Court or the High Court in revision shall not inflict a greater punishment than might have been inflicted by the court by which the offender was found guilty.[61]

A probation officer under the Probation of Offenders Act, 1958 shall be a person appointed to be a probation officer by the State Government or recognised as such by the State Government; or a person provided for this purpose by a society recognised in this behalf by the State Government; or in any exceptional case, any other person whom in the opinion of the court, is fit to act as a probation officer in the special circumstances of the case.[62]

A court which passes an order or the District Magistrate of the district in which the offender for the time being resides may, at any time, appoint any probation officer in the place of the person named in the supervision order.

"A presidency town shall be deemed to be a district and Chief Presidency Magistrate shall be deemed to be the District Magistrate of that district."

A probation officer, in the exercise of his duties under this

---

60. *Ibid.*, Sec. 9(3).
61. *Ibid.*, Sec. 11.
62. *Ibid.*, Sec. 13(1).

Act, shall be subject to the control of the District Magistrate of the district, in which the offender for the time being resides.[63]

A probation officer shall, subject to such conditions and restrictions, as may be prescribed—inquire, in accordance with any directions of a court, into the circumstances or home surroundings of any person accused of all offence with a view to assist the court ill determining the most suitable method of dealing with him and submit reports to the court; supervise probationers and other persons placed under his supervision and, where necessary, endeavour to find them suitable employment; advise and assist offenders in the payment of compensation or costs ordered by the court; advise and assist, in such cases and in such manner as may be prescribed, persons who have been released; and perform such other duties as may be prescribed.[64]

Every probation officer and every other officer appointed shall be deemed to be public servants within the meaning of Section 21 of the Indian Penal Code.[65]

No suit or other legal proceeding shall lie against the State Government or any probation officer or any other officer appointed in respect of anything which is in good faith done or intended to be done in pursuance of any rules or orders.[66]

The State Government may, with the approval of the Central Government, by notification in the official Gazette make rules to carry out the purposes of the Probation of Offenders' Act.

In particular, and without prejudice to the generality of the foregoing power such rules may provide for all or any of the following matters,[67] namely:

(a) Appointment of probation officers, the terms and conditions of their service and the area within which they are to exercise jurisdiction;
(b) Duties of probation officers under this Act and the submission of reports by them;

---

63. *Ibid.*, Sec. 13(3).
64. *Ibid.*, Sec. 14.
65. *Ibid.*, Sec. 15.
66. *Ibid.*, Sec. 16.
67. *Ibid.*, Sec. 17(2).

(c) The payment of remuneration and expenses to probation officers or of a subsidy to any society which provides probation officers; and

(e) Any other matter which is to be, or may be, prescribed.

All rules made shall be subject to the condition of previous publication and shall, as soon as may be after they are made, be laid before the State Legislature.

(D) Juvenile and Criminal Justice System

The child of today is the citizen of tomorrow, the criminal traits of the youngsters must be suppressed in time so as to prevent them from becoming hardened criminals in future. It is with this aim in view that most of the countries of the world are engaged in handling the problem of juvenile delinquents on priority basis.

Early penology did not recongise any discrimination between adult and the juvenile offenders so far punishment to them was concerned. Therefore, the problem of juvenile delinquency is essentially a recent origin. The movement for special treatment to juvenile offenders started by the end of 18th century. Prior to that, even young boys were equally punished to death like adults under the law.[68] The great majority of historians have celebrated the court's mission as savior of unfortunate youth and portrayed is as the greatest achievement of a generation whose solicitous concern for children marked a revolution in human sensibility.[69]

Juvenile delinquency refers to conduct of children or youths that is either violative of the prohibitions of the criminal law or is otherwise regarded as deviant and inappropriate. The juvenile justice system is an alternative to the criminal justice system.[70] The term 'delinquency' has been derived from the Latin word 'delinquer' which means 'to omit'. The Romans used the term to refer to the failure of a person to perform the

---

68. See, *supra* note 39, p. 192.
69. See, Sanford H. Kadish, *Encyclopedia of Crime and Justice,* (1983), p. 450.
70. See, Sanford H. Kadish, *Encyclopedia of Crime and Justice*, Vol. 2, (1983), p. 583.

assigned task or duty. In simpler words it may be said that delinquency is a form of behaviour or rather misbehaviour or deviation from the general accepted norms of conduct of the society. [71]

Juvenile delinquency is a gateway to adult crime, since a large percentage of criminal careers had their roots in childhood. It is a problem that has been causing a serious concern all over the world. In recent years, children and their problems have been receiving attention both of the Government and also of the society. Like any other countries of the world, India have also envisaged to tackle the problem of juvenile delinquency on two fundamental principles that the young offenders should not be 'tried' but they should rather be 'corrected' and they should not be 'punished' but 'reformed'. [72] To attain this objective adequate provisions under Sections 82 and 83 of the Indian Penal Code, 1860 have been made. [73] Again, Section 360 of the Code of Criminal Procedure, 1973 provides that "when any person who is below twenty-one years of age is convicted of an offence punishable with fine only or with imprisonment for a term of seven years or less, or when any person under twenty-one years of age or any woman is convicted of an offence not punishable with death or imprisonment for a life and no previous conviction is proved against the offender." Section 27 of the Code of Criminal Procedure also suggests that a lenient treatment to juveniles has already received statutory recognition in the Indian law. The Section provides that if a person below sixteen years of age commits an offence other than the one punishable with death of imprisonment for life, he should be awarded a lenient punishment depending on his previous history, character and circumstances which led him to commit the crime. His sentence can further be commuted for good behaviour during the term of his imprisonment. [74]

To provide for the care, protection, treatment, development and rehabilitation of neglected or delinquent juveniles and for the adjudication of certain matters relating to, and disposition

---

71. See, *supra* note 47, p. 486.
72. See, *supra* note 39, p. 196.
73. For details see, the Indian Penal Code, 1860, Ss. 82 and 83.
74. See, Ahmad Siddique, *Criminology*, (2005), p. 574.

of, delinquent juvenile the Juvenile Justice Act, 1986 was enacted by Parliament. Several provisions of the Constitution including Clause (3) of Article 15, Clause (e) and (f) of Article 39, Article 45 and Article 47 also impose on the State a primary responsibility of ensuring that all the needs of children are met and that their basic human rights are fully protected. On 20th November, 1989 General Assembly of the United Nations adopted the Convention on the Rights of the Child wherein a set of standards to be adhered to by all State parties in securing the best interests of the child has been prescribed. The Convention emphasizes social reintegration of child victims, to the extent possible, without resorting to judicial proceedings. The Government of India, having ratified the Convention, has found it expedient to re-enact the existing law relating to juveniles bearing in mind the standards prescribed in the Convention of the Rights of the Child, the United Nations Standard Minimum Rules for the Administration of Juvenile Justice, 1985, the United Nations Rules for the Protection of Juveniles Deprived of their Liberty 1990, and all other relevant international instruments. To achieve this object the Juvenile Justice (Care and Protection of Children) Bill was introduced in Parliament and it came on the statute book as the Juvenile Justice (Care and Protection of Children) Act, 2000.

Where an inquiry has been initiated against a juvenile in conflict with law or a child in need of care and protection and during the course of such inquiry the juvenile or the child ceases to be such, then, notwithstanding anything contained in this Act or in any other law for the time being in force, the inquiry may be continued and orders may be made in respect of such person as if such person had continued to be a juvenile or a child.[75]

Notwithstanding anything contained in the Code of Criminal Procedure, 1973, the State Government may, by notification in the Official Gazette, constitute for a district or a group of districts specified in the notification, one or more Juvenile Justice Boards for exercising the powers and discharging the duties conferred or imposed on such Boards in relation to juveniles in conflict with law.[76]

---

75. The Juvenile Justice (Care and Protection of Children) Act, 2000.
76. *Ibid.*, Sec. 4(1).

A Board shall consist of a Metropolitan Magistrate or a Judicial Magistrate of the first class, as the case may be, and two social workers of whom at least one shall be a woman, forming a Bench and every such Bench shall have the powers conferred by the Code of Criminal Procedure, 1973, on a Metropolitan Magistrate or, as the case may be, a Judicial Magistrate of the first class and the Magistrate on the Board shall be designated as the principal Magistrate.[77]

No Magistrate shall be appointed as a member of the Board unless he has special knowledge or training in child psychology or child welfare and no social worker shall be appointed as a member of the Board unless he has been actively involved in health education, or welfare activities pertaining to children for at least seven years.

The term of office of the members of the Board and the manner in which such member may resign shall be such as may be prescribed.[78]

The appointment of any member of the Board may be terminated after holding inquiry, by the State Government,[79] if:

(i) He has been found guilty of misuse of power vested,

(ii) He has been convicted of an offence involving moral turpitude, and such conviction has not been reversed or he has not been granted full pardon in respect of such offence, and

(iii) He fails to attend the proceedings of the Board for consecutive three months without any valid reason or he fails to attend less than three-fourth of the sittings in a year.

The Board shall meet at such times and shall observe such rules of procedure in regard to the transaction of business at its meetings, as may be prescribed. A child in conflict with law may be produced before an individual member of the Board, when the Board is not sitting.

A Board may act notwithstanding the absence of any member of the Board, and no order made by the Board shall be

---

77. *Ibid.*, Sec. 4(2).
78. *Ibid.*, Sec. 4(4).
79. *Ibid.*, Sec. 4(5).

invalid by reason only of the absence of any member during any stage of proceedings: Provided that there shall be at least two members including the principal Magistrate present at the time of final disposal of the case.

In the event of any difference of opinion among the members of the Board in the interim or final disposition, the opinion of the majority shall prevail, but where there is no such majority, the opinion of the principal Magistrate shall prevail.[80]

Where a Board has been constituted for any district or a group of districts, such Board shall, notwithstanding anything contained in any other law for the time being in force but save as otherwise expressly provided in this Act, have power to deal exclusively with all proceedings relating to juvenile in conflict with law.

The powers conferred on the Board by or may also be exercised by the High Court and the Court of Session, when the proceeding comes before them in appeal, revision or otherwise.[81]

When any Magistrate not empowered to exercise the powers of a Board is of the opinion that a person brought before him is a juvenile or the child, he shall without any delay record such opinion and forward the juvenile or the child and the record of the proceeding to the competent authority having jurisdiction over the proceeding.

The competent authority to which the proceeding is forwarded shall hold the inquiry as if the juvenile or the child had originally been brought before it.[82]

Any State Government may establish and maintain either by itself or under an agreement with voluntary organisations, observation homes in every district or a group of districts, as may be required for the temporary reception of nay juvenile in conflict with law during the pendency of any inquiry regarding them.

Where the State Government is of opinion that any institution other than a home established or maintained, is fit for the temporary reception of juvenile in conflict with law

---

80. *Ibid.*, Sec. 5.
81. *Ibid.*, Sec. 6.
82. *Ibid.*, Sec. 7.

during the pendency of any inquiry regarding them under this Act, it may certify such institution as an observation home.

The State Government may provide for the management of observation homes, including the standards and various types of services to be provided by them for rehabilitation and social integration of a juvenile, and the circumstances under which, and the manner in which, the certification of an observation home may be granted or withdrawn.[83]

Every juvenile who is not placed under the charge of parent or guardian and is sent to an observation home shall be initially kept in a reception unit of the observation home for preliminary inquiries, care and classification for juveniles according to his age group, such as seven to twelve years, twelve to sixteen years and sixteen to eighteen years, giving due considerations to physical and mental status and degree of the offence committed, for further induction into observation home.[84]

Any State Government may establish and maintain either by itself or under an agreement with voluntary organisations, special homes in every district or a group of districts, as may be required for reception and rehabilitation of juvenile in conflict with law.

Where the State Government is of opinion that any institution other than a home established or maintained, is fit for the reception of juvenile in conflict with law to be sent there, it may certify such institution as a special home.

The State Government may, provide for the management of special homes, including the standards and various types of services to be provided by them which are necessary for re-socialisation of a juvenile, and the circumstances under which, and the manner in which, the certification of a special home may be granted or withdrawn.

The rules may also provide for the classification and separation of juvenile in conflict with law on the basis of age and the nature of offences committed by them and his mental and physical status.[85]

---

83. *Ibid.*, Sec. 8(3).
84. *Ibid.*, Sec. 8(4).
85. *Ibid.*, Sec. 9.

Any person in whose charge a juvenile is placed in pursuance of the Juvenile Justice Act shall, while the order is in force have the control over the juvenile as he would have if he were his parents, and shall be responsible for his maintenance, and the juvenile shall continue in his charge for the period stated by competent authority, notwithstanding that he is claimed by his parents or any other person.[86]

When any person accused of a bailable or non-bailable offence, and apparently a juvenile, is arrested or detained or appears or is brought before a Board, such person shall, notwithstanding anything contained in the Code of Criminal Procedure, 1973 or in any other law for the time being in force, be released on bail with or without surety but he shall not be so released if there appear reasonable grounds for believing that the release is likely to bring him into association with any known criminal or expose him to moral, physical or psychological danger or that his release would defeat the ends of justice.

When such person having been arrested is not released on bail by the officer-in-charge of the police station, such officer shall cause him to be kept only in an observation home in the prescribed manner until he can be brought before a Board.

When such person is not released on bail by the Board it shall, instead of committing him to prison, make an order sending him to an observation home or a place of safety for such period during the pendency of the inquiry regarding him as may be specified in the order.[87]

Where a juvenile is arrested, the officer-in-charge of the police station or the special juvenile police unit to which the juvenile is brought shall, as soon as may be after the arrest, inform:[88]

(a) The parent or guardian of the juvenile, if he can be found of such arrest and direct him to be present at the Board before which the juvenile will appear; and

(b) The probation officer of such arrest to enable him to obtain information regarding the antecedents and

---

86. *Ibid.*, Sec. 11.
87. *Ibid.*, Sec. 12.
88. *Ibid.*, Sec. 13.

family background of the juvenile and other material circumstances likely to be of assistance to the Board for making the inquiry

Where a juvenile having been charged with the offence is produced before a Board, the Board shall hold the inquiry in accordance with the provisions of this Act and may make such order in relation to the juvenile as it deems fit: Provided that an inquiry shall be completed within as period of four months from the date of its commencement, unless the period is extended by the Board having regard to the circumstances of the case and in special cases after recording the reasons in writing for such extension.[89]

Where a Board is satisfied on inquiry that a juvenile has committed an offence, then, notwithstanding anything to the contrary contained in any other law for the time being in force, the Board may, if it thinks so fit:[90]

(a) Allow the juvenile to go home after advice or admonition following appropriate inquiry against and counselling to the parent or the guardian and the juvenile;

(b) Direct the juvenile to participate in group counselling and similar activities;

(c) Order the juvenile to perform community service;

(d) Order the parent of the juvenile or the juvenile himself to pay a fine, if he is over fourteen years of age and earns money;

(e) Direct the juvenile to be released on probation of good conduct and placed under the care of any parent, guardian or other fit person, on such parent, guardian or other fit person executing a bond, with or without surety, as the Board may require, for the good behaviour and well-being of the juvenile for any period not exceeding three years;

(f) Direct the juvenile to be released on probation of good conduct and placed under the care of any fit institution

---

89. *Ibid.*, Sec. 14.
90. *Ibid.*, Sec. 15(1).

for the good behaviour and well-being of the juvenile for any period not exceeding three years;

(g) Make an order directing the juvenile to be sent to a special home:

    (i)   In the case of juvenile, over seventeen years but less than eighteen years of age for a period of not less than two years; and

    (ii)   In case of any other juvenile for the period until he ceases to be a juvenile: Provided that the Board may, if it is satisfied that having regard to the nature of the offence and the circumstances of the case it is expedient so to do, for reasons to be recorded, reduce the period of stay to such period as it thinks fit.

The Board shall obtain the social investigation report on juvenile either through a probation officer or a recognised voluntary organisation or otherwise, and shall take into consideration the findings of such report before passing an order.

Where an order is made, the Board may, if it is of opinion that in the interests of the juvenile and of the public, it is expedient so to do, in addition make an order that the juvenile in conflict with law shall remain under the supervision of a probation officer named in the order during such period, not exceeding three years as may be specified therein, and may in such supervision order impose such conditions as it deems necessary for the due supervision of the juvenile in conflict with law: Provided that if at any time afterwards it appears to the Board on receiving a report from the probation officer or otherwise, that the juvenile in conflict with law has not been of good behaviour during the period of supervision or that the fit institute on under whose care the juvenile was placed is no longer able or willing to ensure the good behaviour and well-being of the juvenile it may, after making such inquiry as it deems fit, order the juvenile in conflict with law to be sent to a special home.[91]

---

91. *Ibid.*, Sec. 15(3).

The Board shall while making a supervision order, explain to the juvenile and the parent, guardian or other fit person or fit institution, as the case may be, under whose care the juvenile has been placed, the terms and conditions of the order and shall forthwith furnish one copy of the supervision order to the juvenile, the parent, guardian or other fit person or fit institution, as the case may be, the sureties, if any, and the probation officer.[92]

Notwithstanding anything to the contrary contained in any other law for the time being in force, any police officer may take charge without warrant of a juvenile in conflict with law who has escaped from a special home or an observation home or from the care of a person under whom he was placed, and shall be sent back to the special home or the observation home or that person, as the case may be; and no proceeding shall be instituted in respect of the juvenile by reason of such escape, but the special home, or the observation home or the person may, after giving the information to the Board which passed the order in respect of the juvenile, take such steps in respect of the juvenile as may be seemed necessary.[93]

Whoever, having the actual charge of or control over, a juvenile or the child, assaults, abandons, exposes or wilfully neglects the juvenile or causes or procures him to be assaulted, abandoned, exposed or neglected in a manner likely to cause such juvenile or the child unnecessary mental or physical suffering shall be punishable with imprisonment for a term which may extend to six months, or fine, or with both.[94]

Whoever, employs or uses any juvenile or the child for the purpose or causes any juvenile to beg shall be punishable with imprisonment for a term which may extend to three years and shall also be liable to fine.

Whoever, having the actual charge of, or control over, a juvenile or the child abets the commission of the offence punishable, shall be punishable with imprisonment for a term which may extend to one year and shall also be liable to fine.[95]

The State Government may, by notification in Official Gazette, constitute for every district or group of districts,

92. *Ibid.*, Sec. 15(4).
93. *Ibid.*, Sec. 22.
94. *Ibid.*, Sec. 23.
95. *Ibid.*, Sec. 24.

specified in the notification, one or more Child Welfare Committees for exercising the powers and discharge the duties conferred on such Committees in relation to child in need of care and protection.[96]

The Committee shall consist of a Chairperson and four other members as the State Government may think fit to appoint, of whom at least one shall be a woman and another, an expert on matters concerning children.

The qualifications of the Chairperson and the members, and the tenure for which they may be appointed shall be such as may be prescribed.[97]

The Committee shall function as a Bench of Magistrates and shall have the powers conferred by the Code of Criminal Procedure, 1973 on a Metropolitan Magistrate or, as the case may be, a Judicial Magistrate of the first class.

The Committee shall meet at such times and shall observe such rules of procedure in regard to the transition of business at its meetings, as may be prescribed.

A child in need of care and protection may be produced before an individual member for being placed in safe custody or otherwise when the Committee is not in session.

In the event of any difference of opinion among the members of the Committee at the time of any interim decision, the opinion of the majority shall prevail but where there is no such majority the opinion of the Chairperson shall prevail.

The Committee may act, notwithstanding the absence of any member of the Committee, and no order made by the Committee shall be invalid by reason only of the absence of any member during any stage of the proceeding.[98]

The Committee shall have the final authority to dispose of cases for the care, protection, treatment, development and rehabilitation of the children as well as to provide for their basic needs and protection of human right.

Where a Committee has been constituted for any area, such Committee shall, notwithstanding anything contained in any other law for the time being in force but save as otherwise

---

96. *Ibid.*, Sec. 29(1).
97. *Ibid.*, Sec. 29(3).
98. *Ibid.*, Sec. 30.

expressly provided have the power to deal exclusively with all proceedings relating to children in need of care and protection.[99]

Any child in need of care and protection may be produced before the Committee by one of the following persons:

(i) Any police officer or special juvenile police unit or a designated police officer;

(ii) Any public servant;

(iii) Child line, a registered voluntary organisation or by such other voluntary organisation or an agency as may be recognised by the State Government;

(iv) Any social worker or a public spirited citizen authorised by the State Government; or

(v) By the child himself.

The State Government may make rules provide for the manner of making the report to the police and to the Committee and the manner of sending and entrusting the child to children's home pending the inquiry.[100]

The Committee or any police officer or special juvenile police unit or the designated police officer shall hold an inquiry, may pass an order to send the child to the children's home for speedy inquiry by a social worker or child welfare officer. Manner and the Committee, on its own or on the report from any person.

The inquiry shall be completed within four months of the receipt of the order or within such shorter period as may be fixed by the Committee: Provided that the time for the submission of the inquiry report may be extended by such period as the Committee may, having regard to the circumstances and for the reasons recorded in writing, determine.

After the completion of the inquiry if the Committee is of the opinion that the said child has no family or ostensible support, it may allow the child to remain in the children's home or shelter home till suitable rehabilitation is found for him or till he attains the age of eighteen years.[101]

---

99. *Ibid.*, Sec. 31.
100. *Ibid.*, Sec. 32.
101. *Ibid.*, Sec. 33.

The State Government may establish and maintain either by itself or in association with the voluntary organisations, children's homes, in every district or group of districts, as the case may be, for the reception of child in need of care and protection during the pendency of any inquiry and subsequently for their care, treatment, education, training, development and rehabilitation.

The State Government may, by rules made under this Act, provide for the management of children's homes including the standards and the nature of services to be provided by them, and the circumstances under which, and the manner in which, the certification of a children's home or recognition to a voluntary organisation may be granted or withdrawn.[102]

The State Government may appoint inspection committees for the children's homes (hereinafter referred to as the inspection committees) for the State, a district and city, as the case may be, for such period and for such purposes as may be prescribed.

The inspection committee of a State, district or of a city shall consist of such number of representatives from the State Government, local authority, Committee, voluntary organisations and such other medical experts and social workers as may be prescribed.[103]

The rehabilitation and social reintegration of a child shall begin during the stay of the child in a children's home or special home and the rehabilitation and social reintegration of children shall be carried out alternatively by:[104]

   (i) Adoption,
  (ii) Foster care,
 (iii) Sponsorship, and
 (iv) Sending the child to an after-care organisation.

The primary responsibility for providing care and protection to children shall be that of his family.

Adoption shall be resorted to for the rehabilitation of such children as are orphaned, abandoned, neglected and abused through institutional and non-institutional methods.

---

102. *Ibid.,* Sec. 34.
103. *Ibid.,* Sec. 35.
104. *Ibid.,* Sec. 40.

In keeping with the provisions of the various guidelines for adoption issued from time to time by the State Government, the Board shall be empowered to give children in adoption and carry out such investigations as are required for giving children in adoption in accordance with the guidelines issued by the State Government from time to time in this regard.

The children's homes or the State Government run institutions for orphans shall be recognised as an adoption agencies both for scrutiny and placement of such children for adoption in accordance with the guidelines.[105]

The State Government may make rules to ensure effective linkages between various governmental, non-governmental, corporate and other community agencies for facilitating the rehabilitation and social reintegration of the child.[106]

The modern criminal jurisprudence has recognised that no one is a born criminal and many crimes are the product of socio-economic conditions and compulsions. Although no much can be done for hardened criminals, considerable stress has been laid on braining about reform of younger offenders, not guilty of very serious offences and of preventing their association with habitual and incorrigible offenders who have taken to crime as a profession for their existence, on whom reformative theory of punishment has absolutely no impact. The modern reformative theory of criminal justice system makes a psycho-analytical study of the social background and economic status of the criminal and takes punishment as a means to a social end and the emphasis is that punishment is not an end itself, but as a means to an end. Reform the criminal and not punish him is the consensus of the opinion of the modern criminologists all over the world.

III. DRAWBACKS IN PRESENT CRIMINAL JUSTICE SYSTEM IN INDIA

The primary task of any government is to protect the personal rights of the people. Security of the person and property of the people is an essential requisite of good

---

105. *Ibid.*, Sec. 41(4).
106. *Ibid.*, Sec. 45.

governance and this can be achieved by the criminal justice system. Prof. Harvart Wachsler has rightly observed:

"Whatever views are held about the penal law, no one will question its importance in society. This is the law on which men place their ultimate reliance for protection against all the deepest injuries that human conduct can inflict on individuals and institutions. By the same token, penal law governs the strongest force that we permit official agencies to bring to bear on individuals its promise as an instrument of safety is matched only by its power to destroy. If penal law is weak or ineffective, basic human interests are in jeopardy. If it is harsh or arbitrary in its impact, it works gross injustice to those caught within its coils. The law that carries such responsibilities should surely be as rational and just as law can be. Nowhere in the entire legal field is more at stake for the community or for the individual."[107]

Effective, efficient and just criminal system of a nation is the backbone of its very foundation. An effective system not only deliver justice but also deliver it in time. India has inherited and borrowed from colonial power system of criminal law and procedures, as well as rules of evidence, courts, police and correctional system. How far this system of criminal justice has succeeded to achieve its two primary goals, the control of crime of individual rights. Crime control implies orderly and efficient method for arresting, prosecuting, convicting and punishing the guilty and for deterring crime by others. The protection of individuals' rights is a necessity to guard the accused against the arbitrary exercise of power by the State. The rising crime rate and the high rate of recidivism clearly indicate that the system is not effective deterrent.[108] Today, cases of murder, rape, theft, assault, robbery, disorderly conduct, corruption and bride burning occur much more than in the past. The open violation of laws, bribery of police, pressure of professional criminals, intimidation of victims and witnesses are experienced in day-to-day life.

---

107. Quoted by Dr. Bharat B. Das, *In Criminal Law Journal*, Journal Section (2005), p. 215.
108. See, Subhash Chander Singh, *Criminal Justice : An Overview*, CrLJ (Journal Section) (1999), p. 45.

Today, what we understand by criminal justice system is somewhat fractured and a centrifugal system with all the segments of the system forcing away from each other leaving at its very focal point. The criminal justice today plagued with many drawbacks :

1. The most important drawback of the system was the ever decreasing rate of conviction in India. Efficacy of criminal justice system in any country is primarily judged on the basis of the conviction rate as it is the ultimate result of the combined efforts of the system. In India, the conviction rate is far from the satisfactory and in a serious matter from overall maintenance of law and order in the society.

2. As a result of poor cooperation between the police, prosecution and the judiciary, the number of cases pending trial has been increasing at a tremendous rate. Cases number few lakhs are estimated to be pending in the various courts in the country.[109] A direct result of this is corresponding increase in the number of under-trial prisoners in the jail and subsequent problems associated with it.

3. It is well known that in States where the criminal justice system was enable to deliver the goods, the unauthorized groups like private army, militant organisations, underworld gangs, etc. have taken over the task of grievance removal at their level. Many States in India are the glaring examples of this fact.[110]

4. Lack of commitment and decreasing coordination and cooperation among various functionaries of the criminal justice system result in failure not only on the part of the police to deliver justice to the victim, but also by the judiciary. This, many time, forces the police to resolve to third degree methods on he suspects. In its enthusiasm to provide fast relief, policemen are slowly falling prey to the shortcut methods.

---

109. 2.87 crore cases in all courts in all types till 30th June, 2004. For more details see, the *Tribune* 25 October, 2005.
110. Ranvir Sena in Bihar, People War Group in Andhra, Daud Gang in Bombay and various militant gangs in Punjab and North-East States.

5. The increasing corruption in the system also attracts attention. As a result of lack of commitment of effective control over functionaries it is not much easier to find the weak link. The corruption in the various levels of the criminal justice system is the direct result of the different units working in isolation and the complete lack of accountability, on the part of functionaries.

6. Due to lack of joint effort on the part of different functionaries, the prison has no longer remained the centre for the reformation of the criminals. Rather all times crime breeds from the prison, as is the experience in number of cases.

7. Increasing lawlessness and decreasing fear of the law in the Indian society are the result of the failure of the criminal justice system to punish the criminals. The fear of punishment as deterrence of committing a crime has evaporated, as a general impression is that nothing serious can happen in the existing system to a law breaker. The criminal justice system in India has failed to establish the certainty of punishment for crime.

8. The lack of commitment shown by the witnesses and advocates, particularly defence council to the goal of criminal justice system has totally vitiated the system. Their cooperation is vital for the just operation of the system.

9. The Governmental functionaries have not realised the importance of non-governmental organisations or voluntary organisations for the success of the criminal justice system. Not seeking their cooperation has resulted in denial of their assistance in solving the problems concerning the operation of criminal justice system cropping up in the practices.

10. The result of the whole chaos is that the people are losing faith in the criminal justice system and this attitude is dangerous for any civilized society and country like India.

IV. SUM-UP

Indian criminal justice system has two primary responsibilities, i.e. prevention and control of crime and the protection of civil rights. The most important factor in preventing and determining crime is the certainty of punishment the efficiency with which who commits crime is arrested, prosecuted, convicted and punished. Efforts should be made to improve the management of prosecution in order to increase the certainty of conviction and punishment for most serious offenders and repeaters. For better administration of criminal justice, recidivists, career criminals and violent offenders need to be prosecuted expeditiously in a selective manner, because these offenders pose a serious threat to the society.

In India, the police, the courts and other correctional agencies tend to be isolated from each as well as from other communities groups, welfare agencies and human- rights institutions. It appears that the administrators of police, courts prisons, and probation services tend to maintain their *status-quo*. As agents and organs of the Government, the police and courts conform to traditional practices and often have relatively little latitude in which and how to operate. The primary goals of criminal justice system can best be secured only through proper co-ordination between the different wings of criminal justice agencies.

Criminal Justice Administration and Judicial Attitude

I. INTRODUCTION

The democratic constitutional systems have always assigned high prestige to the judiciary especially in view of the challenging tasks entrusted to it. The notion of functional independence of the law courts in a democratic country also makes the judiciary too sensitive to its position *vis-a-vis*, other branches of government and the extra-constitutional structures which the democratic system creates for its sustenance.[1] The court system being somewhat away and above the democratic din and bustle, characteristic of the legislatures can play an objective guarding.

The Indian judicial system has a long and glorious history of functional accomplishments and admirable social purpose. The ancient and mediaeval period of Indian history made

---

1. See, P.D. Sharma, *Police and Criminal Justice Administration in India*, (1985), p. 117.

innovations in the field of administration of justice, but, what free India today, has in the name of judicial system is a proud legacy of the British Raj. Notwithstanding, all their hunches and precautionary susceptibilities the Britishers evolved a system of judiciary and criminal justice in country which was a queer-mixture of Anglo-Saxon principles.[2]

The Republican Constitution of India while proclaiming its faith in Western liberalism and parliamentary democracy treated its judiciary with utmost respect and sensitivity. The Supreme Court of India and the High Courts in each States are the apex of the judicial reforms of the country which, for the purposes of dealing with criminal cases consist of a number of courts presided over by Sessions Judges, Metropolitan Magistrates and Judicial Magistrates at different places in each State.[3] With coming into force, the Code of Criminal Procedure, 1973, the judiciary has been separated from the executive as envisaged in Article 50 of the Constitution of India and effect of separation has been established throughout the country.[4]

The functioning of our courts is linked with the image of our judicial system. The image of the courts depends not upon the architectural beauty and the spaciousness of the courts buildings. It also does not depend upon the finally cut robes of the members of the Bench and Bar, not upon the other trappings of the courts. Likewise, the image of the courts does not depend upon long arguments, the number of authorities cited and the erudition displayed in judgements.[5] It depends in the final analysis, upon the way the cases are handled upon the extent of confidence the courts inspire in the parties to the case before upon the promptness or absence of delay in the disposal of cases and upon the approximation of the judicial findings of fact with the realities of the matters.

Administration of criminal justice is provided by a wide range of legislative measures of diverse kinds. But in recent time

---

2. *Ibid.*

3. See, B.S. Sherawal, *Criminal Courts and Justice Delivery System,* Indian Bar Review, Jan-March, 2001, p. 21.

4. For details see, Article 50 of the Constitution of India, 1950.

5. See, H.R. Khanna, *Self-Reflection on Criminal Justice,* Journal of the Indian Law Institute, Vol. 17, No. 4, Oct.-Dec., 1975, p. 508.

judiciary, particularly at the appellate level, has played a vital role in giving creative interpretations leading to broadening and evolving new concepts of criminal justice system. Such judicial role is a marked feature of judicial process, particularly, emanating from the Supreme Court. In this way it would be useful to refer to certain judicial enunciations that go in to make the character of contemporary criminal justice administration.[6] Such enunciations relate to certain vital impacts on the processes of criminal justice administration in India.

II. JUDICIAL CONTROL ON POLICE POWERS

The Indian judiciary led by Supreme Court has exhibited a judicial activism in recognizing and enforcing the laws.

Commenting on the role of legal profession and lawyers in the judicial system, Mr. Justice H.R. Khanna, former Judge of the Supreme Court of India observed that *"the legal profession is designed to be a profession of service . . . service to the community. The important duty of the profession is to act as an interpreter, guide and faithful servant of the community."*

(A) First Information Report, Police Custody and Charge Sheet

The police has been trying to build up an image as a ruthless, oppressive machinery to create terror and thus to prevent crimes. The attitude does not work well and adoption results in the loss of reputation as an effective force in carrying out the task assigned to it. The law responded to the situation by giving more and more safeguards to the accused. The Supreme Court has got an opportunity to dwell on the need for adding more protective rights to the accused in view of the chances of abuse of power by police.

It was held by the Supreme Court in *Thulia Kaili* v. *State of Tamil Nadu*[7] that :

The FIR in Section 154 in the criminal case is an extremely

---

6. See. K.I. Vibhute, *Criminal Justice*, (2004), p. 107.
7. AIR 1973 SC 501.

vital and valuable piece of evidence for the purpose of corroborating the oral evidence adduced at the trial. The importance of the report can hardly be overestimated from the standpoint of the accused. The object of insisting upon prompt lodging of the report to the police in respect of commission of an offence is to obtain early information regarding the circumstances in which the crime was committed. The names of the actual culprits and the part played by them as well as the names of the eye witnesses present at the scene of occurrence. Delay in lodging the F.I.R quite often results in embellishment which is a creature of after thought on account of delay, the report not only get bereft of the advantage of spontaneity. Danger creeps into the introduction of coloured version, exaggerated account or concocted story as a result of deliberation and consultation. It is, therefore, essential that the delay in the lodging the FIR report should be satisfactorily explained.

Supreme Court in *Apren Joseph alias Current Kun Jukunju* v. *State of Kerala*,[8] held that :

the receipt and recording of information report by the police is not a condition precedent to the setting in motion of a criminal investigation. Nor does the statute provide that such information report can only be made by an eye witness. FIR under Section 154 is not even considered a substantive piece of evidence. It can only be used to corroborate or contradict the informant's evidence in court. But this information when recorded is the basis of the case set-up by the informant. It is very useful if recorded before there is time and opportunity to embellish or before the informant's memory fades. Undue or unreasonable delay in lodging the F.I.R., therefore, inevitably gives rise to suspicion which puts the court on guard to look for the possible motive and the explanation for the delay and consider its effect on trustworthiness or otherwise of the prosecution version. No duration of time in the abstract

---

8. AIR 1973 SC 1.

can be fixed as reasonable for giving information of a crime to the police, the question of reasonable time being a matter for determination by the court in each case. Mere delay in lodging the F.I.R. report with the police is, therefore, not necessarily, as a matter of law, fatal to the prosecution. The effect of delay in doing so in the light of the plausibility of the explanation forthcoming for such delay accordingly must fall for consideration on all the facts and circumstances of a given case. It can be used as a previous statement for the purpose of corroboration or contradiction of its maker under Section 157 and Section 145 of the Indian Evidence Act.

In *Hallu* v. *State of M.P.*[9] the Apex Court refused to attach any importance to the circumstance that the names of the appellants were not mentioned in the report on the ground that though it was earliest in point of time it could not be treated as the First Information Report under Section 154 of the Criminal Procedure Code. In this view the Apex Court clearly held that Section 154 does not require that the Report must be given by a person who has personal knowledge of the incident reported. The section speaks of an information relating to the commission of a cognizable offence given to an officer-in-charge of a police station.

In *Pudda Narayana* v. *State of Andhra Pradesh,*[10] the learned counsel appearing for the appellants tried to support the judgment of the learned Additional Sessions Judge and pointed out a number of circumstances which according to him cast a serious doubt on the veracity of the prosecution case. In the first place, it was argued that the learned Additional Sessions Judge rightly held that as the F.I.R., did not contain the overt acts attributed to each of the accused, the story of the prosecution must be held to be an afterthought. Dealing with this aspect of the matter, the High Court pointed out that the F.I.R. was lodged soon after the occurrence and there was no occasion for the informant to have mentioned all the material particulars in the F.I.R. which had to be narrated and proved at the trial.

---

9. AIR 1974 SC 1936.
10. AIR 1975 SC 1252.

Another point taken by the learned Additional Sessions Judge was that in the inquest report details of the overt acts committed by the various accused have not been mentioned in the relevant column. The learned Judge in fact has assumed without any legal justification that because the details were not mentioned in the requisite column of the in-quest report, therefore, the presumption will be that the eye witnesses did not mention the overt acts in their statements before the police. To begin with it seems that the learned Additional Sessions Judge's approach is legally erroneous. A statement recorded by the police during the investigation is not at all admissible and the proper procedure is to confront the witnesses with the contradictions

In *Balaka Singh* v. *State of Punjab*,[11] the brief statements of the facts of the case mentioned in the inquest report are based on the report lodged by Banta Singh. In this brief statement, however the names of Inder Singh, Sucha Singh, Teja Singh and Makhan Singh accused are not mentioned as culprits, specifically. It is correct that in the brief facts mentioned in the body there is no reference of the names of these four men.

Thus even the A.S.I. while admitting that the names of the four accused were not mentioned by Banta Singh has not chosen to give any explanation for this deliberate omission to that effect. According to the prosecution the names of the four accused who have been acquitted by the High Court had already been mentioned in the F.I.R. which was lodged 4/5 hours before the inquest report was prepared. Any Investigating Officer possessing some intelligence would have at once questioned Banta Singh as to how it is that while he had named the four accused in the F.I.R. He had not referred to them in his brief statement in the inquest report. In these circumstances, therefore, the High Court was fully justified in holding that the omission of the names of the four accused acquitted by the High Court in the inquest report was a very important circumstance which went in favour of the four accused. This omission has a two-fold reaction. In the first place it throws doubt on the complicity of the four accused acquitted by the High Court and secondly it casts serious doubt on the veracity and authenticity

---

11. AIR 1975 SC 1962.

of the F.I.R. itself. It is not understandable as to why the four accused who are alleged to have taken an active part in the assault on the deceased were not at all mentioned in the inquest report and in the brief statement of the very person who had lodged the F.I.R. four hours before. Counsel for the State tried to justify this omission on the ground that in the inquest report the names of all the nine accused appear to have been mentioned at the top of that document. There is, however, no column for mentioning the names of the accused and therefore, there was no occasion for the Investigating Officer to have mentioned the names of the accused in that particular place.

Finally, the Investigating Officer Teja Singh admitted in his evidence that he had prepared the inquest report and that he had read out the same to Banta Singh and Harnam Singh but later tried to say that he did not recollect whether he had read out the inquest report to Banta Singh and Harnam Singh before getting their thumb impressions on the inquest report. This circumstance speaks volumes against the prosecution case. If, therefore, it is once established that the names of the four accused were deliberately added in the inquest report at the instance of the prosecution there is no guarantee regarding the truth about the participation in the assault on the deceased by the appellants.

Another finding which demolishes the entire edifice and fabric of the prosecution case is that the F.I.R. itself was not written at 10 P.M. as alleged by the informant Banta Singh but it was written out after the inquest report was prepared by the A.S.I. and after the names of the four accused acquitted by the High Court were inserted in the inquest report. If this is true then the entire case of the prosecution becomes extremely doubtful. The High Court has also derived support from another important circumstance to come to the conclusion that the F.I.R. was not written at 10 P.M. as alleged by the prosecution but after the preparation of the inquest report at about 2-30 A.M. The High Court points out that according to the prosecution the special report reached the Ilaqa Magistrate at 11 A.M. on September 2, 1966, i.e. more than 12 hours after the F.I.R. was lodged at the police station whereas it should have been delivered to the Ilaqa Magistrate during the night or at least in the early morning. Counsel appearing for the appellants submitted that under the High Court Circulars and the Police Rules it was incumbent upon the Inspector who recorded the F.I.R. to send a copy of the F.I.R. to the Ilaqa Magistrate immediately without any loss of time and the delay in sending the F.I.R. has not been properly explained by the prosecution as rightly held by the High Court. It is, therefore, clear that the F.I.R. itself was a belated document and came into existence during the small hours of September 2, 1966. Indeed if this was so, then there was sufficient time for the prosecution party who are undoubtedly inimical to the accused to deliberate and prepare a false case not only against the four accused who have been acquitted, but against the other five appellants also. The High Court also found that the best person to explain the delay in sending the special report to the Ilaqa Magistrate was the Police Constable who had carried the F.I.R. to the Ilaqa Magistrate but the Constable has not been examined by the prosecution. On this point the High Court observed as follows :

> The delay with which the special report was made available to the Ilaqa Magistrate is indicative of the fact that the first information report did not come into existence probably till about sunrise by when the dead body had already been dispatched for the purpose of post-mortem examination to Patiala along with the inquest report, so that the Investigating Officer was no longer in a position to make alterations in the body of that report and all that he could do was to add later on the names of the said four appellants to its heading.

This finding of the High Court is based on cogent materials and convincing reasons, but unfortunately the High Court has not considered the effect of this finding on the truth of the prosecution case with regard to the participation of the appellants. In our opinion, in view of the finding given by the High Court it has been dearly established that the F.I.R. was lodged not at 10 P.M. as alleged by the prosecution but some time in the early morning of September 2, 1966. If this was so, then the F.I.R. lost its authenticity. If the prosecution could go to the extent of implicating four innocent persons by inserting their names in the inquest report and in the F.I.R. which was written subsequent to the inquest report they could very well have put in the names of the other five appellants also because they were equally inimical to the prosecution party, and there could be no difficulty in doing so because it is found by the High Court that all the prosecution witnesses belonged to one party who are on inimical terms with the accused.

In *Sarwan Singh* v. *State of Punjab*,[12] the court was of the view that it is well settled that mere delay in despatch of the F.I.R. is not a circumstance which can throw out the prosecution case in its entirety. The matter was also considered by the Apex Court in *Pola Singh* v. *State of Punjab*,[13] where the Court observed as follows:

> But when we find in this case that the F.I.R. was actually recorded without delay and the investigation started on the basis of that F.I.R. and there is no other infirmity brought to our notice, then, however improper or objectionable the delayed receipt of the report by the Magistrate concerned it cannot by itself justify the conclusion that the investigation was tainted and the prosecution insupportable.

In these circumstances, therefore, the learned Judges held that the Additional Sessions Judge was not at all justified in rejecting the prosecution case on the ground of the delay in despatch of the F.I.R. in the peculiar circumstances of this case.

In *Kurukshetra University* v. *State of Haryana*,[14] the Kurukshetra University filed a first information report through its Warden with regard to an incident which is alleged to have taken place on the night between 25th and 26th of Sep., 1975 in one of the University hostels. Acting on that report, the police registered a case under Sections 448 and 452, Indian Penal Code, against respondent 2, Vinay Kumar. But before any investigation could be done by the police respondent 2 filed a petition in the High Court of Punjab and Haryana praying that the First Information Report be quashed. The High Court, without

---

12. AIR 1976 SC 2304; (1976) 4 SCC 369.
13. AIR 1972 SC 2679.
14. AIR 1977 SC 2229.

issuing notice to the University, quashed the First Information Report by its judgment dated December 22, 1975 and directed respondent 1, the State of Haryana to pay a sum of Rs. 300 by way of costs to respondent 2. The University asked for a review of the order since it had no notice of the proceedings, but that application was dismissed by the High Court, giving rise to this appeal.

The Apex Court held that the High Court in the exercise of its inherent powers under Section 482 of the Code of Criminal Procedure, it could quash a First Information Report. The police had not even commenced investigation into the complaint filed by the Warden of the University and no proceeding at all was pending in any court in pursuance of the F.I.R. It ought to be realized that inherent powers do not confer an arbitrary jurisdiction on the High Court to act according to whim or caprice. That statutory power has to be exercised sparingly, with circumspection and in the rarest of rare cases.

While quashing the F.I.R. the High Court went out of its way and made observations concerning the University's power to enforce discipline in its campus. The High Court seems to feel that outsiders can with impunity flout the University's rule that no outsider shall stay in a University hostel. Such a view is plainly calculated to subvert discipline in a sphere where it is most needed. We are clear that the High Court ought not to have made these observations without, at least, giving a hearing to the University.

The Supreme Court, therefore, allowed the appeal and set aside the judgment of the High Court including the order asking the State of Haryana to pay the costs amounting to Rs. 300 to the respondent.

It was held by Fazil Ali, Patanjali Sastri, S.R. Dass and Vivan Base, JJ., in *Tara Singh* v. *State*[15] that, Section 173(1)(a) requires that as soon as the police investigation under Chapter XIV is complete, the police should forward to the Magistrate a report in the prescribed form setting forth the names of the parties, the nature of the information and the names of the persons who appear to be acquainted with the circumstances of case. Where, therefore, the first report made by the police to a

---

15. AIR 1951 SC 441.

Magistrate, though called incomplete challan, contain all these particulars and a second report called a supplementary challan is filed subsequently, giving the names of certain witnesses who are merely formal witnesses, the First Report is in fact, a complete report as required by Section 173(1)(a) and it is not necessarily vitiated by the mere fact that a supplementary challan is subsequently filed. The conviction and sentence are set aside and the case is sent back to the High Court with a direction that court will order a retrial *denovo* in the Session Court, treating committal as good.

In *H.N. Rishbud* v. *State of Delhi*,[16] it was held by the Supreme Court of India that, Section 155(2) prohibits the police from investigating a non-cognizable case without the order of a Magistrate. A Magistrate should not order investigation in a non-cognizable offence arbitrarily or capriciously. He must apply his mind to the facts and must before ordering for investigation see whether there are reasonable grounds for believing that the offence as complained has been committed. An order for investigation cannot be passed in the belief that an offence is likely to be committed in future. Section 155(2) is mandatory and, therefore, an investigation into a non-çognizable case without order of Magistrate is illegal. But invalidity of investigation does not affect the competence of the court unless there is miscarriage of justice.

In *Baladen and others* v. *State of U.P.*[17] the Supreme Court observed that :

> Ordinarily accused persons are entitled to challenge the testimony of witnesses examined in court with reference to the statement said to have been made by them before the investigating police officer.

It was further observed by the court that :

> the record made by a police investigating officer has to be considered by the court only with a view to weigh the evidence actually adduced in the court. If the police record

16. AIR 1955 SC 196.
17. AIR 1956 SC 181.

becomes suspect on unreliable on the ground that it was deliberately perfunctory or dishonest, it looses much of its value and the court in judging the case of a particular accused has to weigh the evidence given against him in court. Statement made by prosecution witnesses before the investigating police officer being the earliest statement made by them with reference to the facts of the occurrence are valuable material for testing the veracity of the witness examined in court, with particular reference to those statements which happened to be at variance with their earlier statements, but the statements made during police investigation are not substantive evidence.

In *Deoman Upadhyaya* v. *State of Uttar Pradesh,*[18] S.K. Das, Kapur, Hidayatullah and Shah, JJ. observed that :

By the combined operation of Section 27 of the Evidence Act and Section 162 of the Cr.P.C., the admissibility in evidence against a person in a Cr.P.C. of a statement made to a police officer leading to the discovery of a fact depends for its determination on the question whether he was in custody at the time of making the statement, it is provable if he was not in custody at the time when he made it, otherwise it is not.

It was further observed that the accused approached a police officer investigating the offence. He offered to give information leading to the discovery of fact and also having a bearing on the charge which might be made against him. The Supreme Court held that he had been submitted to the custody by action within the meaning of Sub-Section (1) of the Section 46.[19]

---

18. See, AIR 1960 SC 1125; also see AIR 1922 PC 342, AIR 1933 Pat 149.
19. *Ibid.*
   Note : In accordance with the opinion of the majority the appeal is allowed Sec. 27 of the Evi. Act and Sec. 162 (2) of the Cr.P.C. in so far as "that Sec. 27 of the Evidence Act" are *intra vires* and do not offend Article 14 of the Constitution of India. The order of High Court acquitting the respondent is also set aside and the order of the Court of Session convicting the accused (respondent) under Section 302 of the Indian Penal Code and sentencing him to death is restored.

Bachawat, J. in *Aghnoo Nagesia* v. *State of Bihar*[20] held that :

The First Information Report recorded under Section 154, Cr.P.C. as such is not a substantive evidence, but may be used to corroborate the informant under Section 157 of the Evidence Act, or to contradict him under Section 145 of the Act. If the informant is called as a witness. Where the accused himself gives the first information, the fact of his giving the information is admissible against him as evidence of his conduct under Section 8 of the Evidence Act. If the information is non-confessional, it is admissible against the accused as an admission under Section 21 of the Evidence Act and is relevant. But a confessional First Information Report by the accused to a police officer cannot be used against him in view of Section 25 of the Evidence Act, where the F.I.R. is given by the accused to a police officer and amounts to a confessional statement, proof of the confession is prohibited by Section 25. The confession includes not only the admission of the offence but all other admissions of incriminating facts related to the offence contained in the confessional statement is receivable in evidence except to the extent that the ban 25 is lifted by 27. The test of severeability, namely, that if a part of the report is properly severable from the strict confessional part, then the severable part could be tendered in evidence, is misleading and the entire confessional statement is hit by Section 25 and save and except as provided by Section 27 and save and except the formal part identifying the accused as the maker of the report, no part of it could be tendered in evidence.

In *Tula Ram* v. *Kishore Singh*[21] case the court observed that:

In these circumstances we are satisfied that the action taken by the magistrate was fully supportable in law and he did not commit any error in recording the statement of the

---

20. AIR 1966 SC 119; also see, AIR 1964 SC 1850, AIR 1957 SC 366; AIR 1964 Pat 210, AIR 1952 SC 343.
21. AIR 1977 SC 2401; See also AIR 1976 SC 1672, AIR 1968 SC 117.

complainant and the witnesses and thereafter, issuing process against the appellants. The High Court has discussed the points involved threadbare and has also cited number of decisions and we entirely agree with the view taken by the High Court."

Fazal Ali, J. further held that :

"Thus on careful consideration of the facts and circumstances of the case the following legal proposition emerges :

(1) That the Magistrate can order investigation under Section 156(3) only at the pre-cognizance stage, that is to say before taking cognizance under Section 190, 200 and 204 and where a Magistrate decides to take cognizance under the provisions of Chapter XIV he is not entitled in law to order any investigation under Section 156(3). Though in cases not falling within the proviso of Section 202 he can order an investigation by police which would be in the nature of an enquiry as contemplated by Section 202 of the Code.

(2) Where a Magistrate chooses to take cognizance he can adopt any of the following alternative :

    (a) He can pursue the complaint and is satisfied that there are sufficient grounds for proceedings he can straight away issue process to the accused but before he does so he must comply with the requirements of Section 200 and record the evidence of the complainant of his witnesses.

    (b) The Magistrate can postpone the issue of process and direct an enquiry by himself.

    (c) The Magistrate can postpone the issue of process and direct an enquiry by any other person or an investigation by the police.

(3) In case the Magistrate after considering the statement of the complainant and the witnesses or as a result of

the investigation and the enquiry ordered is not satisfied that there are sufficient grounds for proceedings he can dismiss the complaint.

(4) Where a Magistrate orders investigation by the police before taking cognizance under Section 156(3) of the Code and receives the report and discharge the accused or straightway issue process against the accused or apply his mind to the complaint filed before him and take action under Section 190 as described above.

(5) The present case we find no merit in his appeal which is accordingly dismissed.[22]

V.R. Krishna Iyer, J., in *Nandini Sathpathy* v. *P.L. Dhani*[23] held that:

Every litigation has a touch of human crisis and, as here, it is but a legal projection of life's vicissitudes. A Complaint was filed by the D.S.P., Vigilance Cuttack, against the appellant, the former Chief Minister of Orissa, under Section 179 IPC, before S.D. Judicial Magistrate, Sadar, Cuttack, alleging offending facts which we will presently explain. Thereupon the Magistrate took cognizance of the offence and issued summons for appearance against the accused. Aggrieved by the action of the Magistrate urging that the complaint did not and could not disclose an offence, the agitated accused appellant moved the High Court under Article 226 of the Constitution as well as Section 401 of the Cr.P.C., challenging the validity of the magisterial proceedings. The broads submission unsuccessfully made before the High Court, was that the charge rested upon a failure to answer interrogation by the police but this charge unsustainable because the umbrella of Article 20(3) of the Constitution and the immunity under Section 161(2) of the Cr.P.C. were wide enough to shield her in her refusal. We have declared the law on a thorny constitutional question where the amber light from

---

22. *Ibid.*
23. AIR 1978 SC 1025.

American rulings and beacon beams from Indian precedents have aided us in our decision. Where, however, the accused person is a woman and the police constantly insists on the woman to appear at the police station, it will amount to flagrant contravention of the provisions of Section 160(1) of the Code of Cr.P.C. In view of Supreme Court such deviance must be visited with prompt punishment since police men may not be a law into themselves expecting others to obey the law.

In *Hussainara Khatoon* v. *Home Secretary, Bihar*,[24] P.N. Bhagwati, J. held that :

When an undertrial prisoner is produced before a Magistrate and he has been in detention for 90 days or 60 days, as the case may be, the Magistrate must, before making an order of further remand to judicial custody, point out the under-trial prisoner that he is entitled to be released on bail. If there are adequate grounds to Magistrate may extend the period—not excluding 60 days, for detention of an accused in the police custody. On the expiry of the period person should be released on the bail.

In *Harpal Singh* v. *State of H.P.*[25] a Special Leave directed against the judgment of the High Court of Himachal Pradesh, S.M. Fazal Ali, J. held as under :

The appellants have been convicted under Section 376 of the I.P.C. and sentenced to rigorous imprisonment for four years each. The central evidence in the case consists of the testimony of Saroj Kumari, the girl who is said to have been raped by the appellant and other who was acquitted by the trial court. The occurrence according to the prosecutrix, took place on the night intervening the 20th and 21st August, 1972. The F.I.R. was lodged on 31st August, 1972. The complainant had given reasonable

---

24. AIR 1979 SC 1377.
25. AIR 1981 SC 361.

explanation for lodging it after ten days of the occurrence. She stated that as honour of the family was involved, its members had to decide whether to take the matter to the court or not. The police can't refuse to report the F.I.R.

Gurnam Kaur v. *Bakshish Singh.*[26] In this case the High Court had discarded the evidence of eye witnesses on superficial and unsubstantial grounds. Apart from the fact that there were no justifiable grounds for rejecting their testimony. The Apex Court greatly impressed by the evidence of and the substantial corroboration received by it from the First Information Report and the medical and the expert evidence and observed that an examination of the First Information Report shows that Bakshish Singh was responsible for firing two shots at Karam Singh and one shot at Gurdeep Singh. He was alleged to have shot once at the legs and later again at the neck of Karam Singh and once on the right thigh of Gurdeep Singh. The medical evidence supports the evidence of and what is more important the medical evidence is in tune with the First Information Report. The empty cartridges which were found at the scene of occurrence show that two of them found near Karam Singh and one found near Gurdeep Singh were shot from the pistol of Bakshish Singh. The manner in which the medical evidence and the expert evidence fit in with the earliest version given in the First Information Report

In *Sevi* v. *State of Tamil Nadu,*[27] one of the disturbing features of the case was the strange conduct of the Sub-Inspector of Police. According to him he was told by a person on the telephone that there was some rioting at Kottaiyur and that some persons were stabbed. He made an entry in the general diary and proceeded to Kottaiyur taking with him the F.I.R. book, the hospital Memo book, etc. This was indeed very extraordinary conduct on the part of the Sub-Inspector of Police. If he was not satisfied with the information that any cognizable offence had been committed he was quite right in making an entry in the general diary and proceeding to the village to verify the information without registering any F.I.R. But, we have yet not come across any case where an Officer Incharge of a Police

---

26. AIR 1981 SC 631.
27. AIR 1981 SC 1230.

Station has carried with him the F.I.R. Book. The First Information Report book is supposed to be at the Police Station House all the time. If the Sub-Inspector is not satisfied on the information received by him that a cognizable offence has been committed and wants to verify the information his duty is to make an entry in the general diary, proceed to the village and take a complaint at the village from someone who is in a position to give a report about the commission of a cognizable offence. Thereafter, the ordinary procedure is to send the report to the Police Station to be registered at the Police Station by the Officer Incharge of the Police Station. But, indeed, we have never come across a case where the Station House Officer has taken the First Information Report Book with him to the scene of occurrence. According to the suggestion of defence the original First Information Report which was registered was something altogether different from what has now been put forward as the First Information Report and that the present report is one which has been substituted in the place of another which was destroyed. To substantiate their suggestion the defence requested the Sessions Judge to direct the Sub-Inspector to produce the First Information Report Book in the Court so that the counterfoils might be examined. The Sub-Inspector was unable to produce the relevant F.I.R. Book in Court notwithstanding the directions of the Court. The F.I.R. book, if produced, would have contained the necessary counterfoils corresponding to the F.I.R. produced in Court. The Sub-Inspector when questioned stated that he searched for the counterfoil book but was unable to find it. Though he claimed that relevant entries had been made in the general diary at the Station. But the Sub-Inspector did not produce the general diary in Court. The production of the general diary would have certainly dispelled suspicion. In the circumstances we think that there is great force in the submission of the learned counsel for the accused that the original F.I.R. has been suppressed and, in its place some other document has been substituted. If that is so, the entire prosecution case becomes suspect. All tne eye-witnesses are partisan witnesses and notwithstanding the fact that four of them were injured we are unable to accept their evidence in the peculiar circumstances of the case. Where the entire evidence is of a partisan character impartial investigation can lend assurance to the Court to enable it to accept such partisan evidence. But where the investigation itself is found to be tainted the task of the Court to shift the evidence becomes very difficult indeed. Another feature of the case which doubt the credibility of the witnesses is the photographic and somewhat dramatic account which they gave of the incident with minute details of the attack on each of the victims. According to the account of the witnesses it was as if each of the victims of the attack came upon the stage one after the other to be attacked by different accused in succession, each victim and his assailant being followed by the next victim and the next assailant. Surely the account of the witnesses is too dramatic and sounds obviously invented to allow each witness to give evidence of the entire attack. But the witnesses themselves admit in cross-examination that they were all attacked simultaneously. If so, it was impossible for each of them to have noticed the attack on everyone else.

Having regard to all these special features of this case the Court held that the High Court was justified in setting aside the acquittal of the appellants and convicting them. The appeals are, therefore, allowed. The appellants, if not on bail, will be released forthwith. If they are on bail their bail bonds will stand cancelled.

In *State (Delhi Administration)* v. *Dharampal and others,*[28] it was observed by the court that, so far as authorisation of the police custody of accused under Section 167(2) is concerned, it is legislative mandate that in no way the detention of accused in police custody can be authorised for any time after expiry of the period of first fifteen days remand. The Magistrate may allow the detention other than custody in police till 90(60) days, as the case may be. The Magistrate is competent to authorise detention of any accused in police custody for a specific period on adequate ground on in the first fifteen days and that detention in police custody or judicial custody or *vice-versa* can be authorised only within first fifteen days. After fifteen days detention the accused cannot be sent to police custody at all except in other cases in which remand of first fifteen days has not started. It was stated in the above citation that the words

---

28.   1982 CrLJ 1103.

'from time to time' occurring in Section show that several orders can be passed under Sec. 167(1) and that the nature of custody can be altered from judicial custody to police custody and vice-versa during the first period of 15 days mentioned in Sec. 167(2) of Code of Criminal Procedure and that after fifteen days the accused could only be kept in judicial custody or in any other custody as ordered by the Magistrate but not in the custody of police.

Y.V. Chandrachud CJ, A. Varadarajan and Amarendra Nath Sen, J.J., held in *State of W.B.* v. *Swapan Kumar Guha*[29] case that :

> usually, in case of cognizable offences, the investigation is initiated by giving of information under Section 154 to a police officer-in-charge of a police station. However, such first information report is not an indispensable requisite for the investigation of crime. Even without any F.I.R., if a police officer-in-charge of a police station has reason to suspect the commission of a cognizable offence, he can proceed to investigate the offence under Section 157(1). The police, of course, have to unfettered discretion to commence investigation under Section 157. They can exercise the power of investigation only if FIR or other relevant material *prima facie* discloses the commission of a cognizable offence.

In *Darshan Singh* v. *State of Punjab*,[30] the First Information Report lodged by Mohinder Singh mentions the names of some accused only. The fact that the names of the other accused are not mentioned in the F.I.R. was at least a circumstance which the prosecution had to explain, though no rule of law stipulates that an accused whose name is not mentioned in a F.I.R. is entitled to an acquittal. But instead of considering the circumstances in which, and the reasons for which, Mohinder Singh did not mention the names of the other accused in the F.I.R., the High Court took the view that the omission in the F.I.R. was a matter of little consequence since it was made good by the fact that

---

29. (1982) 1 SCC 561.
30. AIR 1983 SC 554.

Sohan Singh had mentioned the names of all the accused in his dying declaration.

According to Tulzapurkar, J., observations, in *State of U.P.* v. *Gokaran and others*[31] case, it is not that as if every delay in sending a delayed special report to the District Magistrate under Section 157, Cr.P.C., would necessarily lead to the inference that the F.I.R. has not been lodged at the time stated or has been antetimed or antedated or that the investigation is not fair and fortnight. Where the steps in investigation by way of drawing inquest report and other panchanamas started soon which could only follow the handing over of FIR, the delayed receipt of special report by District Magistrate would not enable the court to dub the investigation as tainted one nor could FIR be regarded as antetimed and antedated.

According to Ahmadi, J., explanation in *Prithichand* v. *State of Himachal Pradesh*,[32] case, the learned counsel for the appellant submitted that there was delay in filing the first information report. We do not think so, immediately after the incident was narrated to the mother and other ladies, a decision was taken to await the return of the father before deciding on the course of action. On the arrival of the father the Sarpanch was contacted, who advised that police should be informed about the incident. The Sarpanch, however, stated that he would accompany them next morning since it was already dark. The girl was taken to Palampur Station next morning and the F.I.R. was lodged. We, therefore, do not think that there was any delay in reporting the matter to the police.

In *Gurbachan Singh* v. *Satpal*[33] case Sabyasachi Mukharji, J., observed that :

the evidentiary value of F.I.R. is reduced if it is made after such delay which is unexplained. We do not find any infirmity in this finding and we also held on consideration and appraisement of the evidences as well as the circumstances set out herein before that it was a case of suicide committed by the deceased Ravinder Kaur being

---

31. 1985 CrLJ, 511.
32. AIR 1989 SC 702.
33. AIR 1989 SC 378.

constantly abused, taunted for bringing less dowry and also being defamed for carrying on illegitimate child. It is pertinent to mention that in the appeal before the High Court it was not urged on behalf of the accused that the case of suicide was not proved and such there was no finding by the High Court on this score. In such circumstances this argument is totally devoid of merit and as such it is not sustainable.

In *State of U.P.* v. *R.K. Srivastava*[34] the Court expressed that, it is a well settled principle of law that if the allegations made in the FIR are taken at their face value and accepted in their entirety do not constitute an offence, the criminal proceedings instituted on the basis of such F.I.R. should be quashed. The question is whether the facts disclosed in the F.I.R. constitute the offences with which the accused have been charged. It is manifestly clear from the allegations in the F.I.R. that the respondent or the other accused had no intention whatsoever to make any wrongful gain or to make any wrongful loss to the Bank. They had accepted the said three cheques amounting to Rs. 54,600 and sent the same for clearance after debiting the LOC account. The said cheques have been encashed and the money was received by the State Bank of India. The Court further observed that, the High Court has rightly held that the allegations made in the F.I.R. do not constitute any offence of cheating, nor do they constitute any offence of forgery. No document has been referred to in the F.I.R. as the outcome of forgery.

Finally the Supreme Court observed that the High Court has rightly held that as the criminal proceedings have been started against the respondent on the basis of a F.I.R. which does not contain any definite accusation, it amounts to an abuse of process of the Court and, as such, is liable to be quashed.

It was observed by the Supreme Court in *Tara Singh* v. *State of Punjab*[35] case, that delay in giving the F.I.R by itself cannot be ground to doubt the prosecution case. In the instant case, the names of the accused were consistently mentioned throughout.

---

34. AIR 1989 SC 2222.
35. 1990 CrLJ 2681 SC.

There was absolutely no ground to hold that the F.I.R. was brought into existence subsequently during the investigation and the mere delay in lodging the report by itself could not give scope for an adverse inference leading to rejection of the prosecution case outright. The evidence of the eye-witnesses was consistent and corroborated by the medical evidence. There was no inordinate and unexplained delay in filing F.I.R.

In *State of Andhra Pradesh* v. *P.V. Pavithran*,[36] The High Court has quashed the First Information Report on the ground that there was inordinate delay in the investigation. Aggrieved by that judgment, the State has preferred this criminal appeal.

Mr. Madhava Reddy, learned senior counsel appearing on behalf of the appellant took an exception to the observation of the learned single Judge of the High Court reading:

> ". . . . hold that wherever there is an inordinate delay on the part of the investigating agency in completing investigation, the case merits quashing of the First Information Report even. Generally, this Court will not quash the F.I.R. because it amounts to stopping of investigation, but where there is an inordinate delay, the same is a ground to quash even the F.I.R." and contended that the above observation is too wide a proposition and it would be detrimental to the prosecution in future under all circumstances, regardless of the reasons therefor."

Observation of the High Court makes it necessary to examine the question whether a mere delay in the investigation of a criminal proceeding will by itself serve as a sufficient ground for quashing the proceedings in pursuance of the registration of the case notwithstanding whatever may be the reasons for the delay. This question has come up for determination in a number of cases wherein this Court has examined the right of an accused for a speedy investigation and trial in a criminal case in the light of Article 21 of the Constitution of India.

There is no denying the fact that a lethargic and

---

36. AIR 1990 SC 1266; Also see *Raghuvir Singh* v. *State of Bihar*, AIR 1987 SC 149.

lackadaisical manner of investigation over a prolonged period makes an accused in a criminal proceedings to live every moment under extreme emotional and mental stress and strain and to remain always under a fear psychosis. Therefore, it is imperative that if investigation of a criminal proceeding staggers on with tardy pace due to the indolence or inefficiency of the investigating agency causing unreasonable and substantial delay resulting in grave prejudice or disadvantage to the accused, the Court as the protector of the right and personal liberty of the citizen will step in and resort to the drastic remedy of quashing further proceedings in such investigation.

While so, there are offences of grave magnitude such as diabolical crimes of conspiracy or clandestine crimes committed by members of the underworld with their tentacles spread over various parts of the country or even abroad. The very nature of such offences would necessarily involve considerable time for unearthing the crimes and bringing the culprits to book. Therefore, it is not possible to formulate inflexible guidelines or rigid principles of uniform application for speedy investigation or to stipulate any arbitrary period of limitation within which investigation in a criminal case should be completed.

The determination of the question whether the accused has been deprived of a fair trial on account of delayed or protracted investigation would also, therefore, depend on various factors including whether such delay was unreasonably long or caused deliberately or intentionally to hamper the defence of the accused or whether such delay was inevitable in the nature of things or whether it was due to the dilatory tactics adopted by the accused. The Court, in addition, has to consider whether such delay on the part of the investigating agency has caused grave prejudice or disadvantage to the accused.

The assessment of the above factors necessarily vary from case to case. It would, therefore, follow that no general and wide proposition of law can be formulated that whenever there is inordinate delay on the part of the investigating agency in completing the investigation, such delay, *ipso facto*, would provide ground for quashing the First Information Report or the proceedings arising therefrom.

It follows from the above observations that no general and wide proposition of law can be formulated that wherever there is any inordinate delay on the part of the investigating agency in completing the investigation, such delay is a ground to quash the F.I.R.

Ratnavel Pandian, J., in *State of Haryana* v. *Ch. Bhajan Lal and others*,[37] observed that :

> The king is under no man, but under God and the law' was the reply of the Chief Justice of England, Sir Edward Coke when James-I once declared, 'then I am to be under the law. It is a treason to affirm it'—so wrote Henry Bracon who was a Judge of the King's Bench.

> The words of Bracton in his treatise in Latin 'quod rex non debat esse sub homine sed sub deo et lege' (that the King should not be underman, but under God and the law) were quoted time and time again when the stuart king claimed to rule by divine right. We would like to quote and requote those words of Sir Edward Coke even at the threshold. In our democratic polity under the Constitution based on the concept of 'Rule of Law' which we have adopted and given to ourselves and which serves as an aorta in the anatomy of our democratic system. The law is supreme. Everyone whether the individually or collectively is unquestionably under the supremacy of the law. Whoever he may be, however, high he is, he is under the law. No matter how powerful he is and how rich he may be.

It was further held by the Supreme Court that :

> If any information disclosing a cognizable offence is laid before an officer-in-charge of a police station satisfying the requirements of Section 154(1) of the Code, the said police-officer has no other option except to enter the substance thereof in the prescribed form, that is to say, to register a case on the basis of such information. The commencement of investigation in a cognizable offence by a police officer is subject to condition:
>
> (1) the police officer should have reason to suspect the commission of a cognizable offence as required by

---

37. AIR 1992 SC 604.

Section 157(1).

(2) Secondly, the police officer should subjectively satisfy himself as to whether there is sufficient ground for entering on an investigation even before he starts an investigation into the facts and circumstances of the case as contemplated under Clause (b) of the proviso to Section 157(1).

Further, as Clause (b) of the proviso permits the police officer to satisfy himself about the sufficiency of the ground even before entering on an investigation, it postulates that the police officer has to draw his satisfaction only on the material which were placed before him at that stage, namely, the first information together with the documents, if any, enclosed. In other words, the police officer has to satisfy himself only on the allegations mentioned in the F.I.R. before he enters on an investigation as to whether those allegations do constitute a cognizable offence warranting an investigation.[38]

In *Joginder Kumar* v. *State of U.P.*,[39] the petitioner, a young advocate of 28 years, was called by the SSP, Ghaziabad, U.P., in his office for making enquiries in some cases. It was alleged that on 7.1.1994 at about 10 O'clock he personally along with his brother appeared before the SSP, at about 12.55 p.m. The brother of the petitioner sent a telegram to the Chief Minister of U.P. apprehending the petitioner's false implication in some criminal cases and his death in fake encounter. In the evening it came to be known that the petitioner was detained in the illegal custody of SHO. Next day the SHO instead of producing the petitioner before a Magistrate, asked the relatives to approach the SSP. On 9.1.1994 in the evening the relatives of the petitioner came to know that the petitioner had been taken to some undisclosed destination. Under these circumstances the writ petition under Article 32 was preferred for release of the petitioner, the Supreme Court on 11.1.1994 ordered notice to the State of U.P. as well as SSP Ghaziabad. The SSP along with the petitioner appeared before the court on 14.1.1994 and stated that the petitioner was not in detention at all and that his help was taken

---

38. *Ibid.*
39. (1994) 4 SCC 260.

for detecting some cases relating to abduction and the petitioner was helpful in cooperating with the police, therefore, there was no question of detaining him.

The M.N. Venkatachalia, CJ., S. Mohan and Dr. A.S. Anand, J.J., of the Supreme Court held that :

> The right of the arrested person to have some one informed, upon request and to consult privately with a lawyer was recognized by Section 56 (1) of the Police and Criminal Evidence Act, 1984. These rights are inherent in Articles 21 and 22(1) of the Constitution of India and required to be recognised and scrupulously protected. For effective enforcement of these fundamental rights the following requirements are issued :
>
> (1) An arrested person being held in custody is entitled, if he so requests to have one friend, relative or other person who is known to him or likely to take an interest in his welfare told as far as is practicable that he has been arrested and where he is being detained.
> (2) The police officer shall inform the arrested person when he is brought to the police station of this right.
> (3) An entry shall be required to be made in the diary as to who was informed of the arrest. These protection from power must be held to flow from Articles 21 and 22(1) and enforced strictly.

It shall be the duty of the Magistrate, before whom the arrested person is produced, to satisfy himself that these requirements have been complied with.[40]

Bar Association v. *State*[41] was a case, in which a practicing lawyer, his wife and child were abducted and murdered and the lawyers fraternity were not satisfied with investigation and demanded judicial enquiry. The Supreme Court held that :

> When investigation was completed a charge-sheet filed, it is not for the Supreme Court to ordinarily direct the re-

---

40. *Ibid.*
41. 1994 CrLJ 1368 SC.

opening of investigation. However, in the facts and circumstances of the case to do complete justice in the matter and to install confidence in public mind, the Supreme Court directed fresh investigation by the CBI.

According to Dr. A.S. Anand and Faizanuddin, J.J. in a judgement delivered in *Bhiru Singh* v. *State of Rajasthan*.[42]

The FIR is given by an accused himself to a police officer and amounts to a confessional statement, proof of the confession is prohibited by Section 25 of the Evidence Act. The Section 164 provides that 'no confession made to a police officer shall be proved as against a person accused of any offence'. If the FIR given by the accused is non-confessional, it may be admissible in evidence against the accused as an admission under Section 21 of the Evidence Act or as showing his conduct under Section 8 of the Evidence Act.

In *Girish Yadav* v. *State of M.P.*[43] the Learned senior counsel for the appellants invited the attention to the decision of the Apex Court in the case of *Meharaj Singh (L/Nk.)* v. *State of U.P.*,[44] wherein Dr. A.S. Anand, J. sitting with Faizan Uddin, J. had to consider a similar grievance regarding the alleged ante-timing of FIR, In this connection the following pertinent observations were made :

> FIR in a criminal case and particularly in a murder case is a vital and valuable piece of evidence for the purpose of appreciating the evidence led at the trial. The object of insisting upon prompt lodging of the FIR is to obtain the earliest information regarding the circumstance in which the crime was committed, including the names of the actual culprits and the parts played by them, the weapons, if any, used, as also the names of the eye-witnesses, if any. Delay in lodging the FIR often results in embellishment, which is a creature of an afterthought. On account of delay, the FIR not only gets benefit of the advantage of spontaneity, danger also creeps in of the introduction of a coloured version or exaggerated story. With a view to

---

42. (1994) 2 SCC 467.
43. AIR 1996 SC 3098; (1996)8 SCC 186.
44. (1994) 5 SCC 188 : (1994 AIR SCW 2210).

determine whether the FIR was lodged at the time it is
alleged to have been recorded, the Courts generally look
for certain external checks. One of the checks is the receipt
of the copy of the FIR, called a special report in a murder
case, by the local Magistrate. If this report is received by
the Magistrate late it can give rise to an inference that the
FIR was not lodged at the time it is alleged to have been
recorded, unless, of course, the prosecution can offer a
satisfactory explanation for the delay in despatching or
receipt of the copy of the FIR by the local Magistrate. The
second external check equally important is the sending of
the copy of the FIR along with the dead body and its
reference in the inquest report. Even though the inquest
report, prepared under Section 174, Cr.P.C., is aimed at
serving a statutory function, to lend credence to the
prosecution case, the details of the FIR and the gist of
statements recorded during inquest proceedings get
reflected in the report. The absence of those details is
indicative of the fact that the prosecution story was still in
an embryo state and had not been given any shape and
that the FIR came to be recorded later on after due
deliberations and consultations and was then ante-timed to
give it the colour of a promptly lodged FIR.

In *Baldev Singh* v. *State of Punjab*,[45] the Supreme Court held
that :

The FIR is not a substantive piece of evidence, it is only
relevant in judging the veracity of prosecution case and the
value to be attached to it depends on the facts of each case.
Only the essential or broad picture need be stated in the
FIR and all minute details need not be mentioned therein.
It is not a verbatim summary of the prosecution case. It

45. AIR 1996 SC 372 and also see *Ram Kumar* v. *State of M.P.*, AIR 1975 SC
1026; *Bishan Das* v. *State of Punjab*, AIR 1975 SC 573; *Podda Narayana* v.
State of A.P., AIR 1975 SC 1252; *Gurnam Kaur* v. *Bakshish Singh*, AIR 1981
SC 631; *State of Haryana* v. *Sher Singh*, AIR 1981 SC 1021; *State of U.P.* v.
Ballabh Das, AIR 1985 SC 1384); *Jagtar Singh* v. *State of Punjab*, AIR 1988
SC 628 and *Baldev Singh* v. *State of Punjab*, (1990) 4 SCC 692: (AIR 1991 SC
31).

need not contain details of the occurrence as if it were an "encyclopaedia" of the occurrence. It may not be even necessary to catalogue the overt acts therein. Non-mentioning of some facts or vague reference to some others are not fatal.

In *Rupan Deol Bajaj* v. *Kanwar Pal Singh Gill*[46] case Justice M. K. Mukherjee, observed that :

We are constrained to say that in making the observations the High Court has flagrantly disregarded—unwittingly we presume—the settled principle of law that at the stage of quashing an FIR or complaint the High Court is not justified in embarking upon an enquiry as to the probability, reliability or genuineness of the allegation made therein. It has been pointed out in *Bhajan Lal's case*[47] an FIR or a complaint may be quashed if the allegations made therein are so absurd and inherently improbable that no prudent person can ever reach a just conclusion that there is sufficient ground for proceeding against the accused but conducted investigation in a fair and impartial manner and apprehending that the police would conclude the investigation by treating the case was untraced, he was filing the complaint. On the receipt of the complaint the Chief Judicial Magistrate transferred it to a Judicial Magistrate for disposal and the latter, in view of the fact that an investigation by the police was in progress in relation to the same offences called for a report from the investigating officer in accordance with Section 210 of Cr.P.C. In mean time on December 6, 1988 to be precise Mr. Gill moved the High Court by filing a petition under Section 482 Cr.P.C. for quashing the FIR and the complaint. On that petition an interim order was passed staying the investigation into the FIR lodged by Mrs. Bajaj. Resultantly the learned Judicial Magistrate proceeded with the complaint and the witnesses produced by them. The

---

46. 1996 CrLJ 381 SC; Also see, 1994 AIR SCW 3699; (1994) 4 SCC 602; AIR 1994 SC 2623; AIR 1966 SC 1773; AIR 1967 SC 63.
47. 1992 AIR SC 604.

petition earlier filed by Mr. Gill under Section 482 Cr.P.C. came up for haring before the High Court thereafter and was allowed by its order and both the FIR and complaint were quashed. The above two orders of the High Court are under challenge under these appeals at the instance of Mr. and Mrs. Bajaj of the two appeals were first proceed the High Court has not recorded such a finding, obviously because on the allegation in the FIR is not possible to do so. For the reasons aforesaid we must hold that the High Court has committed a gross error of law in quashing the FIR and the complaint. Accordingly, we set aside the impugned judgment and dismiss the petition filed by Mr. Gill in the High Court under Section 482 Cr.P.C. Before we part with this judgment we wish to mention that in the course of his arguments, Mr. Sanghi, suggested that matter may be given a quietness if Mr. Gill was to express regret for his alleged misbehaviour. That is a matter for the parties to consider for the offences in question are compoundable with the permission of the court.

S. Saghir Ahmad, J. in *State of Orissa* v. *Sharat Chandra Sahu*[48] case held that :

(1) When information is given to an officer-in-charge of a police station of a commission within the limits of such station of a non-cognizable offence, he shall enter or cause to be entered the substance of the information in a book to be kept by such officer in such form as the State Government may prescribe in this behalf, and refer the informant to the Magistrate.

(2) No police officer shall investigate a non-cognizable case without the order of a Magistrate having power to try such case or commit the case for trial.

(3) Any police officer receiving such order may exercise the same power in respect of the investigation (except the power of arrest without warrant) as an officer-in-charge of a police station may exercise in a cognizable case.

---

48. (1996) 6 SCC 435.

(4)   Where a case relates to two or more offences of which at least one is cognizable, the case shall be deemed to be a cognizable case, notwithstanding that the other offences are non-cognizable.

In a situation where a criminal case consists of both cognizable and non-cognizable offences. To meet such a situation Sec. 155(4) provides that where a case relates to two or more offences of which at lease one is cognizable, the case shall be deemed to be a cognizable case, notwithstanding that the other offences are non-cognizable. A case alleging commission of offences under Section 494 and 498-A IPC could be investigated by the police, though offences under Section 494 is a non-cognizable offence, by virtue of Section 155(4).

In *Bandlamuddi Atchuta Ramaiah and others* v. *State of A.P.*,[49] the legal position was that a statement contained in the FIR furnished by one of the accused in the case cannot, in any manner, be used against another accused. Even as against the accused who made it, statement cannot be used if it is inculpatory in nature nor can it be used for the purpose of corroboration or contradiction unless its maker offers himself as a witness in the trial. The very limited use of it is an admission under section 21 of the Evidence Act against its maker alone unless the admission does not amount to confession. The Supreme Court observed that :

A first information report is not a substantive piece of evidence and can only be used to corroborate the statement of the maker under Sec. 157, Evidence Act, or to contradict it under Sec. 145 of that Act. It cannot be used as evidence against the maker at the trial if he himself becomes an accused, nor to corroborate or contradict other witnesses.

The Supreme Court in *Rattan Chand* v. *State of H.P.*,[50] held that:

---

49.   AIR 1997 SC 496.
50.   AIR 1997 SC 768; Also see *Podda Narayana* v. *State of Andhra Pradesh*, AIR 1975 SC 1252; *Sone Lal* v. *State of Uttar Pradesh*, AIR 1978 SC 1142; *Gurnam Kaur* v. *Bakshish Singh*, AIR 1981 SC 631.

Criminal Courts should not be fastidious with mere omissions in First Information Statement, since such Statements cannot be expected to be a chronicle of every detail of what happened, nor to contain an exhaustive catalogue of the events which took place. The person who furnishes first information to authorities might be fresh with the facts but he need not necessarily have the skill or ability to reproduce details of the entire story without anything missing therefrom. Some may miss even important details in a narration. Quite often the Police Officer, who takes down the first information, would record what the informant conveys to him without resorting to any elicitatory exercise. It is the voluntary narrative of the informant without interrogation which usually goes into such statement.

The Supreme Court in *State of W.B.* v. *Mirmohammad Omar*[51] emphasized that:

Castigation of investigation unfortunately seems to be regular practice when the trial courts acquit accused in criminal cases. Where investigation was conducted completely flawless or absolutely foolproof, the function of the criminal courts should not be wasted in picking out these lapses in investigation. The Police officer in the present system, the ill-equipped machinery. They have to cope with, and the traditional apathy of respectable persons to come forward for giving evidences in criminal cases which are the realities of the police force have to confront with while conducting investigation in almost every case. Before an investigating officer is impacted with castigation remarks the courts should not overlook the fact that usually such officer is not heard in respect of such remarks made against them. In overview the court need to make such deprecatory remarks only when it is absolutely necessary in particular case, it is possible by keeping in mind the broad realities indicated above.

---

51. AIR 2000 SC 2988.

It was observed by the Supreme Court in *Munshi Prasad and others* v. *State of Bihar*[52] that :

> The appellants contended that delayed receipt of the FIR in the Court of the Chief Judicial Magistrate cannot but be viewed with suspicion. While it is true that Section 157 of the Cr.P.C. makes it obligatory on the officer-in-charge of the police station to send a report of the information received to a Magistrate forthwith, but that does not mean an imply to denounce and discard and otherwise positive and trustworthy evidence on record. If the court is otherwise convinced and has come to a conclusion as regards the truthfulness of the prosecution case, merely delay, which can otherwise be ascribed to be reasonable, would not itself demolish the prosecution case.

In *Rajesh* v. *State of Gujarat,*[53] the trial court in its judgment dealt with the aspect that merely non-mentioning of the number of crime registered upon FIR or name of prosecution witness would not lead the court to believe that the FIR had been ante-timed in view of the unequivocal, reliable and confidence inspiring testimony.

The Supreme Court in *Narayan Rao* v. *State of A.P.*[54] held that:

> In order to simplify commitment proceedings preceding the trial of accused persons by a Court of Session, Sec. 207-A was added by way of amendment of the Code in 1955. From Sub-Sections (3) and (4) of that Section it is clear that in cases exclusively triably by a Court of Session. It is the duty of the Magistrate while holding a preliminary inquiry, to satisfy himself that the documents referred in Sec. 173 have been furnished to the accused and if he found that the police officer concerned had not carried out his duty in that behalf, the Magistrate should see to it that is done. The provisions contained in Sec. 173(4) and Section 207-A(3) have been introduced by amending the Act of 1955, in

---

52. (2001) CrLJ 4708 SC.
53. AIR 2002 SC 1412.
54. AIR 1957 SC 737; Also see AIR 1927 PC 44(V14), AIR 1947 PC 67 (V 34).

order to simplify the procedure in respect of inquiries leading upto a Session trial, and at the same time, to safeguard the interests of accused persons by enjoining upon police officers concerned and Magistrates before whom such proceedings are brought, to see that all the documents, necessary to give the accused persons all the information for the proper conduct of their defence are furnished.

But non-compliance with those provisions has not the result of vitiating those proceedings and subsequent trial. The word 'shall' occurring both in Sub-Section (4) and Sub-Section (3) of Section 207-A, is not mandatory but only directory, because an omission by a police officer, to fully comply with the provisions of Section 173, should not be allowed to have such a far-reaching effect as to render the proceedings including the trial before the court of Session, wholly ineffective.

While delivering the Judgment, Sinha, J. observed that :

The main question for determination in this appeal by Special Leave is whether and, if so, how far non-compliance with the provisions of Section 173(4) and 207-A(3) of the Code of Cr.P.C. has affected the legality of the proceedings and the trial resulting in the conviction of the appellant.

After carefully considering the argument advanced on behalf of the appellant, we have come to the conclusion that the proceedings and the trial have not been vitiated by the admitted non-compliance with the provisions aforesaid, of the Code, and that the irregularity is curable by reference to Section 537 of Code, as no case of prejudice has been made out.

In the Section 46 of the Cr.P.C. in making an arrest, the police officer or other persons making the same shall actually touch or confine the body of the person to be arrested, unless there be a submission to the custody by word or action.

If such person forcibly resists the endeavour to arrest him, or attempts to evade the arrest, such police officer or the person may use all means necessary to effect the arrest.

The words 'all means' used in Sub-Section 2 are wide enough, meaning thereby that assistance from others may be taken in effecting the arrest. Where a public officer arrests a person under warrant he must communicate the substance of it to the person to be arrested or must show the warrant on demand.[55] On this aspect the High Court held that merely, "on account of some irregularities in mentioning the names or noting the timing during the course of investigation, by the prosecution or some discrepancies and contradictions, which are at the micro-level could not be said to be sufficient and efficient to discard and dislodge the otherwise weighty and very important, serious and sound testimony of eyewitness, Rakesh one of the close relatives of the deceased, whose presence was quite natural and whose evidence is, also, found to be quite reliable and dependable and, rightly, accepted by the trial court". After going through the testimony of the prosecution witnesses particularly perusing the record including FIR. The plea of ante-timing of the FIR is the figment of imagination of the defence and not a reality. Assuming that the FIR number and the name of the complainant was known at the time of recording of Panchanama and it was not mentioned therein, such circumstance would not probabilise the defence version that the FIR had been ante-timed, in view of the cogent, reliable and confidence inspiring testimony of Rakesh, Satish and Umaben.

After going through the whole of the evidence, the other record produced in the case and the judgments of the trial court and the High Court, the Apex Court find no reason to interfere in the concurrent findings of fact arrived at against the accused holding them guilty for which they have been convicted and sentenced.

It was observed by the Supreme Court in *Ashok Kumar Pandey* v. *State of Delhi*,[56] that :

---

55. *Ibid.*
56. AIR 2002 SC 1468; Also see, *Rameshwar* v. *State of Rajasthan*, AIR 1953 SC 54; *Dallp Singh and Ors.* v. *The State of Punjab*, AIR 1953 SC 364; *Vadivelu Thevar* v. *State of Madras*, AIR 1957 SC 614; *Masaiti* v. *The State of Uttar Pradesh*, AIR 1965 SC 202; *State of Punjab* v. *Jagir Singh, Baljit Singh and Karam Singh*, AIR 1973 SC 2407 and *Guli Chand and Ors.* v. *State of Rajasthan*, AIR 1974 SC 276.

The occurrence as disclosed by solitary eyewitness, Daya Kant Pandey, who is nobody else than father of one of the victims and father-in-law of the appellant. In his evidence in court, he has supported the case, disclosed in the first information report, that when he along with father of the appellant had gone to terrace of the house for sleeping, on hearing the cries of his daughter, went outside the room, found the same locked from inside, opened it by giving a kick and found that the appellant was inflicting knife blows upon his daughter Neelam and Annu, his daughter's daughter, was lying in the room on the ground in a pool of blood. When this witness shouted in horror, the appellant came towards him with a knife and this witness moved aside and started crying loudly whereupon the accused took to his heels. In the meantime, Sita Ram Pandey, father of the appellant, also came there from the terrace and landlord Hira Nand, arrived at first floor of the house. The witness stated that with the help of father of the appellant, and the landlord, the injured persons were brought to the ground floor and a three wheeler was hired in which this witness and took the injured persons to the hospital where the doctor declared them brought dead. He further stated that the police went to the hospital and recorded his *fard beyan* there. Thereafter, he went to the police station and from there to the place of occurrence. This witness has consistently supported the prosecution case. It has been pointed out on behalf of the appellant that when the witness had seen that the appellant was inflicting injury upon his daughter, he did not take any steps to rescue her which is not natural conduct of a human being, especially when he is father of the deceased and the same shows that this witness was never present at the place of occurrence, had never seen any occurrence and arrived at the hospital after having received the information at Ghaziabad where he was residing. It appears that before the witness arrived, the appellant had inflicted injuries on different parts of the body of his daughter who was lying on ground in a pool of blood and when he arrived on hearing the cries of his daughter, the appellant was found giving indiscriminate dagger blows to Neelam, daughter of this witness, on different parts of her body and when this witness protested, he ran towards him. In these circumstances, it cannot be said to be unnatural if he could not take any step to save the life of his daughter as he being unarmed, as an ordinary normal human being, could not have taken risk of his life at the hands of the appellant which was so imminent. It was pointed out that no reliance should have been placed upon the evidence the solitary interested eyewitness, as he being father of the deceased lady and grand-father of the deceased child, chances of false implication of the appellant, who was not liked by this witness, could not be ruled out. It is well-settled that evidence of a witness cannot be discarded merely on the ground that he is either partisan or interested or both, if otherwise the same is found to be credible.

It was held by the Supreme Court in *Ramsinah B. Judeja* v. *State*[57] that:

Under Sections 154 and 162 any telephonic information about commission of a cognizable offence, if any, irrespective of the nature and details of such information cannot be treated as first information report. If a telephonic message is cryptic in nature and the officer-in-charge proceeds to the place of occurrence on the basis of that information to find out the details of the nature of the offence, if any, then it cannot be said that the information which had been received by him on telephone shall be deemed to be FIR. The object and purpose of giving such telephonic message is not to lodge the FIR but to make an officer-in-charge of the police station to reach the place of occurrence. On the other hand, if the information given on telephone is not cryptic and on the basis of that information the officer-in-charge is *prima facie* satisfied about the commission of a cognizable offence and he proceeds from the police station after recording such information to investigate such offences then any statement made by any person in respect of the said

---

57. AIR 2003 SCW 5050.

offence including about the participant shall be deemed to be a statement made by a person to the police officer in the course of investigation covered by Section 162. In the instant daily diary entry showing that unknown person had given information on telephone about a vehicle hitting the deceased. Thus, it would not constitute FIR and, therefore, the written report lodged by eye-witness was not hit by Section 162 Cr.P.C.

It was observd by the Supreme Court in *Sohan Lal alias Sohan Singh* v. *State of Punjab,*[58] that :

The F.I.R. is only a report about the information as to the commission of an offence. It is not substantive evidence, as the police has yet to investigate the offence. If Bansi Ram's was the testimony in support of the prosecution, then perhaps the counsel's was right. The statement made by Kamlesh Rani under Section 161 of the Cr.P.C. recorded on 7.4.1996 by Satnam Singh, ASI, both of which can be treated as dying declarations.

It was held by the Supreme Court in *Jogender Nath Gharei* v. *State of Orissa,*[59] that :

A cumulative reading of the provisions of the Cr.P.C. makes it clear that Magistrate, who on receipt of a complaint orders an investigation under Section 156(3) and receives a police report under Section 173(1) may thereafter do one of three things viz. :

(1) He may decide that there is no sufficient ground for proceeding further and drop the case.
(2) He may take cognizance of an offence under Section 190(1)(b) on the basis of the original complaint and proceed to examine upon oath the complainant and his witnesses under Section 200.
(3) He may take cognizance of an offence under Section

---

58. 2003 CrLJ 456 SC.
59. 2003 CrLJ 3953 SC.

190(1)(b) on the basis of the original complaint and proceed to examine upon oath the complainant and his witnesses under Section 200.

If he adopts the third alternative, he may hold or direct an enquiry under Section 202, if he thinks fit. Thereafter he may dismiss the complaint or issue process, as the case may be.

The Supreme Court observed in *Jandel Singh* v. *State of M.P.,*[60] that :

> Investigating officer reached the spot at about 10.00 p.m. He did not carry the investigation further at night due to darkness. He did not make any effort to search for the accused though their houses were a few steps away from the place of occurrence. It is unbelievable that an investigating officer who is going for the investigation of a murder case at night would not carry torch with him or try to procure some other source of light to carry on with the investigation. There were houses all around and could have easily arranged for some light. He did not send a copy of the First Information Report to the Jurisdictional Magistrate. Cumulatively all these facts put a doubt on the prosecution version and it leaves an impression that the prosecution has not come out with the truth. All probability the commission of crime came to notice in the morning and thereafter the investigation started. If that be so, the presence of eye-witnesses become very much doubtful.

In *Krishnan and another* v. *State,*[61] the Supreme Court observed that :

> The fact that FIR was given almost immediately, rules out any possibility of deliberation to falsely implicate any person. All the materials particulars implicating the four appellant were given. It has to be noted that both the trial courts and High Court have analysed in great detail.

---

60. 2003 CrLJ 3528 SC.
61. AIR 2003 SC 2978.

Prosectuion witness evidence to form the basis for conviction. Therefore, the trial court and the High Court rightly acted upon the evidence the highly hypothetical imaginative story advance by the defence to contend that his family members killed the deceased is to hollow to be accepted. If that was really so, they would not have been chosen the place and the time for doing so. There is not even a shadow of material to substantive the plea.

It was observed by the Supreme Court in *State of Maharashtra* v. *Christian Community Welfare Council of India and another,*[62] that:

Herein we notice the mandate issued by the High Court to prevent the police from arresting a lady without the presence of the lady constable, said direction also prohibits the arrest of a lady after sunset and before sunrise under any circumstances. While we do agree with the object behind the direction issued by the High Court in Cl. (vii) of operative part of its judgment, we think a strict compliance of the said direction, in a given circumstance, would cause practical difficulty in investigating agencies and might even give room for evading the process of law by unscrupulous accused. While it is necessary to protect the female sought to be arrested by the police from police misdeed, it may not be always possible and practical to have to the presence of a lady constable when the necessity for such arrest arises, therefore, we think this direction issued requires some modifications without disturbing the object behind the same. We think the object will be served if a direction is issued to the arresting authority that while arresting a female person, all efforts should be made to keep a lady constable present but in circumstances where the arresting officer is reasonably satisfied that such presence of a lady Constable is not available or possible and/or the delay in arresting caused by securing the presence of a lady constable would impede the course of investigation such arresting officer for reasons to be

---

62.　AIR 2004 SC 7.

recorded either before the arrest or immediately after the arrest be permitted to arrest female person for lawful reasons at any time of the day or night depending on the circumstances of the case even without the presence of a lady constable. We also direct that with the above modification is regarded to the direction issued by the High Court in Cl. (vii) of this appeal, this appeal is disposed off.

It was further observed by the Supreme Court in *Vidyadharan* v. *State of Kerala*[63] that :

We shall first deal with the plea about false implication. It is seen that though there were some delay in lodging the FIR, it is but natural in a traditional bound society to avoid embarrassment which is inevitable when reputation of a woman is concerned. Delay in every case cannot be a ground to arouse suspicion. It can only be so when the delay is unexplained. In the instant case the delay has been properly explained. A charge sheet under Section 354 is one which is very easy to make and is very difficult to rebut. It would however, be unusual in a conservation society that a woman would be used as pawn to wreck vengeance. When a plea is taken about false implications. Courts have a duty to make deeper scrutiny of the evidence and decide acceptability or otherwise of the accusation.

Subba Rao, J. speaking for Court in *State rep. by Inspector of Police Vigilance and Anti-corruption Tiruchirapalli, Tamil Nadu* v. *Jaya Pal*[64] observed that :

The police officer, who laid/recorded the FIR regarding the suspected commission of certain cognizable offences by the respondent is competent to investigate the case and submit the final report to the court of Special Judge. There is nothing in the provisions of the Cr.P.C. which preclude the Inspector of Police, vigilance from taking up to the

63. 2004 CrLJ 605 SC.
64. 2004 CrLJ 1819 SC.

investigation. The fact that the said police officer prepared the FIR on the basis of the information received by him and registered the suspected crime does not disqualify him from taking up the investigation of the cognizable offence. A *suo-motu* move on the part of the police officer to investigate a cognizable offence impelled by the information received from some source is not outside the purview of the provisions contained in Sections 154 to 157 of the Code of Criminal Procedure or any other provisions of the Code. The proceedings cannot be quashed on premise that the investigation by the same officer who 'lodged' the FIR would prejudice the accused in as much as the investigating officer cannot be expected to act fairly and objectively. There is no principle or binding authority to held that the moment the competent police officer on the basis of information received, makes out an FIR incorporating his name as informant, he forfeits his right to investigate. A *suo-motu* move on the part of the police officer to investigate a cognizable offence impelled by the information received from some sources not outside the purview of provision of Sections 154 to 157, the scheme was Sections 154, 156 and 157 was clarified thus by the court.

The Supreme Court in *Inspector of Police* v. *N.M.T. Joy Immaculate*,[65] highlighted that :

The Section 167 Cr.P.C. empowers a Judicial Magistrate to authorise the detention of an accused in the custody of police. Section 209 Cr.P.C. confers powers upon a magistrate to remand an accused to custody until the case has been committed to the court of Sessions and also until the conclusion of the trial. Section 309 Cr.P.C. confers power upon a court to remand an accused to custody after taking cognizance of an offence or during commencement of trial when he finds it necessary to adjourn the enquiry or trial. The order of the remand has no baring on the proceedings of the trial itself nor it can have any effect on

---

65. 2004 CrLJ 215 SC.

the ultimate decision of the case. If an order of remand is found to be illegal, it cannot result in acquittal of the accused or in termination of proceedings. A remand order cannot affect the progress of the trial or its decisions in any manner. It cannot be categorized even as an 'intermediate order'. The order is, therefore, a pure and simple interlocutory order and in view of the bar created by sub-Section (2) of Section 397(2) Cr.P.C., a revision against the said order is not maintainable.

(B) Investigation

The investigation of an offence is the field exclusively reserved for the police whose powers in that field are unfettered so long as the power to investigate into the cognizable offense is legitimately exercised in strict compliance with the provision falling under the Criminal Procedure Code.

In _Ram Kishan Mithan Lal Sharma_ v. _State of Bombay_,[66] the Supreme Court observed that in order to resolve the conflict of opinion one has to examine the purpose of test identification parades. These parades are held by the police in the course of their investigation for the purpose of enabling witnesses to identify the properties which are the subject-matter of the offence or to identify the persons who are concerned in the offence. They are not held merely for the purpose of identifying property or persons irrespective of their connection with the offence. Whether the police officers interrogate the identifying witnesses or the Panch witnesses who are procured by the police do so, the identifying witnesses are explained the purpose of holding these parades and are asked to identify the properties which are the subject-matter of the offence or the persons who are concerned in the offence.

The Apex Court further held that an attempt has been made to argue before us that while the evidence of the police officer may be inadmissible, the evidence of the Panch witness as well as of the identifying witnesses themselves, relating to the fact of the prior identification, as an item of corroborative evidence is admissible. I agree that on the evidence given in this

---

66. AIR 1955 SC 104.

case, there is no scope for such differentiation and that the entire evidence relating to the prior identification parades concerning the 4th accused is in substance, evidence only of the prior statements of the identifying witnesses to the police officer and is hence inadmissible. But I wish to guard myself against being understood as having assented to the suggestion that in law a differentiation can be made in such cases between the three classes of evidence, viz. (1) of the police officer, (2) of the Panch witness, and (3) of the identifying himself, in so far as they speak to a prior identification at a parade held by the police officer. I am inclined to think that such differentiation is unsound and inadmissible. The legal permissibility of the proof is a matter of importance because, though the evidence of prior identification is only corroborative evidence, still such corroboration is of considerable value in cases of the kind.

In *A. C. Sharma* v. *Delhi Administration,*[67] the Supreme Court observed that the investigation in the present case by the Deputy Superintendent of Police cannot be considered to be in any way unauthorised or contrary to law. In this connection it may not be out of place also to point out that the function of investigation is merely to collect evidence and any irregularity or even illegality in the course of collection of evidence can scarcely be considered by itself to affect the legality of the trial by an otherwise competent Court of the offence so investigated. In *H. N. Rishbud & Inder Singh* v. *State of Delhi,*[68] it was held that an illegality committed in the course of investigation does not affect the competence and jurisdiction of the Court for trial and where cognizance of the case has in fact been taken and the case has proceeded to termination the invalidity of the preceding investigation does not vitiate the result unless miscarriage of justice has been caused thereby. When any breach of the mandatory provisions relating to investigation is brought to the notice of the Court at an early stage of the trial the Court will have to consider the nature and extent of the violation and pass appropriate orders for such reinvestigation as may be called for, wholly or partly.

The Apex Court further held that, notwithstanding anything in the Police Act, 1861, the Central Government may

---

67. AIR 1973 SC 913; (1973) 1 SCC 726.
68. (1955) 1 SCR 1150; AIR 1955 SC 196.

constitute a special Police force to be called the Delhi Special Police Establishment for the investigation in any Union territory of offences notified under Section 3. Subject to any orders which the Central Government may make in this behalf, members of the said Police establishment shall have throughout any Union territory in relation to the investigation of such offences and arrest of persons concerned in such offences, all the powers, duties, privileges and liabilities which Police officers of that Union territory have in connection with the investigation of offences committed therein. Any member of the said Police establishment of or above the rank of Sub-Inspector may, subject to any orders which the Central Government may make in this behalf, exercise in any Union territory any of the powers of the officer-in-charge of a Police Station in the area in which he is for the time being and when so exercising such powers shall, subject to any such orders as aforesaid, be deemed to be an officer-in-charge of a Police Station discharging the functions of such an officer within the limits of his Station.

In *State of Bihar and another v. JAC Saldanha and others*,[69] the Supreme Court observed as under:

> There is a clear-cut and well demarcated sphere of activity in the field of crime detection and crime punishment. Investigation of an offence is the field exclusively reserved for the executive through the police department the superintendence over which vests in the State Government. The executive which is charged with a duty to keep vigilance over law and order situation is obliged to prevent crime and if an offence is alleged to have been committed it is its bounden duty to investigate into the offence and bring the offender to book. Once it investigates and finds an offence having been committed it is its duty to collect evidence for the purpose of proving the offence. Once that is completed and the investigating officer submits report to the Court requesting the Court to take cognizance of the offence under Section 190 of the Code its duty comes to an end. On a cognizance of the offence being taken by the Court the police function of investigation comes to an end

---

69. 1980(1) SCC 554.

subject to provision contained in Section 173(8), there commences the adjudicatory function of the judiciary to determine whether an offence has been committed and if so, whether by the person or persons charged with the crime by the police in its report to the Court, and to award adequate punishment according to law for the offence proved to the satisfaction of the Court. There is thus a well defined and well demarcated function in the field of crime detection and its subsequent adjudication between the police and the Magistrate.

In *State of Rajasthan* v. *Bhawani and others*[70] the High Court has extensively relied upon the site plan prepared by the investigating officer for discarding the prosecution case and for this purpose has referred to the place from where the accused are alleged to have entered the Nohara, the place from where they are alleged to have fired upon the deceased and also has drawn an inference that the place wherefrom the accused are alleged to have fired upon the deceased, the shot could not have hit the houses on the eastern side of the Nohara. Many things mentioned in the site plan have been noted by the investigating officer on the basis of the statements given by the witnesses. Obviously, the place from where the accused entered the Nohara and the place from where they resorted to firing is based upon the statement of the witnesses. These are clearly hit by Section 162 Cr.P.C. What the investigating officer personally saw and noted alone would be admissible. This legal position was explained in *Tori Singh and another* v. *State of U.P.*,[71] in following words :

A rough sketch map prepared by the sub-inspector on the basis of statements made to him by witnesses during the course of investigation and showing the place where the deceased was hit and also the places where the witnesses were at the time of the incident would not be admissible in evidence in view of the provisions of S. 162 of the Code of Criminal Procedure, for it is in effect nothing more than the

---

70. AIR 2003 SC 4230.
71. AIR 1962 SC 399.

statement of the Sub-Inspector that the eye-witnesses told him that the deceased was at such and such place at the time when he was hit. The sketch-map would be admissible so far as it indicates all that the Sub-Inspector saw himself at the spot; but any mark put on the sketch-map based on the statements made by the witnesses to the Sub-Inspector would be inadmissible in view of the clear provisions of S. 162 of the Code of Criminal Procedure as it will be no more than a statement made to the police during investigation. Therefore, such marks on the map cannot be used to found any argument as to the improbability of the deceased being hit on that part of the body where he was actually injured, if he was standing at the spot marked on the sketch-map.

The Apex Court held that the findings recorded by the High Court on the basis of the site plan prepared by the investigating officer whereby it discarded the prosecution case is clearly illegal being based upon inadmissible evidence and has to be set aside.

In *Union of India* v. *Prakash P. Hinduja*,[72] the principal question requiring consideration was whether the Court can go into the validity or otherwise of the investigation done by the authorities charged with the duty of investigation under the relevant statutes and whether any error or illegality committed during the course of investigation would so vitiate the charge-sheet so as to render the cognizance taken thereon bad and invalid.

The Supreme Court referred to in several decisions and gave its view as under:

> In India as has been shown there is a statutory right on the part of the police to investigate the circumstances of an alleged cognizable crime without requiring any authority from the judiciary authorities, and it would, as their Lordships think, be an unfortunate result if it should be held possible to interfere with those statutory rights by an exercise of the inherent jurisdiction of the Court. The

---

72. AIR 2003 SC 2612.

functions of the judiciary and the police are complementary not overlapping and the combination of individual liberty with a due observance of law and order is only to be obtained by leaving each to exercise its own function, always, of course, subject to the right of the Court to intervene in an appropriate case when moved under Section 491, Criminal Procedure Code, to give directions in the nature of *habeas corpus*. In such a case as the present, however the Court's functions begin when a charge is preferred before it and not until then.

(C) Arrest

Our criminal justice system appears to revolve round, the pivotal institution of judiciary. From the very moment of infraction of the right to freedom of movement of a citizen by way of arrest, the judiciary oversees everything at every stage in the criminal justice process.

The Supreme Court in *Joginder Kumar* v. *State of U.P. and others*[73] held that :

No arrest can be made because it is lawful for the Police Officer to do so. The existence of the power to arrest is one thing. The justification for the exercise of it is quite another. The Police Officer must be able to justify the arrest apart from his power to do so. Arrest and detention in police lock-up of a person can cause incalculable harm to the reputation and self-esteem of a person. No arrest can be made in a routine manner on a mere allegation of commission of an offence made against a person. It would be prudent for a Police Officer in the interest of protection of the constitutional rights of a citizen and perhaps in his own interest that no arrest should be made without a reasonable satisfaction reached after some investigation as to the genuineness and bonafides of a complaint and a reasonable belief both as to the person's complicity and even so as to the need to effect arrest. Denying a person of his liberty is a serious matter. The recommendations of the

---

73. AIR 1994 SC 1349; 1994 CrLJ 1981.

Police Commission merely reflect the constitutional concomitants of the fundamental right to personal liberty and freedom. A person is not liable to arrest merely on the suspicion of complicity in an offence. There must be some reasonable justification in the opinion of the officer effecting the arrest that such arrest is necessary and justified. Except in heinous offences, an arrest must be avoided if a police officer issues notice to person to attend the Station House and not to leave Station without permission would do.

The Court further observed that :

A realistic approach should be made in this direction. The law of arrest is one of balancing individual rights, liberties and privileges, on the one hand, and individual duties, obligations and responsibilities on the other; of weighing and balancing the rights, liberties and privileges of the single individual and those of individuals collectively; of simply deciding what is wanted and where to put the weight and the emphasis; of deciding which comes first— the criminal or society, the law violator or the law abider.

The quality of a nation's civilisation can be largely measured by the methods it uses in the enforcement of criminal law. The Apex Court in *Smt. Nandini Satpathy* v. *P.L. Dani*,[74] quoting Lewis Mayers stated:

To strike the balance between the needs of law enforcement on the one hand and the protection of the citizen from oppression and injustice at the hands of the law-enforcement machinery on the other is a perennial problem of statecraft. The pendulum over the years has swung to the right.

The Apex Court while quoting the National Police Commission's Third Report referring the quality of arrests by the Police in India mentioned power of arrest as one of the chief

---

74. AIR 1978 SC 1025.

sources of corruption in the police. The report suggested that, by and large, nearly 60% of the arrests were either unnecessary or unjustified and that such unjustified police action accounted for 43.2% of the expenditure of the jails. The said Commission in its Third Report observed that:

> It is obvious that a major portion of the arrests were connected with very minor prosecutions and cannot, therefore, be regarded as quite necessary from the point of view of crime prevention. Continued detention in jail of the persons so arrested has also meant avoidable expenditure on their maintenance. In the above period it was estimated that 43.2 per cent of the expenditure in the connected jails was over such prisoners only who in the ultimate analysis need not have been arrested at all.

Lastly the Supreme Court held that effective enforcement of the fundamental rights granted under Articles 21 and 22(1) of the Constitution and required to be recognised and scrupulously protected. For effective enforcement of these fundamental rights, the court issued the following requirements:

1. An arrested person being held in custody is entitled, if he so requests to have one friend, relative or other person who is known to him or likely to take an interest in his welfare told as far as is practicable that he has been arrested and where is being detained.
2. The Police Officer shall inform the arrested person when he is brought to the police station of this right.
3. An entry shall be required to be made in the Diary as to who was informed of the arrest. These protections from power must be held to flow from Articles 21 and 22(1) and enforced strictly.

In *Sajan Abraham* v. *State of Kerala*[75] the Apex Court observe that an obligation is cast on the prosecution while making an arrest or seizure, the officer should make full report of all

---

75. AIR 2001 SC 3190; (2001) 6 SCC 692.

particulars of such arrest or seizure and send it to his immediate superior officer within 48 hours of such arrest or seizure. The submission is, this has not been done. It is true that the communication to the immediate superior has not been made in the form of a report, which is also recorded by the High Court that has sent copies of FIR and other documents to his superior officer which is not in dispute. The copies of the FIR along with other records regarding the arrest of appellant and seizure of the contraband articles were sent to his superior officer immediately after registering the said case. So, all the necessary information to be submitted in a report was sent. This constitutes substantial compliance and mere absence of any such report cannot be said it has prejudiced the accused. This section is not mandatory in nature. When substantial compliance has been made, as in the present case it would not vitiate the prosecution case.

In *State of Punjab* v. *Balbir Singh*,[76] the Supreme Court held that :

> The provisions of Sections 52 and 57 of the Code of Criminal Procedure, which deal with the steps to be taken by the officers after making arrest or seizure under Sections 41 to 44 are by themselves not mandatory.

In *D.K. Basu* v. *State of West Bengal*[77] the Supreme Court considered it appropriate to issue the following requirements to be followed in all cases of arrest or detention till legal provisions are made in that behalf as preventive measures:

(1) The police personnel carrying out the arrest and handling the interrogation of the arrestee should bear accurate, visible and clear identification and name tags with their designations. The particulars of all such police personnel who handle interrogation of the arrestee must be recorded in a register.

(2) That the police officer carrying out the arrest of the arrestee shall prepare a memo of arrest at the time of arrest and such memo shall be attested by at least one

---

76. (1994) 3 SCC 299; AIR 1994 SC 1872.
77. AIR 1997 SC 610; 1997 CrLJ 743.

witness, who may be either a member of the family of the arrestee or a respectable person of the locality from where the arrest is made. It shall also be countersigned by the arrestee and shall contain the time and date of arrest.

(3) A person who has been arrested or detained and is being held in custody in a police station or interrogation centre or other lock-up, shall be entitled to have one friend or relative or other person known to him or having interest in his welfare being informed, as soon as practicable, that he has been arrested and is being detained at the particular place, unless the attesting witness of the memo of arrest is himself such a friend or a relative of the arrestee.

(4) The time, place of arrest and venue of custody of an arrestee must be notified by the police where the next friend or relative of the arrestee lives outside the district or and through the Legal Aid Organisation in the District and the police station of the area concerned telegraphically within a period of 8 to 12 hours after the arrest.

(5) The person arrested must be made aware of this right to have someone informed of his arrest or detention as soon as he is put under arrest or is detained.

(6) An entry must be made in the diary at the place of detention regarding the arrest of the person which shall also disclose the name of the next friend of the person who has been informed of the arrest and the names and particulars of the police officials in whose custody the arrestee is.

(7) The arrestee should, where he so requests, be also examined at the time of his arrest and major and minor injuries, if any, present on his/her body, must be recorded at that time. The "Inspection Memo" must be signed both by the arrestee and the police officer effecting the arrest and its copy provided to the arrestee.

(8) The arrestee should be subjected to medical examination by a trained doctor every 48 hours during his detention in custody by a doctor on the panel of

approved doctors appointed by Director, Health Services of the concerned State or Union Territory, Director, Health Services should prepare such a panel for all Tehsils and Districts as well.

(9) Copies of all the documents including the memo of arrest, referred to above, should be sent to the (sic) Magistrate for his record.

(10) The arrestee may be permitted to meet his lawyer during interrogation, though not throughout the interrogation.

(11) A police control room should be provided at all district and State headquarters, where information regarding the arrest and the place of custody of the arrestee shall be communicated by the officer causing the arrest, within 12 hours of effecting the arrest and at the police control room it should be displayed on a conspicuous police board.

The Court further held that these directions are in addition to the constitutional and statutory safeguards and do not detract from various other directions given by the Courts from time to time in connection with the safeguarding of the rights and dignity of the arrestee.

III. CRIMINAL COURTS PROCEEDING AND JUDICIAL INTERPRETATION

The Trial Court Judges and Magistrates is one of the most important factors to ensure the efficient working of our judicial system. The quality of justice, it needs to be stressed, depends not merely upon having well worded codes and statutes, but much more so upon the way they are administered and enforced. In an evaluation is to be made of the role of the different functionaries who play their parts in the administration of justice, the top position would necessarily have assigned to the trial court. The image of the judiciary for the common man is projected by the trial court and this in turn depends upon their intellectual, moral and personal qualities.

(A) Charge

Framing of charges is the concern of the court under the criminal justice system. However, it is generally complained that courts accept the charges framed by police in the report under Section 173 of Cr.P.C. Though the power to discharge is conferred on courts, it is seen that ordinarily courts do not discharge an accused as they can find *prima facie* case against the persons reported upon by the police under Sec. 173 of Cr.P.C.

In *Municipal Corporation of Delhi* v. *Ram Kishan Rohtagi,*[78] the Supreme Court held that where the allegations set out in the complaint did not constitute any offence and the High Court quashed the order passed by the Magistrate taking cognizance of the offence there would be no bar to the Court's discretion under Section 319, Cr. P.C. if it was made out on the additional evidence laid before it. Section 319 gives ample powers to any Court to take cognizance against any person not being an accused before it and try him along with the other accused. This Court clearly observed that:

In these circumstances, therefore, if the prosecution can at any stage produce evidence which satisfied the Court that the other accused or those who have not been arrayed as accused against whom proceedings have been quashed have also committed the offence the Court can take cognizance against them and try them along with the other accused. But we would hasten to add that this is really an extraordinary power which is conferred on the Court and should be used very sparingly and only if compelling reasons exist for taking cognizance against the other person against whom action has not been taken. More than this we would not like to say anything further at this stage. We leave the entire matter to the discretion of the Court concerned so that it may act according to law. We would, however, make it plain that the mere fact that the proceedings have been quashed against respondents will not prevent the Court from exercising its discretion if it is fully satisfied that a case for taking cognizance against them has been made out on the additional evidence led before it.

---

78. AIR 1983 SC 67.

In *Sohan Lal* v. *State of Rajasthan*[79] the Supreme Court held that:

> Add to any charge means the addition of a new charge. An alteration of a charge means changing or variation of an existing charge or making of a different charge. Addition to and alteration of a charge or charges implies one or more existing charge or charges.

In *Niranjan Singh Karam Singh Punjabi* v. *Jitendra Bhimraj Bijjaya*,[80] after considering the provisions of Sections 227 and 228, Code of Criminal Procedure, the Court posed a question, whether at the stage of framing the charge, trial Court should marshal the materials on the record of the case as he would do on the conclusion of the trial? The Court held that at the stage of framing the charge inquiry must necessarily be limited to deciding if the facts emerging from such materials constitute the offence with which the accused could be charged. The Court may peruse the records for the limited purpose, but it is not required to marshal it with a view to decide the reliability thereof. The Court referred to earlier decisions[81] in and held thus:

> It seems well settled that at the Sections 227-228 stage the Court is required to evaluate the material and documents on record with a view to finding out if the facts emerging therefrom taken at their face value disclose the existence of all the ingredients constituting the alleged offence. The Court may for this limited purpose shift the evidence as it cannot be expected even at the initial stage to accept all that the prosecution states as gospel truth even if it is opposed to common sense or the broad probabilities of the case.

---

79. AIR 1990 SC 2158.
80. AIR 1990 SC 1962 : 1990 Cri LJ 1869.
81. *State of Bihar* v. *Ramesh Singh*, (1977) 4 SCC 39 : (AIR 1977 SC 2018 : 1977 Cri LJ 1606); *Union of India* v. *Prafulla Kumar Samal*, (1979) 3 SCC 4 : (AIR 1979 SC 366 : 1979 Cri LJ 154) and *Supdt. and Remembrancer of Legal Affairs, West Bengal* v. *Anil Kumar Bhunja*, (1979) 4 SCC 274 : (AIR 1980 SC 52 : 1979 Cri LJ 1390).

If the Court is satisfied that a prima facie case is made out for proceeding further then a charge has to be framed. Per contra, if the evidence which the prosecution proposes to produce to prove the guilt of the accused, even if fully accepted before it is challenged by the cross-examination or rebutted by the defence evidence, if any, cannot show that accused committed the particular offence then the charge can be quashed.

In the case of *Minakshi Bala* v. *Sudhir Kumar*,[82] the Apex Court considered the question of quashing of charge by the High Court in invoking its inherent jurisdiction under Sec. 482, Code of Criminal Procedure. In that context, this Court made the following pertinent observations :

> ". . . . To put it differently, once charges are framed under Sec. 240, Cr.P.C. the High Court in its revisional jurisdiction would not be justified in relying upon documents other than those referred to in Sections 239 and 240, Cr.P.C.; nor would it be justified in invoking its inherent jurisdiction under Sec. 482, Cr.P.C. to quash the same except in those rare cases where forensic exigencies and formidable compulsions justify such a course. We hasten to add even in such exceptional cases the High Court can look into only those documents which are unimpeachable and can be legally translated into relevant evidence.

Apart from the infirmity in the approach of the High Court in dealing with the matter which the Supreme Court has already noticed, further find that instead of adverting to and confining its attention to the documents referred to in Sections 239 and 240, Cr.P.C. the High Court has dealt with the rival contentions of the parties raised through their respective affidavits at length and on a threadbare discussion thereof passed the impugned order. The course so adopted cannot be supported; firstly, because finding regarding commission of an offence cannot be recorded on the basis of affidavit evidence and secondly, because at the stage of framing of charge the Court cannot

---

82. (1994) 4 SCC 142.

usurp the functions of a trial Court to delve into and decide upon the respective merits of the case.

In *State of M.P.* v. *Mohan Lal Soni*,[83] the High Court in revision quashed the charges accepting the contentions raised by the accused after detailed consideration of material produced on record. Having regard to the facts and circumstances of the case and referring to earlier decisions of the Apex Court held thus :

> In our view, it is apparent that the entire approach of the High Court is illegal and erroneous. From the reasons recorded by the High Court, it appears that instead of considering the *prima facie* case, the High Court has appreciated and weighed the materials on record for coming to the conclusion that charge against the respondents could not have been framed. It is settled law that at the stage of framing the charges, the Court has to *prima facie* consider whether there is sufficient ground for proceeding against the accused. The Court is not required to appreciate the evidence and arrive at the conclusion that the materials produced are sufficient or not for convicting the accused. If the Court is satisfied that a *prima facie* case is made out for proceeding further then a charge has to be framed. The charge can be quashed if the evidence which the prosecutor proposes to adduce to prove the guilt of the accused, even if fully accepted before it is challenged by cross-examination or rebutted by the defence evidence, if any, cannot show that accused committed the particular offence.

In *State of M.P.* v. *S.B. Johari*,[84] the Supreme Court, adverting to the question of quashing of charges in the light of the provisions contained in Sections 227 and 288, 401 and 397 and 482, Cr.P.C. did not favour the approach of the High Court in meticulously examining the materials on record for coming to the conclusion that the charge could not have been framed for a particular offence.

---

83. AIR 2000 SC 2583.
84. (2000) 2 SCC 57; AIR 2000 SC 665.

In *Roy, V.D.* v. *State of Kerala*[85] the Supreme Court held that, it is well settled that the power under Section 482 of the Cr.P.C. has to be exercised by the High Court, *inter alia,* to prevent the abuse of the process of any Court or otherwise to secure the ends of justice. Where criminal proceedings are initiated based on illicit material collected on search and arrest which are *per se* illegal and vitiate not only a conviction and sentence based on such material but also the trial itself, the proceedings cannot be allowed to go on as it cannot be but amount to abuse of the process of the Court in such a case not quashing the proceedings would perpetuate abuse of the process of the Court resulting in great hardship and injustice to the accused. In our opinion, exercise of power under Section 482 of the Cr.P.C. to quash proceedings in a case like the one on hand, would indeed secure the ends of justice.

In *State of Delhi* v. *Gyani Devi,*[86] the Supreme Court, while quashing and setting aside the order passed by the High Court, made the following observations:

> ". . . After considering the material on record, learned Sessions Judge framed the charge as stated above. That charge is quashed by the High Court against the respondents by accepting the contention raised and considering the details of the material produced on record. The same is challenged by filing these appeals. In our view, it is apparent that the entire approach of the High Court is illegal and erroneous. From the reasons record by the High Court, it appears that instead of considering the *prima facie* case, the High Court has appreciated and weighed the materials on record for coming to the conclusion that charge against the respondents could not have been framed. It is settled law that at the stage of framing the charge, the Court has to *prima facie* consider whether there is sufficient ground for proceeding against the accused. The Court is not required to appreciate the evidence and arrive at the conclusion that the materials produced are sufficient or not for convicting the accused. If the Court is satisfied

---

85. AIR 2001 SC 137.
86. AIR 2001 SC 40; (2000) 8 SCC 239.

that a *prima facie* case is made out for proceeding further then a charge has to be framed. The charge can be quashed if the evidence which the prosecutor proposes to adduce to prove the guilt of the accused, even if fully accepted before it is challenged by cross-examination or rebutted by defence evidence, if any, cannot show that the accused committed the particular offence. In such case, there would be no sufficient ground for proceeding with the trial . . ."

The Court further Judged in the light of the settled position of law as reiterated in the decisions noted above, the order under challenge in the present case does not stand the scrutiny. The High Court has erred in its approach to the case as if it was evaluating the medical evidence for the purpose of determining the question whether the charge under Sec. 304/34, I.P.C. framed against the accused respondents was likely to succeed or not. This question was to be considered by the trial Judge after recording the entire evidence in the case. It was not for the High Court to pre-judge the case at the stage when only a few witnesses (doctors) had been examined by the prosecution and that too under the direction of the High Court in the revision petition filed by the accused. The High Court has not observed that the prosecution had closed the evidence from its side. There is also no discussion or observation in the impugned order that the facts and circumstances of the case make it an exceptional case in which immediate interference of the High Court by invoking its inherent jurisdiction under Sec. 482, Cr.P.C. is warranted in the interest of justice. On consideration of the matter we have no hesitation to hold that the order under challenge is vitiated on account of erroneous approach of the High Court and it is clearly unsustainable.

In *Munna Devi* v. *State of Rajasthan*,[87] the Apex Court held that the revision power under the Code of Criminal Procedure cannot be exercised in a routine and casual manner. While exercising such powers, the High Court has no authority to appreciate the evidence in the manner as the trial and the appellate courts are required to do. Revisional powers could be exercised only when it is shown that there is a legal bar against

---

87. AIR 2002 SC 107.

the continuance of the criminal proceedings or the framing of charge or the facts as stated in the first information report even if they are taken at the face value and accepted in their entirety do not constitute the offence for which the accused has been charged.

In the instant case, the learned judge ignored the basic principles which conferred the jurisdiction upon the High Court for exercise of revisional powers. It was premature for the High Court to say that the material placed before the trial court was insufficient for framing the charge or that the statement of the prosecutrix herself was not sufficient to proceed further against the accused-respondent.

As the impugned order has been passed against the settled position of law, it is unsustainable and is accordingly set aside. The order of framing the charge passed by the trial court against the accused is upheld with directions to proceed with the trial of the case and dispose of the same on merits in accordance with law.

(B) Bail

As far as granting of bail is concerned the broad guidelines laid down in the Criminal Procedure Code, 1973, but the courts have evolved certain standards. For the purpose of cancellation of bail the courts have also evolved certain guidelines. These are generally found in judgements of various High Courts and Supreme Court.

It was observed by Krishna Iyer, J., in *Gudikanti Narasimhulu v. Public Prosecutor, High Court of Andhra Pradesh*[88] that :

the issue of bail is one of liberty, justice, public safety and burden of the public treasury, all of which insist that a developed jurisprudence of bail is integral to a socially sensitized judicial process. After all, personal liberty of an accused or convict is fundamental, suffering lawful eclipse only in terms of procedure established by law. The last four words of Art. 21 are the life of that human right.

---

88. (1978) 1 SCC 240; AIR 1978 SC 429.

In *Balchand Jain* v. *State of Madhya Pradesh,*[89] Bhagwati, J. who spoke for himself and A.C. Gupta, J. observed that:

the power of granting "anticipatory bail is somewhat extraordinary in character and it is only in exceptional cases where it appears that a person might be falsely implicated, or a frivolous case might be launched against him, or "there are reasonable grounds for holding that a person accused of an offence is not likely to abscond, or otherwise misuse his liberty while on bail" that such power is to be exercised.

In *Shahzad Hasan Khan* v. *Ishtiaq Hasan Khan & another,*[90] the Supreme Court observed as below :

Had the learned Judge granted time to the complainant for filing counter-affidavit correct facts would have been placed before the court and it could have been pointed out that apart from the inherent danger of tampering with or intimidating witnesses and aborting the case, there was also the danger to the life of the main witnesses or to the life of the accused being endangered as experience of life has shown to the members of the profession and the judiciary, and in that event, the learned Judge would have been in a better position to ascertain facts to act judiciously. No doubt liberty of a citizen must be zealously safeguarded by court, nonetheless when a person is accused of a serious offence like murder and his successive bail applications are rejected on merit there being *prima facie* material, the prosecution is entitled to place correct facts before the court. Liberty is to be secured through process of law, which is administered keeping in mind the interests of the accused, the near and dear of the victim who lost his life and who feel helpless and believe that there is no justice in the world as also the collective interest of the community so that parties do not lose faith in the institution and indulge in private retribution. Learned

89. AIR 1977 SC 366.
90. 1987 (2) SCC 684.

Judge was unduly influenced by the concept of liberty, disregarding the facts of the case.

Kashmira Singh v. *Duman Singh,*[91] the appellant, Kashmira Singh was arrested subsequent to the registration of an F.I.R. upon a complaint filed by the respondent, Duman Singh. The accused and his family members had been involved in a long standing dispute over a certain piece of land. Being apprehensive of a quarrel, the local police had initiated proceedings under Section 145 of the Code of Criminal Procedure, 1973. In the F.I.R., the complainant alleges that he was led to believe that the accused and his family members had, on 28-5-1993, violated the Tehsildar's order, not to interfere with the land and had ploughed the land and sown a paddy crop. To verify whether this was true, the complainant and a few others went to the village of the accused. He alleges that after having confirmed the news, he and five others were returning in their vehicles when they came upon the accused, his three brothers and his father, who were armed and were standing near the village chowk. The complainant and his party stopped their vehicles and, one member of the complainant's party, who was armed with a Dang, went up to the accused's party to enquire why they had violated the Tehsildar's order. According to the complainant, the accused's brother reacted by attacking that person, whereupon an altercation ensued between both sides. The members of both parties were armed with Dangs, Sotis and rifles. The skirmish resulted in the death of some of the persons present. (The F.I.R. records the death of two members of the complainant's party while the impugned judgment states that one member of the accused's party was also killed).

In the impugned judgment, the learned Judge states that while seeking bail, the accused had concealed material facts from the Court in that he had only relied on the fact that Chamkaur Singh had not pressed his application for bail on 14-9-1993, without mentioning that Chamkaur Singh's applications for bail were later rejected on two occasions. Moreover, the learned Judge stated that while granting bail, he had been under the impression that there were two cross versions and both

---

91. AIR 1996 SC 2176.

parties had been challenged by the police whereas, in fact, only one challan, against the accused party, had been issued. For these reasons, the learned Judge saw it fit to cancel the bail granted to the accused.

The Supreme Court in *Kashi Nath Roy v. State of Bihar*[92] held that the criminal jurisprudence obtaining in this country, Courts exercising bail jurisdiction normally do and should refrain from indulging in elaborate reasoning in their orders in justification of grant or non-grant of bail. For, in that manner, the principle of "presumption of innocence of an accused" gets jeopardized; and the structural principle of "not guilty till proved guilty" gets destroyed, even though all same elements have always understood that such views are tentative and not final, so as to affect the merit of the matter. Here, the appellant has been caught and exposed to a certain adverse comment and action solely because in reasoning he had disclosed his mind while granting bail.

In *Chandraswami v. Central Bureau of Investigation*,[93] the complaint relates to an offence alleged to have been committed by the appellants nearly 16 years ago. Not much progress has taken place in the conduct of the proceedings but the examination-in-chief and a part of the cross-examination of the complainant, the main witness, has been completed. The appellants have been in custody since 2-5-1996. The only reason put forth by the trial Court, as well as the High Court, for not releasing the appellants on bail is that there is an apprehension that they are likely to influence the witnesses or tamper with the evidence. The main witness in the present case is the complainant himself, who has been zealously pursuing this case since 1987. It is his perseverance throughout these long years that has made it possible for the case to reach the stage at which it presently stands. His commitment to see the prosecution reach its logical end is strong and he is not likely to be influenced by the accused. In spite of our query at the hearing, the learned Additional Solicitor General was unable to point out any evidence which could now be tampered or influenced by the accused. We are, therefore, not satisfied that if the appellants

---

92. AIR 1996 SC 3240.
93. AIR 1997 SC 2575; (1996) 6 SCC 751.

are released on bail, they would be in a position to influence the witnesses, the main witness being the complainant himself, or tamper with the evidence.

In *State of Maharashtra* v. *Ramesh Taurani*[94] the only evidence collected against the respondent was that he handed over an amount of Rs. 25 lacs to the contract killers (who according to the prosecution committed the murder of Gulshan Kumar). Apart from the fact that in the context of the prosecution case, the above circumstance incriminates the respondent in a large way, the Apex Court find that the Investigating Agency has collected other incriminating materials also against the respondent, to make out a strong *prima facie* case against him. It is trite that among other considerations which the Court has to take into account in deciding whether bail should be granted in a non-bailable offence is the nature and gravity of the offence. The Supreme Court therefore was of the opinion that the High Court should not have granted bail to the respondent considering the seriousness of the allegations levelled against him, particularly at a stage when investigation is continuing.

In *Dolat Ram* v. *State of Haryana*,[95] the Supreme Court while drawing a distinction between rejection of bail in a non-bailable case at the initial stage and the cancellation of bail already granted, opined:

> Very cogent and overwhelming circumstances are necessary for an order directing the cancellation of the bail, already granted. Generally speaking, the grounds for cancellation of bail, broadly (illustrative and not exhaustive) are : interference or attempt to interfere with the due course of administration of justice or evasion or attempt to evade the due course of justice or abuse of the concession granted to the accused in any manner. The satisfaction of the Court, on the basis of material placed on the record of the possibility of the accused absconding is yet another reason justifying the cancellation of bail. However, bail once granted should not be cancelled in a mechanical manner without considering whether any

---

94. AIR 1998 SC 586.
95. (1995) 1 SCC 349.

supervening circumstances have rendered it no longer conducive to a fair trial to allow the accused to retain his freedom by enjoying the concession of bail during the trial. These principles, it appears, were lost sight of by the High Court when it decided to cancel the bail, already granted. The High Court it appears to us overlooked the distinction of the factors relevant for rejecting bail in a non-bailable case in the first instance and the cancellation of bail already granted.

In *Ram Govind Upadhyay* v. *Sudarshan Singh,*[96] undoubtedly, considerations applicable to the grant of bail and considerations for cancellation of such an order of bail are independent and do not overlap each other, but in the event of non-consideration of considerations relevant for the purpose of grant of bail and in the event an earlier order of rejection available on the records, it is a duty incumbent on to the High Court to explicitly state the reasons as to why the sudden departure in the order of grant as against the rejection just about a month ago. The subsequent FIR is on record and incorporated therein are the charges under Sections 323 and 504 IPC in which the charge-sheet have already been issued, the Court ought to take note of the facts on record rather than ignoring it. In any event, the discretion to be used shall always have to be strictly in accordance with law and not de-hors the same. The High Court thought it fit not to record any reason far less any cogent reason as to why there should be a departure when in fact such a petition was dismissed earlier not very long ago. The consideration of the period of one year spent in jail cannot in the view of the Apex Court be a relevant consideration in the matter of grant of bail more so by reason of the fact that the offence charged is that of murder under Section 302 IPC having the punishment of death or life imprisonment. It is a heinous crime against the society and as such the Court ought to be rather circumspect and cautious in its approach in a matter which stands out to be a social crime of very serious nature.

The Apex Court held that grant of bail though being a discretionary order—but, however, calls for exercise of such a

---

96. AIR 2002 SC 1475; (2002)3 SCC 598.

discretion in a judicious manner and not as a matter of course. Order for Bail bereft of any cogent reason cannot be sustained. Needless to record, however, that the grant of bail is dependent upon the contextual facts of the matter being dealt with by the Court and facts however do always vary from case to case. While placement of the accused in the society, though may be considered but that by itself cannot be a guiding factor in the matter of grant of bail and the same should and ought always be coupled with other circumstances warranting the grant of bail. The nature of the offence is one of the basic consideration for the grant of bail—more heinous is a crime, the greater is the chance of rejection of the bail, though, however, dependent on the factual matrix of the matter.

The Court further held that apart from the above, certain other conditions which may be attributed to be relevant considerations may also be noticed at this juncture though however, the same are only illustrative and nor exhaustive neither there can be any. The considerations being: (a) While granting bail the Court has to keep in mind not only the nature of the accusations, but the severity of the punishment, if the accusation entails a conviction and the nature of evidence in support of the accusations. (b) Reasonable apprehensions of the witnesses being tampered with or the apprehension of there being a threat for the complainant should also weigh with the Court in the matter of grant of bail. (c) While it is not accepted to have the entire evidence establishing the guilt of the accused beyond reasonable doubt but there ought always to be a *prima facie* satisfaction of the Court in support of the charge. (d) Frivolity in prosecution should always be considered and it is only the element of genuineness that shall have to be considered in the matter of grant of bail and in the event of there being some doubt as to the genuineness of the prosecution, in the normal course of events, the accused is entitled to an order of bail.

The Supreme Court in *Uday Mohanlal Acharya* v. *State of Maharashtra*,[97] held that:

There is no provision in the Criminal Procedure Code authorising detention of an accused in custody after the

---

97. AIR 2001 SC 1910.

expiry of the period indicated in the proviso to sub-section (2) of S. 167 excepting the contingency indicated in Explanation I, namely, if the accused does not furnish the bail. It is in this sense it can be stated that if after expiry of the period, an application for being released on bail is filed, and the accused offers to furnish the bail, and thereby avail of his indefeasible right and then an order of bail is passed on certain terms and conditions but the accused fails to furnish the bail, and at that point of time a challan is filed then possibly it can be said that the right of the accused stood extinguished. But so long as the accused files an application and indicates in the application to offer bail on being released by appropriate orders of the Court then the right of the accused on being released on bail cannot be frustrated on the oft chance of Magistrate not being available and the matter not being moved, or that the Magistrate erroneously refuses to pass an order and the matter is moved to the higher forum and a challan is filed in interregnum. This is the only way how a balance can be struck between the so-called indefeasible right of the accused on failure on the part of the prosecution to file challan within the specified period and the interest of the society, at large, in lawfully preventing an accused for being released on bail on account of inaction on the part of the prosecuting agency. On the aforesaid premises, we would record our conclusions as follows :

1. Under sub-section (2) of S. 167, a Magistrate before whom an accused is produced while the police is investigating into the offence can authorise detention of the accused in such custody as the Magistrate thinks fit for a term not exceeding 15 days in the whole.

2. Under the proviso to aforesaid sub-section (2) of S. 167, the Magistrate may authorise detention of the accused otherwise than the custody of police for a total period not exceeding 90 days where the investigation relates to offence punishable with death, imprisonment for life or imprisonment for a term of not less than 10 years, and 60 days where the investigation relates to any other offence.

3. On the expiry of the said period of 90 days or 60 days, as the case may be, an indefeasible right accrues in favour of the accused for being released on bail on account of default by the Investigating Agency in the completion of the investigation within the period prescribed and the accused is entitled to be released on bail, if he is prepared to and furnish the bail, as directed by the Magistrate.

4. When an application for bail is filed by an accused for enforcement of his indefeasible right alleged to have been accrued in his favour on account of default on the part of the investigating agency in completion of the investigation within the specified period, the Magistrate/Court must dispose it of forthwith, on being satisfied that in fact the accused has been in custody for the period of 90 days or 60 days, as specified and no charge-sheet has been filed by the Investigating Agency. Such prompt action on the part of the Magistrate/Court will not enable the prosecution to frustrate the object of the Act and the legislative mandate of an accused being released on bail on account of the default on the part of the Investigating Agency in completing the investigation within the period stipulated.

5. If the accused is unable to furnish bail, as directed by the Magistrate, then the conjoint reading of Explanation I and proviso to sub-section (2) of S. 167, the continued custody of the accused even beyond the specified period in paragraph (a) will not be unauthorised, and therefore, if during that period the investigation is complete and charge-sheet is filed then the so-called indefeasible right of the accused would stand extinguished.

6. The expression 'if not already availed of' used by this Court in *Sanjay Dutt's case* (1994 AIR SCW 3857 : 1995 Cri LJ 477) must be understood to mean when the accused files an application and is prepared to offer bail on being directed. In other words, on expiry of the period specified in paragraph (a) of proviso to sub-section (2) of S. 167 if the accused files an application

for bail and offers also to furnish the bail, on being directed, then it has to be held that the accused has availed of his indefeasible right even though the Court has not considered the said application and has not indicated the terms and conditions of bail, and the accused has not furnished the same.

In *Dr. Bipin Shantilal Panchal* v. *State of Gujarat,*[98] a three-Judge Bench decision, the Supreme Court referred to the proviso to sub-section (2) of S. 167 of the Code of Criminal Procedure and held that though the aforesaid provisions would apply to an accused under NDPS Act, but since charge-sheet had already been filed and the accused is in custody on the basis of orders of remand passed under other provisions of the Code the so-called indefeasible right of the accused must be held to have been extinguished. The Court observed thus:

> Therefore, if an accused person fails to exercise his right to be released on bail for the failure of the prosecution to file the charge-sheet within the maximum time allowed by law, he cannot contend that he had an indefeasible right to exercise it at any time notwithstanding the fact that in the meantime the charge-sheet is filed. But on the other hand if he exercises the right within the time allowed by law and is released on bail under such circumstances, he cannot be rearrested on the mere filing of the charge-sheet.

In *Bharat Chaudhary and another* v. *State of Bihar and another*[99] the Supreme Court held that, when the Court of Session or the High Court is granting anticipatory bail, it is granted at a stage when the investigation is incomplete and, therefore, it is not informed about the nature of evidence against the alleged offender. It is, therefore, necessary that such anticipatory bail orders should be of limited duration only and ordinarily on the expiry of that duration or extended duration, the court granting anticipatory bail should leave it to the regular court to deal with the matter on an appreciation of evidence placed before it after

98. AIR 1996 SC 2897 : 1996 Cri LJ 1652.
99. AIR 2003 SC 4662.

the investigation has made progress or the charge sheet is submitted.

(C) Trial

A criminal trial is not like a fairy tale wherein one is free to give flight to one's imagination and phantasy. It concerns itself with the question as to whether the accused arraigned at the trial is guilty of the crime with which he is charged. Crime is an event in real life and is the product of interplay of different human emotions. In arriving at the conclusion about the guilt of the accused charged with the commission of a crime, the Court has to Judge the evidence by the yardstick of probabilities, its intrinsic worth and the animus of witnesses. Every case in the final analysis would have to depend upon its own facts. Although the benefit of every reasonable doubt should be given to the accused, the Courts should not at the same time reject evidence which is *ex facie* trustworthy on grounds which are fanciful or in the nature of conjectures.[100]

The Court taking the plea of the previous case *State of Maharashtra* v. *Chandraprakash Kewalchand Jain*[101] in which Ahmadi, J., (as the Lord Chief Justice then was) speaking for the Bench summarised the position in the following words:

> A prosecutrix of a sex offence cannot be put on par with an accomplice. She is in fact a victim of the crime. The Evidence Act nowhere says that her evidence cannot be accepted unless it is corroborated in material particulars. She is undoubtedly a competent witness under Section 118 and her evidence must receive the same weight as is attached to an injured in cases of physical violence. The same degree of care and caution must attach in the valuation of her evidence as in the case of an injured complainant or witness and no more. What is necessary is that the Court must be alive to and conscious of the fact that it is dealing with the evidence of a person who is

---

100. *State of Punjab* v. *Jagir Singh Baljit Singh and Karam Singh*, AIR 1973 SC 2407.
101. 1990 (1) SCC 550; AIR 1990 SC 658.

interested in the outcome of the charge levelled by her. If the Court keeps this in mind and feels satisfied that it can act on the evidence of the prosecutrix, there is no rule of law or practice incorporated in the Evidence Act similar to illustration (b) to Section 114 which requires it to look for corroboration. If for some reason the Court is hesitant to place implicit reliance on the testimony of the prosecurtix it may look for evidence which may lend assurance to her testimony short of corroboration required in the case of an accomplice. The nature of evidence required to lend assurance to the testimony of the prosecutrix must necessarily depend on the facts and circumstances of each case. But if a prosecutrix is an adult and of full understanding the Court is entitled to base a conviction of her evidence unless the same is shown to be infirm and not trustworthy. If the totality of the circumstances appearing on the record of the case disclose that the prosecutrix does not have a strong motive to falsely involve the person charged, the Court should ordinarily have no hesitation in accepting her evidence.

As a result of the aforesaid discussion, the Apex Court held that the prosecutrix has made a truthful statement and the prosecution has established the case against the respondents beyond every reasonable doubt. The trial Court fell in error in acquitting them of the charges levelled against them. The appreciation of evidence by the trial Court is not only unreasonable but perverse.

The Supreme Court in *Niranjan Singh Punjabi* v. *Jitendra Bijjaya*,[102] held that at Sections 227 and 228 of Cr.P.C. stage the Court is required to evaluate the material and documents on record with a view to finding out if the facts emerging therefrom taken at their face value disclose the existence of all the ingredients constituting the alleged offence. The Court may, for this limited purpose, sift the evidence as it cannot be expected even at that initial stage to accept all that the prosecution states as gospel truth even if it is opposed to common sense or the broad probabilities of the case. Therefore, at the stage of framing

---

102. (1990) 4 SCC 76.

of the charge the Court has to consider the material with a view to find out if there is ground for presuming that the accused has committed the offence or that there is no sufficient ground for proceeding against him and not for the purpose of arriving at the conclusion that it is not likely to lead to a conviction.

State of Punjab v. *Gurmit Singh.*[103] On 30th March, 1984 the sufferer girl was forcibly abducted by four desperate persons who were out and out to molest her honour. It has been admitted by the prosecutrix that she was taken through the bus adda of Pakhowal via metalled road. It has come in the evidence that it is a busy centre. In spite of that fact she has not raised any alram, so as to attract persons that she was being forcibly taken. The height of her own unnatural conduct is that she was left by the accused at the same point on the next morning. The accused would be the last person to extend sympathy to the prosecutrix. Had it been so, the natural conduct of the prosecutrix was first to reach to the house of her maternal uncle to apprise him that she had been forcibly abducted on the previous day. The witness after her being left at the place of abduction lightly takes her examination. She does not complain to the lady teachers who were deployed to keep a watch on the girl students because these students are to appear in the centre of Boys' School. She does not complain to anybody nor her friend that she was raped during the previous night. She prefers her examination rather than to go to the house of her parents or relations. Thereafter, she goes to `her village Mangal Kalan and informs for the first time her mother that she was raped on the previous night. This part of the prosecution story does not look to be probable.

The trial Court, thus, disbelieved the version of the prosecutrix basically for the reasons; (i) "she is so ignorant about the make etc., of the car that entire story that she was abducted in the car becomes doubtful" particularly because she could not explain the difference between a Fiat car, Ambassador car or a Master car; (ii) the Investigating Officer had "shown pitiable negligence" during the Investigation by not tracing out the car and the driver, (iii) that the prosecutrix did not raise any alarm while being abducted even though she had passed through the bus adda of village Pakhowal; (iv) that "the story of

---

103. AIR 1996 SC 1393.

abduction" has been introduced by the prosecutrix or by father or by the thanedar just to give the gravity of offence; and (v) that no corroboration of the statement of the prosecutrix was available on the record and the the story that the accused had left her near the school next morning was not believable because the accused could have no "sympathy" for her.

In *Vineet Narain* v. *Union of India*,[104] it is settled by the Apex Court that the requirement of a public hearing in a Court of law for a fair trial is subject to the need of proceeding being held in camera to the extent necessary in public interest and to avoid prejudice to the accused. The Apex Court considered it appropriate to mention these facts in view of the nature of these proceedings wherein innovations in procedure were required to be made from time to time to sub-serve the public interest, avoid any prejudice to the accused and to advance the cause of justice.

The Supreme Court in *State of M.P.* v. *Mohan Lal Soni*[105] observed that:

> The object of providing such an opportunity as is envisaged in Section 227 of the Code is to enable the Court to decide whether it is necessary to proceed to conduct the trial. If the case ends there it gains a lot of time of the Court and saves much human efforts and cost. If the materials produced by the accused even at that early stage would clinch the issue, why should the Court shut it out saying that such documents need be produced only after wasting a lot more time in the name of trial proceedings. Hence, we are of the view that Sessions Judge would be within his power to consider even materials which the accused may produce at the stage contemplated in Section 227 of the Code.

In *Shaliendra Kumar* v. *State of Bihar*[106] the Supreme Court was of the view that, in a murder trial it is sordid and repulsive matter that without informing the police station officer-in-charge, the matters are proceeded by the court and by the APP

---

104. AIR 1998 SC 889.
105. AIR 2000 SC 2583; (2000) 6 SCC 338.
106. AIR 2002 SC 270.

and tried to be disposed of as if the prosecution has not led any evidence. From the facts stated above, it appears that accused wants to frustrate the prosecution by unjustified means and it appears that by one way or the other the addl. sessions judge as well as the APP have not taken any interest in discharge of their duties. It was the duty of the sessions judge to issue summons to the investigating officer if he failed to remain present at the time of trial of the case. The presence of investigating officer at the time of trial is must. It is his duty to keep the witnesses present. If there is failure on part of any witness to remain present, it is the duty of the court to take appropriate action including issuance of bailable/non-bailable warrants as the case may be. It should be well understood that prosecution cannot be frustrated by such methods and victims of the crime cannot be left in lurch.

The Apex Court in *Rajendra Prasad* v. *Narcotic Cell*[107] observed that:

> After all, function of the criminal court is administration of criminal justice and not to count errors committed by the parties or to find out and declare who among the parties performed better.

The Supreme Court in *Surender Singh Rautela* v. *State of Bihar*[108] submitted that the High Court was not justified in enhancing the punishment awarded against this appellant from imprisonment for life to death sentence as no appeal under section 377 of the Code of Criminal Procedure, 1973 was filed by the State for enhancement of sentence. It has been further submitted that no opportunity of hearing was afforded to appellant Surendra Singh Rautela against the enhancement of sentence. It is well settled that the High Court, *suo motu* in exercise of revisional jurisdiction can enhance the sentence of an accused awarded by the trial court and the same is not affected merely because an appeal has been provided under section 377

---

107. (1999) 6 SCC 110.
108. AIR 2002 SC 260; Also see *Nadir Khan* v. *The State (Delhi) Administration;* AIR 1976 SC 2205 and *Eknath Shankarrao Mukkawar* v. *State of Maharashtra;* AIR 1977 SC 1177.

of the Code for enhancement of sentence and no such appeal has been preferred.

It has been settled by the Apex Court in previous cases[109] that the *suo motu* powers of enhancement under revisional jurisdiction can be exercised only after giving opportunity of hearing to the accused.

The Supreme Court in *State of Karnataka* v. *M. Devendrappa and others*[110] noted that, the powers possessed by the High Court under Section 482 of the Code are very wide and the very plenitude of the power requires great caution in its exercise. Court must be careful to see that its decision in exercise of this power is based on sound principles. The inherent power should not be exercised to stifle a legitimate prosecution. High Court being the highest Court of a State should normally refrain from giving a *prima facie* decision in a case where the entire facts are incomplete and hazy, more so when the evidence has not been collected and produced before the Court and the issues involved, whether factual or legal, are of magnitude and cannot be seen in their true perspective without sufficient material. Of course, no hard and fast rule can be laid down in regard to cases in which the High Court will exercise its extraordinary jurisdiction of quashing the proceeding at any stage.

The scope of exercise of power under Section 482 of the Code and the categories of cases where the High Court may exercise its power under it relating to cognizable offences to prevent abuse of process of any Court or otherwise to secure the ends of justice were set out in some detail by the Apex Court in *State of Haryana and others vs. Ch. Bhajan Lal and others.*[111] A note of caution was, added by the Apex Court that the power should be exercised sparingly and that too in rarest of rare cases. The illustrative categories indicated by this Court are as follows:

(1) Where the allegations made in the first information report or the complaint, even if they are taken at their face

---

109. *Jayaram Vithoba and Another* v. *The State of Bombay;* AIR 1956 SC 146 and *Bachan Singh and Others* v. *State of Punjab;* AIR 1980 SC 267.

110. AIR 2002 SC 671; Also see, *The Janata Dal etc. vs. H.S. Chowdhary and Ors. etc.,* AIR 1993 SC 892; *Dr. Raghubir Saran vs. State of Bihar & Anr,* AIR 1964 SC 1.

111. AIR 1992 SC 604.

value and accepted in their entirely do not prima facie constitute any offence or make out a case against the accused. (2) Where the allegations in the First Information Report and other materials, if any, accompanying the F.I.R. do not disclose a cognizable offence, justifying an investigation by police officers under Section 156(1) of the Code except under an order of Magistrate within the purview of Section 155(2) of the Code. (3) Where the uncontroverted allegations made in the F.I.R. or complaint and the evidence collected in support of the same do not disclose the commission of any offence and make out a case against the accused. (4) Where the allegations in the F.I.R. do not constitute a cognizable offence but constitute only a non-cognizable offence, no investigation is permitted by a police officer without an order of a Magistrate as contemplated under Section 155(2) of the Code. (5) Where the allegations made in the F.I.R. or complaint are so absurd and inherently improbable on the basis of which no prudent person can ever reach a just conclusion that there is sufficient ground for proceeding against the accused. (6) Where there is an express legal bar engrafted in any of the provisions of the Code or the concerned Act (under which a criminal proceeding is instituted) to the institution and continuance of the proceedings and/or where there is a specific provision in the Code or the concerned Act, providing efficacious redress for the grievance of the aggrieved party. (7) Where a criminal proceeding is manifestly attended with malafide and/or where the proceeding is maliciously instituted with an ulterior motive for wreaking vengeance on the accused and with a view to spite him due to private and personal grudge.

IV. CORRECTIONAL INSTITUTIONS AND JUDICIAL INTERPRETATION

You cannot rehabilitate a man through brutality and disrespect. . . . If you treat a man like an animal, then you must expect him to act like one. For every action there is a reaction. . . . And in order for an inmate, to act like a human being you must trust him as such. . . . You can't spit in his face and expect him to smile and say thank you.

The problem of law, when it is called upon to defend persons hidden by the law is to evolve a positive culture and higher consciousness and preventive mechanisms, sensitized strategies and humanist agencies which will bring healing balm to bleeding hearts. Indeed, counsel on both sides carefully endeavoured to help the Court to evolve remedial processes and personal within the framework of the Prisons Act and the parameters of the Constitution.[112]

(A) Prison

Prisons are built with stones of law, and so it behoves the court to insist that, in the eye of law, prisoners are persons, not animals, and punish the deviant 'guardians' of the prison system where they go berserk and defile the dignity of the human inmate. Prison houses are part of Indian earth and the Indian Constitution cannot be held at bay by jail officials 'dressed in a little, brief authority', when Part III is invoked by a convict. For when a prisoner is traumatized, the Constitution suffers a shock. And when the Court takes cognizance of such violence and violation, it does, like the hound of Heaven, 'But with unhurrying chase. And 'unperturbed pace, Deliberate speed and Majestic instancy' follow the official offender and frown down the outlaw adventure.[113]

In _Gopal Vinayak Godse_ v. _State of Maharashtra_[114] the Supreme Court decided that the Prisons Act does not confer on any authority a power to commute or remit sentences; it provides only for the regulation of prisons and for the treatment of prisoners confined therein. Section 59 of the Prisons Act confers a power on the State Government to make rules, _inter alia_, for rewards for good conduct. Therefore, the rules made under the Act should be construed within the scope of the ambit of the Act. The rules, _inter alia_, provide for three types of remissions by way of rewards for good conduct, namely,

---

112. _Sunil Batra_ v. _Delhi Administration_, AIR 1980 SC 1579.
113. _Ibid._
114. AIR 1961 SC 600.

(i) ordinary, (ii) special, and (iii) State. For the working out of the said remissions, under rule 1419 (c), transportation for life is ordinarily to be taken as 15 years' actual imprisonment. The rule cannot be construed as a statutory equation of 15 years' actual imprisonment for transportation for life. The equation is only for a particular purpose, namely, for the purpose of "remission system" and not for all purposes. The word "ordinarily" in the rule also supports the said construction. The non-obstante clause in sub-rule (2) of rule 1447 reiterates that notwithstanding anything contained in rule 1419 no prisoner who has been sentenced to transportation for life shall be released on completion of his term unless orders of Government have been received on a report submitted to it. This also indicates that the period of 15 years' actual imprisonment specified in the rule is only for the purpose of calculating the remission and that the completion of the term on that basis does not *ipso facto* confer any right upon the prisoner to release. The order of Government contemplated in rule 1447 in the case of a prisoner sentenced to transportation for life can only be an order under S. 401 of the Code of Criminal Procedure, for in the case of a sentence of transportation for life the release of the prisoner can legally be effected only by remitting the entire balance of the sentence. Rules 934 and 937 (c) provide for that contingency. Under the said rules the orders of an appropriate Government under S. 401, Criminal Procedure Code, are a pre-requisite for a release. No other rule has been brought to our notice which confers an indefeasible right on a prisoner sentenced to transportation for life to an unconditional release on the expiry of a particular term including remissions. The rules under the Prisons Act do not substitute a lesser sentence for a sentence of transportation for life.

In *Sunil Batra* v. *Delhi Administration*,[115] the Supreme Court was of the view that prisoners are peculiary and doubly handicapped. For one thing, most prisoners belong to the weaker segment, in poverty, literacy, social station and the like. Secondly, the prison house is a walled-off world which incommunicado for the human world, with the result that the bonded inmates are invisible, their voices inaudible, their

---

115. AIR 1980 SC 1579.

injustices unheeded. So it is imperative, as implicit in Art. 21, that life or liberty, shall not be kept in suspended animation or congealed into animal existence without the freshening flow of fair procedure.

In *Maneka Gandhi* v. *Union of India*,[116] the 'meaning of life' given by the Filed, J. bears exception that:

> Something more than mere animal existence. The inhibition against its deprivation extended to all those limbs and faculties by which life is enjoyed. The provision equally prohibits the mutilation of the body by the amputation of an arm or leg, or the putting out of an eye, or the destruction of any other organ of the body through which the soul communicates with the outer world.

Therefore, inside prisons are persons and their personhood, if crippled by law keepers turning law-breakers, shall be forbidden by the writ of this court from such wrong-doing. Fair procedure, in dealing with prisoners, therefore, calls for another dimension of access of law-provision, within easy reach, of the law which limits liberty to persons who are prevented from moving out of prison gates.

In *Bhuvan Mohan Patnaik* v. *State of A.P.*[117] Chandrachud, J., spelt out the position of prisoners and affirmed that:

> Convicts are not, by mere reason of the conviction, denuded of all the fundamental rights which they otherwise possess. A compulsion under the authority of law, following upon a conviction, to live in a prison-house entails by its own force the deprivation of fundamental freedoms like the right to move freely throughout the territory of India or the right to practise a profession. A man of profession would thus stand stripped of his right to hold consultations while serving out his sentence. But the Constitution guarantees other freedoms like the right to acquire, hold and dispose of property for the exercise of which incarceration can be no impediment. Likewise, even

---

116. (1978) 1 SCC 248; AIR 1978 SC 597.
117. AIR 1974 SC 2092.

a convict is entitled to the precious right guaranteed by Article 21 of the Constitution that he shall not be deprived of his life or personal liberty except according to procedure established by law

In *Sunil Batra* v. *Delhi Administration*[118] the Supreme Court stated and directed constitute the mandatory part of the judgment and shall be complied with by the State. But implicit in the discussion and conclusions are certain directives for which it did not fix any specific time limit except to indicate the urgency of their implementation. The Apex Court spelt out four such quasi-mandates—

1. The State shall take early steps to prepare a Hindi, a Prisoner's Handbook and circulate copies to bring legal awareness home to the inmates. Periodical jail bulletins stating how improvements and habilitative programmes are brought into the prison may crease a fellowship which will ease tensions. A prisoners' wall paper, which will freely ventilate grievances will also reduce stress. All these are implementary of S. 61 of the Prisons Act.

2. The State shall take steps to keep up to the Standard Minimum Rules for Treatment of Prisoners recommended by the United Nations, especially those relating to work and wages, treatment with dignity, community contact and correctional strategies. In this latter aspect the observations we have made of holistic development of personality shall be kept in view.

3. The Prisons Act needs rehabilitation and the Prison Manual total overhaul, even the Model Manual being out of focus with healing goals. A correctional-*cum*-orientation course is necessitous for the prison staff inculcating the constitutional values, therapeutic approaches and tension-free management.

4. The prisoners' rights shall be protected by the court by its writ jurisdiction plus contempt power. To make this jurisdiction viable, free legal services to the prisoner

118. AIR 1980 SC 1579.

programmes shall be promoted by professional organisations recognised by the Court such as for e.g. Free Legal Aid (Supreme Court) Society. The District Bar shall, we recommend, keep a cell for prisoner relief.

On the question whether a sentence of transportation for life could be executed in jails within the country or the same was executable only beyond the seas. The position has been clearly enunciated by the Privy Council in *Pt. Kishori Lal's case*.[119] After considering the history of the sentence of transportation, the relevant provisions of the Penal Code, the Code of Criminal Procedure and the Prisoners' Act, the Privy Council came to the conclusion that the said provisions clearly showed that a sentence of transportation was not necessarily executable beyond the seas. It observed thus:

> These sections make it plain that when a sentence of transportation has been passed it is no longer necessarily a sentence of transportation beyond the seas. Nowhere is any obligation imposed on the Government either of India or of the provinces to Provide any places overseas for the reception of prisoners. It appears that for many years the only place to which they have been sent is the Andaman Islands are now in Japanese occupation. Their Lordships have been referred to various orders and directions of an administrative and not, a legislative character showing what prisoners are, and are not. regarded as fit subjects for transportation thereto and showing also that now-a-days only such of those prisoners sentenced to transportation as may volunteer to undergo, transportation overseas are sent to those islands. . . . But at the present day transportation is in truth but a name given in India to a sentence for life and in a few special cases for a lesser period, just as in England the term imprisonment is applied to all sentences which do not exceed two years and penal servitude to those of 3 years and upwards. . . . So in India, a prisoner sentenced to transportation may be sent to the Andamans

---

119. AIR 1945 PC 641.

or may be kept in one of the jails in India, appointed for transportation prisoners.[120]

It may be pointed out that even thereafter there is no dearth of judicial precedents where, in the matter of nature of punishment. Imprisonment for life has been regarded as equivalent to rigorous imprisonment for life. In *State of Madhya Pradesh* v. *Ahmadulla*,[121] the Apex Court after reversing the judgment of acquittal recorded by the High Court on a charge of murder imposed the following sentence:

> But taking into account the fact that the accused has been acquitted by the Sessions Judge—an order which was affirmed by the High Court—we consider that the ends of justice would be met if we sentence the accused to rigorous imprisonment for life.

In *K.M. Nanavati* v. *State of Maharashtra*,[122] the Bombay High Court had sentenced the accused expressly to "rigorous imprisonment for life" and the Supreme Court while dismissing the appeal upheld the sentence as being correctly awarded.

State of Haryana v. *Ghaseeta Ram*.[123] In the instant case, the respondent was admittedly convicted and sentenced by the Additional Sessions Judge for committing various offences under the Indian Penal Code, while he was undergoing sentence for a previous conviction vide judgment dated 22-2-1986. An order of cancellation of remission under Para 633-A of the Punjab Jail Manual could, therefore, be made only after 22-2-1986. It could not precede his conviction. The punishment of forfeiture of remission as already noticed, was imposed by the Superintendent of Jail on the respondent on 17-9-1984, much before his conviction had been recorded by the trial Court. This certainly was not permissible under Para 633-A of the Punjab Jail Manual. The order of punishment dated 17-9-1984 is, thus, not sustainable on the plain language of Para 633-A of the Punjab Jail Manual. The respondent appears to have been

---

120. *Naib Singh* v. *State of Punjab*, AIR 1983 SC 855.
121. AIR 1961 SC 998.
122. AIR 1962 SC 605.
123. AIR 1997 SC 1868.

punished by the Superintendent Jail under Para 613 of the Punjab Jail Manual for commission of the prison offence and not under Para 633-A of the Punjab Manual. The respondent has, therefore, been punished for the same offence twice—once by the Superintendent of the Jail and the second time by the trial Court on his conviction for the same offence. It could not be done in view of the bar contained in Section 52 of the Prison Act read with Para 627 of the Punjab Jail Manual. The High Court, therefore, committed no error in quashing the order of the Superintendent of Jail dated 17-9-1984.

In *State of Punjab* v. *Nihal Singh*,[124] the respondent Nihal Singh was a convict under section 302 Indian Penal Code sentenced by Court Martial to undergo imprisonment for life and incarcerated in Civil Jail, Sangrur (Punjab). Nihal Singh filed a writ petition in the High Court of Punjab and Haryana seeking to be classified as Class-B prisoner and being allowed the facilities available to such prisoners in accordance with para 576-A of the Punjab Jail Manual. Punjab Jail Manual is a compilation of statutory provisions, rules and executive instructions, referable to prison and prisoners, issued from time to time and is meant to guide the jail administration and the jail officers. Para 576-A contemplates classification of convicted persons into 3 categories, namely, classes A, B and C and catalogues the factors which would be relevant for classification and enumerates the benefits and facilities to which the prisoner would be entitled depending on the classification. The petition came up for hearing before a learned single judge of the High Court of Punjab & Haryana, who formed an opinion that the classification of prisoners into classes A, B and C was violative of Articles 14 and 15(1) of the Constitution, and therefore, declared such classification *ultra vires* of the Constitution. Consequent upon such declaration the petition filed by the respondent was directed to be dismissed.

It is pertinent to note that the question of *ultra vires* of para 576-A of Punjab Jail Manual was not raised by anyone before the High Court. The High Court also, before formulating its opinion as expressed in the impugned order, did not give any indication of its mind that adjudication upon the constitutional

---

124. (2002) 7 SCC 513.

validity of the provision was proposed. None was put on notice. Nobody was afforded an opportunity of bringing on record material relevant for adjudication upon such validity. The advocate general of the state was not put on notice. The procedure adopted by the High Court while invalidating para 576-A of the Punjab Jail Manual was wholly unsatisfactory and unsustainable.

Judgment under appeal was set aside by the Supreme Court and writ petition filed by respondent restored as fresh for hearing again. The Apex court disposed of other two appeals on the ground that other two appeals emerged after decision of High Court. Therefore, as High Court orders were set aside, these appeals become infructuous and disposed of accordingly.

In *State of Maharashtra* v. *Asha Arun Gawali*,[125] doubts at times were entertained about the authenticity of such news having regard to the normal good faith to be reposed in the regularity of officials activities. But the admissions made in the affidavits filed by the Jail Authorities and the officials, accept it as a fact. What is still more shocking is that persons have entered the jail, met the inmates and if the statements of the officials are seen hatched conspiracies for committing murders. The High Court was therefore justified in holding that without the active co-operation of the officials concerned these things would not have been possible. The High Court appears to have justifiably felt aghast at such acts of omissions and commissions of the jail officials which *per se* constituted offences punishable under various provisions of the Indian Penal Code and has, therefore, necessarily directed the launching of criminal prosecution against them, besides mulcting them with exemplary costs.

The Apex Court observed that the High Court noticed correctly that when the names of visitors who allegedly were a part of the conspiracy warranting detention of the detenu were not in the list of visitors during the concerned period, there is a patent admission about people getting unauthorised entry into the jails without their names being recorded in the official records something which would be impossible except with the connivance of those who otherwise should have prevented such

---

125. AIR 2004 SC 2223.

things happening. It was noted by the High Court there was no explanation as to how somebody could gain entry in the Jail and meet the detenu and yet no entry would be made therefor. It is not possible unless the Jail officials are themselves a party to the same. If the criminal activities of the detenu were to be prevented and the recurrence of lapses which are serious on the part of those concerned were to be averted, firm action was necessary which yet was not even taken for reasons best known to themselves. In the aforesaid background the concern exhibited by the High Court as a necessary corollary by imposition of costs cannot at all be found fault with.

(B) Parole

In our country, there are no statutory provisions dealing with the question of grant of parole. The Code of Criminal Procedure does not contain any provision for grant of parole. By administrative instructions, however, rules have been framed in various States, regulating the grant of parole. Thus, the action for grant of parole is generally speaking an administrative action.[126]

In *Poonam Lata* v. *M.L. Wadhwa*,[127] the Supreme Court observed that there is abundance of authority that High Courts in exercise of their jurisdiction under Art. 226 of the Constitution do not release a detenu on bail or parole. There is no reason why a different view should be taken in regard to exercise of jurisdiction under Art. 32 of the Constitution particularly when the power to grant relief to a detenu in such proceedings is exercisable on very narrow and limited grounds. In *State of Bihar* v. *Rambalak Singh*,[128] a Constitution Bench laid down that the release of a detenu placed under detention under Rule 30 of the Defence of India Rules, 1962, on bail pending the hearing of a petition for grant of a writ of *habeas corpus* was an improper exercise of jurisdiction. It was observed in that case that if the High Court was of the view that *prima facie* the

---

126. *State of Haryana* v. *Mohinder Singh*, AIR 2002 SCW 478.
127. AIR 1987 SC 1387; (1987) 3 SCC 247; Also see *Anil Dey* v. *State of West Bengal*, AIR 1974 SC 832 and *Golam Hussain* v. *Commissioner of Police, Calcutta*, AIR 1974 SC 1336.
128. AIR 1966 SC 1441.

impugned order of detention was patently illegal in that there was a serious defect in the order of detention which would justify the release of the detenu, the proper and more sensible and reasonable course would invariably be to expedite the hearing of the writ petition and deal with the merits without any delay rather than direct release of the detenu on bail. The learned Judge observed as under :

> It is appropriate for a democratic Government not merely to confine preventive detention to serious cases but also to review periodically the need for the continuance of the incarceration. The rule of law and public conscience must be respected to the maximum extent risk-taking permits, and it is hoped that the petitioner and others like him will not languish in prison cells for a day longer than the administration thinks is absolutely necessary for the critical safety of society.

In *State of Uttar Pradesh* v. *Jairam*,[129] a three Judges Bench speaking through Chandrachud, C.J., referred to *Rambalak Singh's case* and set aside the order passed by the learned single Judge of the High Court admitting the detenu to bail on the ground that it was an improper exercise of jurisdiction. As to grant of parole, it is worthy of note that in none of the cases this Court made a direction under Art. 32 of the Constitution for grant of parole to the detenu but left it to the executive to consider whether it should make an order in terms of the relevant provision for temporary release of the person detained as under Section 12 of the COFEPOSA, in the facts and circumstances of a particular case.

In *Samir Chatterjee* v. *State of West Bengal*,[130] the Court set aside the order of the Calcutta High Court releasing on parole a person detained under Sec. 3(1) of the Maintenance of Internal Security Act, 1971 and viewed with disfavour the observations made by the High Court that 'it was not often that the State Government lost sight of Sec. 15 of the Act providing for temporary release in such situations' as in its view "long-term

---

129. AIR 1982 SC 942.
130. (1975) 1 SCC 80; AIR 1975 SC 1165.

preventive detention can be self-defeating or criminally counter-productive' and that 'it was fair that persons kept incarcerated and embittered without trial should be given some chance to reform themselves by reasonable recourse to the parole power under Sec. 15'. Alagiriswamy, J. speaking for the Court, said that there was no occasion for the High Court to have made these observations, and added :

> We fail to see that these observations lay down any principle of law. Section 15 merely confers a power on the Government. The power and duty of this Court is to decide cases coming before it according to law. In so doing it may take various considerations into account. But to advise the Government as to how they should exercise their functions or powers conferred on them by statute is not one of this Court's functions. Where the Court is able to give effect to its view in the form of a valid and binding order that is a different matter. Furthermore, S. 15 deals with release on parole and there is nothing to show that the petitioner applied for to be released on parole for any specific purpose. As far as we are able to see, release on parole is made only on the request of the party and for a specific purpose.

In *Babulal Das* v. *State of West Bengal*,[131] Krishna Iyer, J. however struck a discordant note and adopted the observations made by the Calcutta High Court and observed :

> It is fair that persons kept incarcerated and embittered without trial should be given some chance to reform themselves by reasonable recourse to the parole power under S. 15. Calculated risks by release for short periods may, perhaps, be a social gain, the beneficent jurisdiction being wisely exercised.

In *Sunil Fulchand Shah* v. *Union of India*,[132] Apex Court observed that release on parole is only a temporary

---

131. (1975) 3 SCR 193; AIR 1975 SC 606.
132. AIR 2000 SC 1023.

arrangement by which a detenu is released for a temporary fixed period to meet certain situations, it does not interrupt the period of detention and, thus, needs to be counted towards the total period of detention unless the rules, instructions or terms for grant of parole, prescribe otherwise. The period during which parole is availed of is not aimed to extend the outer limit of the maximum period of detention indicated in the order of detention. The period during which a detenu has been out of custody on temporary release on parole, unless otherwise prescribed by the order granting parole, or by rules or instructions, has to be included as a part of the total period of detention because of the very nature of parole. An order made under Section 12 of temporary release of a detenu on parole does not bring the detention to an end for any period—it does not interrupt the period of detention—it only changes the mode of detention by restraining the movement of the detenu in accordance with the conditions prescribed in the order of parole. The detenu is not a free man while out on parole. Even while on parole he continues to serve the sentence or undergo the period of detention in a manner different than from being in custody. He is not a free person. Parole does not keep the period of detention in a state of suspended animation. The period of detention keeps ticking during this period of temporary release of a detenu also because a parolee remains in legal custody of the State and under the control of its agents, subject to any time, for breach of condition, to be returned to custody.

It was further observed by the Apex Court that personal liberty is one of the most cherished freedoms, perhaps more important than the other freedoms guaranteed under the Constitution. It was for this reason that the Founding Fathers enacted the safeguards in Article 22 in the Constitution so as to limit the power of the State to detain a person without trial, which may otherwise pass the test of Article 21, by humanising the harsh authority over individual liberty. Since, preventive detention is a form of precautionary State action, intended to prevent a person from indulging in a conduct, injurious to the society or the security of State or public order, it has been recognised as "a necessary evil" and is tolerated in a free society in the larger interest of security of State and maintenance of public order. However, the power being drastic, the restrictions placed on a person to preventively detain must, consistently with the effectiveness of detention, be minimal. In a democracy governed by the Rule of Law, the drastic power to detain a person without trial for security of the State and/or maintenance of public order, must be strictly construed. This Court, as the guardian of the Constitution, though not the only guardian, has zealously attempted to preserve and protect the liberty of a citizen. However, where individual liberty comes into conflict with an interest of the security of the State or public order, then the liberty of the individual must give way to the larger interest of the nation.

In *Dadu v. State of Maharashtra*,[133] the Supreme Court held that parole is not a suspension of the sentence. The convict continues to be serving the sentence despite granting of parole under the Statute, Rules, Jail Manual or the Government Orders. "Parole" means the release of a prisoner temporarily for a special purpose before the expiry of a sentence, on the promise of good behaviour and return to jail. It is a release from jail, prison or other internment after actually been in jail serving part of sentence.

Grant of parole is essentially an Executive function to be exercised within the limits prescribed in that behalf. It would not be open to the Court to reduce the period of detention by admitting a detenu or convict on parole. Court cannot substitute the period of detention either by abridging or enlarging it. Dealing with the concept of parole and its effect on period of detention in a preventive detention matter, this Court in *Poonam Lata v. M.L. Wadhawan*[134] held:

> There is no denying of the fact that preventive detention is not punishment and the concept of serving out a sentence would not legitimately be within the purview of preventive detention. The grant of parole is essentially an executive function and instances of release of detenus on parole were literally unknown until this Court and some of the High Courts in India in recent years made orders of release on parole on humanitarian considerations.

---

133. AIR 2000 SC 3203.
134. AIR 1987 SC 1383 : 1987 Cri LJ 1130.

Historically 'parole' is a concept known to military law and denotes release of a prisoner of war on promise to return. Parole has become an integral part of the English and American systems of criminal justice intertwined with the evolution of changing attitudes of the society towards crime and criminals. As a consequence of the introduction of parole into the penal system, all fixed term sentences of imprisonment of above 18 months are subject to release on licence, that is, parole after a third of the period of sentence has been served. In those countries, parole is taken as an act of grace and not as a matter of right and the convict prisoner may be released on condition that he abides by the promise. It is a provisional release from confinement, but is deemed to be a part of the imprisonment. Release on parole is a wing of the reformative process and is expected to provide opportunity to the prisoner to transform himself into a useful citizen. Parole is thus a grant of partial liberty of lessening of restrictions to a convict prisoner, but release on parole does not change the status of the prisoner. Rules are framed providing supervision by parole authorities of the convicts released on parole and in case of failure to perform the promise, the convict released on parole is directed to surrender to custody. It follows that parole is the release of a very long-term prisoner from a penal or correctional institution after he has served a part of his sentence under the continuous custody of the State and under conditions that permit his incarceration in the event of mishebaviour.

(C) Probation

The legislation for consideration to gives effect to this penal philosophy of probation recommends rehabilitation of the criminals so that they come out of the prison to return to society as law abiding citizens. Certain classes of prisoners which appear to the Government from their antecedents and their conduct in the prison as likely to abstain from crime and lead a peaceable life, can be released on a "licence" but their conduct outside prison shall be supervised by specified individuals or institutions. The period of release on licence or probation granted to them would give them opportunity to lead a crime free and peaceable life.[135] Such period shall be counted towards the sentence of imprisonment imposed on them. Such licensed releases legislatively sanctioned have been recognised as valid law by the Supreme Court in the case of *Maru Ram v. Union of India.*[136] Release on licence is an experiment with prisoners for open jails or as the Court describes it is an "imprisonment of loose and liberal type."

The Supreme Court has indicated in *Dalbir Singh v. State of Haryana*[137] that benefit of Probation of Offenders Act should not normally be afforded in respect of the offences under Section 304-A, IPC when it involves rash or negligent driving. Those are instances for showing how the nature of the offence could dissuade the Court to give the benefit. However, in a case of trivial nature as the respondent is stated to have committed and keeping in view its peculiar circumstances, we find it to be a fit case where powers under Section 3 of the Probation of Offenders Act can be exercised.

In *Chandra Prakash Shahi v. State of U.P.*[138] the Supreme Court held that the period of probation is two years. The Regulation is silent as to the maximum period beyond which the period of probation cannot be extended. In the absence of this prohibition, even if the appellant completed two years of probationary period successfully and without any blemish, his period of probation shall be treated to have been extended as a 'permanent' status can be acquired only by means of a specific order of confirmation.

In *State of Orissa v. Ram Narayan Das*[139] the Supreme Court observed:

> Where it is proposed to terminate the employment of a probationer, whether during or at the end of the period of probation, for any specific fault or on account of his unsuitability for the service, the probationer shall be apprised of the grounds of such proposal and given an

135. *State of M.P.* v. *Bhola*, (2003) 3 SCC 1.
136. 1981(1) SCC 100.
137. 2000 AIR SCW 1653 : AIR 2000 SC 1677 : 2000 Cri LJ 2283.
138. AIR 2000 SC 1706.
139. AIR 1961 SC 177.

opportunity to show cause against it, before orders are passed by the authority competent to terminate the employment.

In *Commandant 20 BN ITB Police* v. *Sanjay Binjoa*,[140] the Surpeme Court held that Probation of Offenders, Act has been enacted in view of the increasing emphasis on the reformation and rehabilitation of the offenders as a useful and self-reliant members of society without subjecting them to deleterious effects of jail life. The Act empowers the Court to release on probation, in all suitable cases, an offender found guilty of having committed an offence not punishable with death or imprisonment for life or for the description mentioned in Sections 3 and 4 of the said Act.

Section 3 of the Probation of Offenders Act provides :

Power of Court to release certain offenders after admonition—When any person is found guilty of having committed an offence punishable under Section 379 or Section 380 or Section 381 or Section 404 or Section 420 of the Indian Penal Code (45 of 1860), or any offence punishable with imprisonment for not more than two years, or with fine, or with both, under the Indian Penal Code or any other law, and no previous conviction is proved against him and the Court by which the person is found guilty is of opinion that, having regard to the circumstances of the case including the nature of the offence and the character of the offender, it is expedient so to do, then, notwithstanding anything contained in any other law for the time being in force, the Court may, instead of sentencing him to any punishment or releasing him on probation of good conduct under Section 4 release him after due admonition.

Explanation—For the purposes of this section, previous conviction against a person shall include any previous order made against him under this section or Section 4.

---

140. AIR 2001 SC 2058.

The Court further said that it is not disputed that for an offence punishable under Section 10 of the Act, the sentence provided is one year with fine entitling the respondent to claim the benefit of Section 3 of the Probation of Offenders Act. It transpires that both the appellate as well as the High Court, after passing the order of conviction and sentence and having regard to the circumstances of the case including the nature of the offence and character of the offender, thought it expedient to take a lenient view and instead of sending him to jail opted to pass a sentence till the rising of the Court. On the point of sentence, the appellate Court observed :

> I think it justified to consider leniently because the accused Sanjay Binjoa is a young boy and he just took excessive liquor on the alleged liquor day. It is also to be kept in mind that in the Para Military Forces liquor is provided comparatively cheaper to the para military personnels, hence I find that the punishment given to the accused for sentences of 3 months is severe consequently, I reach at the conclusion that the sentence awarded by the lower Court is modified accordingly.

V. SUM-UP

The Supreme Court of India has opened new vistas on 'human rights' movement by liberally interpreting and expanding the meaning of criminal justice system. Apex Court under constitutional scheme is guardian, and protector of fundamental rights of the citizen, to enforce the right, to ensure justice administered to all and protect the individual rights without encroachment on individual liberty and with human dignity. Every effects have been devoted to protect and guard the pre-trial detainees. From the very initial stage of First Information Report, investigation, arrest, search, seizure, bail, legal aid, custodial violence and compensation to the victims the Supreme Court has always played a key role.

Protections of rights are the cardinal importance to the process of criminal justice at all levels of investigation, trial and punishment. The Code of Criminal Procedure in India contains salient features in this respect. In the face of new and divergent crime trends, the public trends to have mixed feeling towards crime prevention, control and punishment. While there appears to be widespread demand for making the criminal justice more fair, there is also a push for stronger deterrents and justice rendered on those responsible for disrupting public order, peace and tranquility or restricting them from criminal acts at the cost of injury to human life.

6

Criminal Justice Administration and Role of Police

I. INTRODUCTION

Police is a service dedicated to the protection of life, liberty and property of citizens and the battle arm of the society to deal with criminals and lawless elements. Power given to them under the law alone will not enable them to perform the duties to the satisfaction of the people. They need the full cooperation and support of the people. The police have a significant role to play in the political development of a society by keeping under check forces of disintegration and disorder.

The role of police in the criminal justice administration as prosecutors is of paramount importance. It is obvious that the requisite legislations, howsoever, well intentioned may not deliver the goods unless and until they are efficiently administered by the organs of the system. In fact, in all civilized societies, it is the primary function of the Government to provide basic security to its citizens. The police today represent *"The coercive power of the State"* against the criminal and the anti-social elements who disturb the peace of the society.[1] The police force traditionally enjoys a wide range of powers to deal with the violators and probable breakers of law even before the occurence of actual crime. They are expected to take preventive measures to prevent criminal menace and create conditions conducive for law abidingness and enjoyment of civil liberties. The law assigns to it the major responsibility of law enforcement which includes prevention of vice and crime in society and maintenance of public order, whenever and wherever it is threatened.

II. ORIGIN AND MEANING OF WORD POLICE

Originally, the word police was used in a wider sense to connote the management of internal economy and the enforcement of governmental regulations in a particular country. With the passage of time, the term began to be used in a restricted sense to men "an agent of the State to maintain law and order situation and to enforce the regulations of criminal Code."[2]

The term 'police' has derived from the Greek word 'politia'. Police is defined in Greek tradition as an organised civil force in a town or city for the prevention of the life, property and health of the community or the enforcement of laws. The Latin word 'politia' which literally stands for 'polis' or 'State'[3] means the condition of a State or government also came in use later. In the past it meant a system of administration, but now it indicates an organised body of civil officers engaged in the preservation of law and order, detection of crime and enforcement of laws.

The term 'police' according to the Oxford dictionary means 'a system of regulation for the preservation of order and the enforcement of law.' According to the Royal Commission on police powers and procedure 1929, a policeman is a person paid

---

1. See, Mohd. Asraf, Police and Administration of Criminal Justice in India : An Appraisal, *CMLJ*. Vol. 36, No. 2, April-July 2000, p. 138.
2. See, N.V. Pranjape, Criminology and Administration of Criminal Justice, p. 10.
3. See, Giri Raj Shah, Encyclopaedia of Crime, Police and Judicial System, (1999), p. 2.

to perform, as a matter of duty, acts, which if he were so minded, he might have done voluntarily.[4]

In ancient times, some institutions or other discharging police duties existed, but it was not given a distinct name. A civil organisation for maintaining peace and providing security to the citizens in their lawful occupations is of great antiquity and finds a place in the Egyptian, Greek and Roman laws alike.[5] Even in the laws of Manu, references to the police system are found, and the chief duty of the king, according to these laws, was to restrain violence and punish the evil doers.[6]

The police has been defined as "that executive civil force of the State to which is entrusted the duty of maintaining order and of enforcing regulations for the prevention and detection of crime." Plato envisaged the policeman as the guardian of law and order, and placed him near the top of his ideal society, endowing him with special wisdom, strength and patience.[7]

Before Peel's Police Act, 1829, the word 'police' did no signify an organised police for force because such a thing hardly existed. It was after the passing of this Act that the word assumed its present meaning and came to imply a body of personnel which maintains civil order, enforces laws and prevents and detects crimes.[8]

According to the Indian Police Act, 1861, and the other local Acts the word 'police' includes all persons enrolled under these Acts. The term 'police' includes all officers appointed to maintain peace and public tranquility.

John Cratman in his book 'Police' has defined police as crystallizing the concept and practice of the maintenance of public peace, safety and security.[9]

The term 'police' and 'law enforcement' were used in a much broader way to connote the whole craft of governing a social order by economic, social and cultural policy. The 'police' in our contemporary sense is seen merely as a small part of the whole business of domestic government and regulation, all of

4. See, S. Meharlaj Begum, District Police Administration, (1996), p. 2.
5. See, Encyclopaedia Britannica, p. 158.
6. See, Rajidner Praser, Police Administration, (1986), p. 9.
7. See, Sankar Sen, Police Today, (1986), p. 28.
8. See, *Supra* note 6.
9. See, Ram Lal Gupta, Guide to Police Laws in India, (1961), p. 22.

which was relevant for the understanding and control of crime and disorder.[10] The 'police' are assumed to be a State agency mainly patrolling public places in special uniforms, with a broad mandate of crime prevention, order maintain, detection and investigation of crime and service functions.

In every State there are a number of laws, rules and regulations clearly lay down the powers of the Police. These powers have been given to the law enforcement agencies so that society can be saved and safeguarded from the forces of lawlessness and disorder. In enforcing law, police can exercise discretion in several fields, i.e. in making arrest, search, detention, submission of charge-sheet, etc.[11] The discretion of police in quasi-judicial matters such as these have got to be exercised very carefully and honestly. Jeremy Bentham, who believed that the object of any good law should be to increase the total happiness of the community further said that "no method of prevention should be employed which is likely to cause a greater mischief than the offence itself."

The police role in the administration of criminal justice is clearly defined. Preservation of public order, safety and welfare generally; and prevention and detection of crime and arrest and prosecution of criminals. The job of the police is neither to make laws nor to administer justice under them.[12] Their job is to enforce all laws, Central and States, to safeguard the lives and property of all inhabitants within their respective jurisdiction.

In India, the term 'police' has the same meaning as in Britain. In Britain the earliest use of the word in its preset day sense appears at the end of the 1790, in the title 'Marine Police', a body of men privately instituted in order to protect shipping in the port of London. It is true that 'Commissioner of Police' were known in Scotland as early as 1714, but the word had not the modern connotation. In July 1890 the House of Commons passed a Bill making the Marine Police a publically financed organization, which ushered a new era of policing. Debate about the creation of a standing police force in England raged during the early part of the 19th century[13] confronted with political

---

10. See, Mohammad Farajiha Ghazvini, Police Protection to Victims of Crime, (2002), p. XX.
11. *Supra* note 7, pp. 73-74.
12. See, S.K. Ghosh, Police in Ferment, (1981), p. 20.
13. See, Encyclopaedia Britannica, Inc. 1994, 2002.

objections and fears of potential abuse Robert Peel (Later Sir Robber Peel) sponsored the first successful Bill creating a bureaucratic police force in England. The Metropolitan Police Act was passed in 1829 as a political compromise. The jurisdiction of the Bill was limited to the Metropolitan London area, excluding the city of London and provinces. All police were to be uniformed; and crime and disorder were to be controlled by preventive patrols. This police were to be paid salaries and no stipends were permitted for successful solutions of crimes or the recovery of stolen property. The Metropolitan Police Act established the principles that shaped modern English policing. First, policing was to be preventive, and the primary means of policing was conspicuous patrolling by uniformed police officers. Second, command and control were to be maintained through a centralized, quasi-military organisational structure. Third, police were to be patient, impersonal, and professional.[14] Finally, the authority of the English constable derived from three officials sources—the crown (not the political party in power), the law, and the consent and cooperation of the citizenry. Early police in the United States, the United States inherited England's Anglo-Saxon common law as well as its system of social obligation and constables. As both countries moved from rural agrarian to urban industrialized economies, urban riots, crime, and disorder followed. Yet Americas, like the English were wary of creating standing police forces. In the early 1800's as the United States became more urban, patterns of ethnic diversity began to erode the social and political hegemony of the original English and Dutch settlers. Not only did rioting, crime and disorder begin to flourish, but the basic life-styles of new German and Irish immigrants offended the moral and social sensitivities of the original settlers. Immigrants and urban behaviour was perceived as a threat to the social, economic and political fabric of American life. The American response were tried, and voluntary citizens' groups were encouraged to try to solve urban problems.[15]

In 1844 New York City created the first police department in the United States, using the London Metropolitan Police as a

---

14. *Ibid.*
15. *Id.*

model. The idea of police spread quickly, and in 10 years cities as far west as Milwaukee had created police departments. Police were organised in a quasi-military command structure; there were no detectives; their task was the prevention of crime and disorder; and they provided a wide array of public services. Each city created its own police department. Since Americans lacked a unifying symbol like the English crown local politics and laws became the primary bases of police authority. The decentralization of the authority for policing was extended to political words and neighbourhoods, which developed relatively autonomous police units.

In every democratic country the role of the police is almost identical. The legislators enacts the laws; the police enforce them; and lawyers, magistrates and judges run the trials with the active participation of the public. The police are the agents of the law and the independence of the judiciary form any arbitrary interference by the executive are the main bulwarks of the democratic way of life.[16] To quote Melville, "The police is the primary constitutional force for the protection of the individual in the enjoyment of their legal rights, designed to stand between the powerful and the weak, to prevent oppression, disorder and crime, and to represent the case of law and order at all times and in all places".

In every society the policemen stands for good citizenship. He is a reality to comprehend upon his impartiality, efficiency and intelligence depend the estimation in which law is held by the masses.[17] August Vollmer in his book, 'The Police and Modern Society' states that, "the real police officer is expected to have the wisdom of Soloman, the courage of David, the strength of Samson, the patience of Jacob, the leadership of Moses, the kindness of the good Samartan, the strategy of Alexader, the faith of Daniel, the diplomacy of Linclon, the tolerance of the Carpenter of Nazareth and finally an intimate knowledge of every branch of natural, biological and social sciences.[18]

---

16. *Supra* note 16, p. 21.
17. *Ibid*.
18. *Supra* note 4, pp. 2-3.

III. HISTORICAL DEVELOPMENT OF THE POLICE ADMINISTRATION IN INDIA

The history of police administration is as old as the history of organized human society and the process of human being settlement. The legacy of police dates back to the pre-historic period. The dawn of organized society, civilization and the community life brought change in the image, structure and function of police. With the revolution of civilization, growth and organisation of societies, acceptance of certain stipulated norms, rules and ideology of living created the need to master and monitor certain laws, regulations and ordeals for the social set-up.

(i) Police System in Ancient India

The birth of policeman in man is to be traced to the early times when man started emerging from his savage animalhood and using his power of reasoning and thought, realized the need for self-implement and the benefit of family and corporate life. As family groups expanded, he covered larger and larger area to grow together with other groups expanding from different directions and formed themselves into tribes. These tribes expanded sometimes by uniting with other or by fighting and absorbing forcibly till races grew with different languages. These further expanded into nations and marked out particular area which they called their countries.[19]

When the groups were small, it was possible for each person to do all that was needed for existence. He could hunt, roast meat, draw water, cut trees, light the fire, etc. But, when it came a controlling force of nature, more specialized skill was necessary and people had to be kept at particular jobs to develop special skills. Then it became necessary to develop codes and conventions of conduct in society and give them more rigidity either by force or religion or of law.[20] An organised police force, is therefore, only a projection of the police functions of all individual members of the society. The

---

19. See, K.K. Mishra, *Police Administration in Ancient India*, (1987), p. 3.
20. *Ibid*.

ability of society to tackle successfully, the innumerable challenges every day from nature and from internal and external sources is entirely dependent on its power to maintain its internal order, in this way the police performed its functions.

The origin of police in India can be traced to the earliest Vedic period of Indian history. The two Vedas the Rig Veda and the Atharva Veda, mention certain kinds of crimes and punishment known to Vedic India.[21] In fact, a well regulated system of police is known to have been in existence even during the ancient period of Indian history. According to Manu, the King's principal duty was to prevent theft, restrain violence and punish the guilty. He appointed in towns and villages a number of sepoys, maintained patrols and police chowkies. In fact, all the King's subject were required to assist him in the criminal administration.[22] Manu also prescribes that "the King should recover from the thief stolen property and restore it to the owner, and if he fails to restore it he should compensate the sufferer from his own treasury."

In the Ramayana of Valmiki, it is found that there were squads of police to captivate Hanuman in Lanka. Even when Lord Rama returned from exile, arrangements by police were made to control the crowd to avoid stampede and in the 'Lanka Kand' there is a graphic description of 'Dandayavadha Dharakas', parading the streets of the little kingdom of Ravana.[23] Right from the Vedic period the Indian political philosophers, the writers of Dharma Sutras and Sastras are found to be anxious from maintenance of an institution for preservations of peace and order and for protection of the weak against capacity of the strong. 'Richhakatikan' (the little clay cart) a Sanskrit drama by Sudrak and the 'Shakuntalam' by Kalidasa present a certain amount of policing force at work in an ancient Indian city during the first few centuries after Christ.[24]

Kautilya's Arthasastra written between 321-200 B.C., during the Mauryan period devotes four chapters giving a

---

21. *Supra* note 6, p. 11.
22. J.C. Madan, Indian Police, (1980), p. 3.
23. *Supra* note 6, p. 11
24. *Supra* note 4, p. 24.

detailed description of the functioning of a network of intelligence system through the institution of spies. These spies were the King's eye.[25] It was stipulated that "the King should learn every day at night from his secret spies the intentions and actions of his subjects and officers, and the opinions of ministers, enemies, soldiers, the members of the assembly, relations and the women in the herem. This book is well described monumental work in the proceedings of the pattern of investigation, agencies of punishment and the devices of controlling the crime. Kautilya classified spies into nine distinct categories, including women spies, who belonged to good families, and were loyal, reliable and well-trained in the art of disguise.[26] 'Arthashastra' provides a basic structural organizational and administrative set-up in logistic and philosophical pursuit on the knowledge of police investigation process, punishment, detection and prevention.

From the period of the Mauryas till the end of the Gupta period in 540 A.D., the King continued to be ultimately responsible for making up all losses due to theft. The village headman was assisted by a council which was to help in apprehending criminals with the aid of police. He also performed the functions of collection of revenue for which he was remunerated with grant of land.[27] During this period a lot of smriti literature was written on state-craft and human conduct giving instructions in the sacred law. These Smritis defined danda as the repression of crime and states that using to the possession of this virtue the king himself is known as danda. It is with this view that he defines dandaniti as the administration of the king and considers the institution responsible for the eradication of crime as the most important one in the State.[28]

(ii) Police System in Medieval India

After the break-up of the Hindu empire, the Afghan and the Mughal rulers, who followed their own concept of police

---

25. *Supra* note 22.
26. *Supra* note 6, p. 12.
27. *Supra* note 22, p. 5.
28. *Supra* note 19, p. 15.

administration. Now there were well organised police force maintained for maintaining law and order within the society. The Delhi Sultans revived and modified the existing structure and organisation of police administration.[29] The Sultan being at the helm of 'Diwan-e-Quadar' used to settle the disputes pertaining to criminal administration and religious conflicts. Followed after the Sultan in the hierarchy of administration was the 'Diwan-e-Muzlim' who dealt with a change of subordinate officials. The Amir-i-dad with the assistance of a 'Muhtarib' co-ordinated and supervised the police work of the 'Kotwals'.[30] The Kotwal was a key police official. The Kotwal was assigned to report and regulate the law and order administration in the towns. He was assisted by a number of subordinates as well as the inhabitants within his jurisdiction. The Kotwal's police force patrolled throughout the city at night and guarded vantage points. He kept himself fully informed about the movements, activities and means to livelihood of all persons in the jurisdiction which extended even to rural areas. He also functioned as a Magistrate.[31]

When the Mughals took over the rule, their main objective was to sustain their empire and authority. They introduced only those changes, which suited their objectives. They made all higher appointments hereditary. The provinces were put under the Subedars or Governors. Subedars were responsible for the administration including the criminal justice and keeping peace and order in his jurisdiction.[32] Under the Subedars, were Faujdars incharge of Sarkars or the Districts. The Faujdar represented the executive authority of Government within the limits of a rural district. He was principally a military officer but also have to function as the chief police officer for the area under his command.[33] Faujdars were appointed by the emperor but were placed under the direction and control of the Subedar. Their responsibility was the suppression of crime and rebellion, keeping peace and providing protection to the law-abiding citizens.[34] The district was divided into a number of parganas

29. *Supra* note 4, p. 25.
30. *Ibid*.
31. *Supra* note 22, p. 6.
32. See, Joginder Singh, Inside Indian Police, (2002), pp. 28-29.
33. *Supra* note 6, p. 12.
34. *Supra* note 32.

and sub-divisions which were under the Shigdars. The Faujdar and his subordinate officers were assisted by Zamindars, who had appropriated the police functions of the village headman because they paid and controlled the village watchman. Each Shigdar had a control over the Thanadars appointed one for every thana. A Thanadar was assisted by a small number of armed guards called Barkandazes.[35]

Each Faujdar had 500 to 1500 Sepoys under his charge, The Mughals were urban people. They did not care much about the rural people. They left them to their own fate, to be governed by their feudal lords or Zamindars. The Chaukidars, or village watchmen, employed by the village community, were expected to maintain peace and provide security.[36] As Faujdars had large areas to supervise, they did not have any effective check control on the village police or the people living there.

Intelligence also formed an important function of the Mughal police organisation. It consisted of different classes of newswriters some of whom enjoyed great confidence of the provincial governors and even of the emperors. An officer known as the Darogah of Dak Chowki (Superintendent of Posts and Intelligence) was attached to the imperial court.[37] He was the head of the intelligence department. Under his supervision and control there were posted a number of intelligencers known as the Wapai-navis, the Sawanih-nigar, the Khufia-navis and Harkarah. The duties of all these persons were to communicate secret written reports to the imperial court.

The police system during the Mughal period was undoubtedly suited to the needs of a simple and homogenous agricultural community, but it could no stand the strain of political disorder and the consequent relaxation of control of the centre. So with the decline of the Mughal empire, this system of administration also collapsed.[38] It broke the police organisational structure into a shamble. The police officials started exploiting the situation to their advantage and became notorious and oppressive. The Zamindars, the headman and the watchmen committed crimes and gave shelter to criminals.

35. *Supra* note 22, p. 7.
36. *Supra* note 32, p. 29.
37. *Supra* note 22, pp. 8-9.
38. *Supra* note 6, p. 13.

Even the highest officials indulged in such practices. Under these circumstances, life and property became very insecure.

(iii) Police System in Modern India

As the Mughal Empire declines, their system of administration began to disappear. The Britishers starting from their trading settlements at Bombay, Calcutta and Madras gradually assumed control of province after province. The administration of justice in the original settlements was based on English law, but in dealing with the Indians, in the jurisdiction of those settlements, due regard was paid to indigenous law and custom. Hence, there was a Qazi as an exponent of Mohammedan law, in the staff of the courts in Bombay from the earliest times until 1860.

The history of police administration in British India between 1757 and 1860 was a long series of experiments.[39] The East India Company's interest was only to collect as much money as possible and expand trading. It did not bother about the people, or the law and order, which continued to deteriorate. Lord Clive, as the Governor-General introduced the system, in which all the power was vested in the Company. However, all the responsibility lay on the Nawab. Warren Hastings came to India as Governor of Bengal in August, 1772.[40] He reorganised the judicial system with the Collector at the district level as the head of Faujdari Adalat and the Presidency Court Sadar Nizamat under the Governor and Council. To combat the unrest, Governor-General Lord Cornwallis took police administration out of the hands of Zamindars in 1792 and established in their place a police force responsible to the agents of the Company. Districts were divided into parts, and a police official, known as Daroga, was appointed in each part to maintain law and order.[41] The Daroga was to raise and direct a force of men known as barkandazes, the 'lightening throwers' as they were armed with guns. The Daroga supervised the police work of the village headman and was accountable to the District

---

39. _Supra_ note 22, pp. 11-12.
40. _Supra_ note 32, pp. 32-33.
41. _Supra_ note 6. p. 14.

Judge. The Kotwal, however, remained in-charge of the police administration in the towns.

Wellesley, after becoming the Governor-General was keen to know the position of the policing in the country. He issued a number of questionnaires for formulating a plan, for the improvement of the police in India. The failure of Daroga system had complicated the problem of an efficient functioning of the police administration.[42] In order to arrest the fast worsening state of affairs, the British authorities now desired to find out some solution which could ensure a stable peace and security of life and property throughout the country. Lord Wellesley's enquiry in Bengal in 1801 was followed by Lord William Bentinck, the Governor of Madras, who had appointed a Committee in 1806 with the object of improving the police system under him. The Police Committee, after taking into consideration the views received, recommended that Daroga, should be appointed by the Magistrate on the recommendations of the Zamindars.[43] He should be paid from the public treasury. The Committee was not in favour, of excluding the Zamindars from police administration. On the basis of the findings of the Committee, they decided to enlist the cooperation of the local people in the preservation of peace, and the Madras Regulation-XI of 1816 was passed. It established a uniform pattern of village police throughout the Presidency.[44] Some improvements were also made by the creation of the office of Superintendent of Police, who is now designated as Inspector General of Police, but the law and order situation continued to be unsatisfactory.[45]

In June 1834, Lord Macaulay came to India as a law member. He was in support of depriving the Collector of the office of the Magistrate and disbanding the post of the Commissioner. In 1837, Lord Auckland got the authority from the Court of Directors to use his discretion gradually to separate the office of the Collector and Magistracy, in Bengal, as and when necessary.[46] In 1843, Sir Charles Napier, who had come to India organised the police system in Sind on the model of royal

42. *Supra* note 22, p. 20.
43. *Supra* note 32, pp. 45-46.
44. *Supra* note 6, p. 15.
45. See, M.S. Parmar, Problems of Police Administration , (1992), p. 37.
46. See, K.K. Sharma, Law and Order Administration, (1985), p. 32.

Irish Constabulary. The Sind scheme was followed by other parts of India during the next few years.

Impressed by the reforms in the police administration in Sind, the Madras Government appointed the Torture Commission in 1858 to examine the existing organisation of Madras Police. The Commission recommended that the Superintendent of Police should be appointed in each district and they should devote their time and energies exclusively to the control and supervision of the police force.[47] The Commission also recommended the appointment of a Commissioner of Police Operations through a centralized administrative agency.

The first war of freedom in 1857 made the Britishers to realize that baton and the gun alone would not enable them to hold on to India for long. Reforms that had been maturing for many years with pragmatic bureaucratic thoroughness were suddenly enshrined in law. In 1860, a Police Commission was appointed to look into the problems of police administration and the product of its deliberations was the Police Act of 1861. The Commission suggested certain remedial measures aimed at simplifying the general police administration. It desired to maintain uniformity and consistency in the police system.[48]

The major recommendations of the Police Commission were incorporated into the Police Act of 1861. The main provisions of the Police Act were neither revolutionary nor particularly novel; they extended to the whole of British India and arrangements which had already been found useful in several provinces.[49] The importance of the Act lay in fact that it provided authoritative answers to the two questions implicit in the British experimentation with police organisation during the last one hundred years, i.e. the relationship between the imperial and rural police and coordination between police administration with the other functions of imperial authority. Another landmark in the history of Indian police during the British period was the appointment of All India Police Commission in 1902, by Lord Curzon, Viceroy of India,

---

47. *Supra* note 6, p. 16.
48. *Supra* note 45, p. 38.
49. *Supra* note 6, pp. 18-19.

comprising seven members including two Indians. The Commission was required to conduct a comprehensive inquiry to secure a reasonable degree of uniformity in the police organisation, training, strength and pay of all ranks of the district police, to improve the performance of police personal and to suggest effective measures to ensure prevention of torture by police, better magisterial supervision over police and several other allied duties.[50] There was no entry of Indians into the Imperial Police and it was thrown open to Indians only after 1920 through entrance examination. Till 1931, Indians were appointed against only 20 percent of the total posts of Superintendents of Police but thereafter more Indians were appointed to Indian police due to non-availability of suitable European candidates. But, after the All India Commission, 1902, nothing concrete was done in the reform of police administration till independence whereas many important changes took place in the social, economic and political life of the country.

In 1947, the colonial rule in India was replaced by representative democracy. The people of India resolved to constitute India into a Sovereign Democratic republic through a new Constitution on 26th January, 1950. It inaugurate a new era in the administration of police in India. The new Constitution assigned the responsibility for law and order to the State, and the existing police system was retained.[51]

The post-independent Police Commission relating to its internal organisation and new law and order discipline had to be reviewed at several places and stages. The fathers of the Indian Constitution terminated the office of the Secretary of State for India, and retained the Indian Police Services. The Union Public Service Commission was empowered to conduct competitive examinations and select those with merit. The All India Services Act of 1951 prescribes the framework for Indian Police Services and Indian Police Service Recruitment Rules were framed jointly by the Union Public Service Commission and the Union Ministry of Home.[52]

---

50. *Supra* note 45, p. 38.
51. *Supra* note 6, p. 34.
52. *Supra* note 4, p. 34.

The Indian police system and structure as presently organised are based on 145 years old the Police Act of 1861. The working of police personal was reviewed twice in India, once in 1902 and the next in 1977 by the National Police Commission. The findings of the National Commission on Police was defective training, inefficiency, lack of public relations, lack of machinery of redressal of grievances of police and finally corrupt and oppression.[53]

Under Article 246 of the Constitution of India which divides the legislative authority between Union and State in three lists – the Union, the State and the Concurrent. The subject of police has been placed under State List at Entry 1.[54] The subjects of administration of justice, prison and reformatories and local administration have also placed under this list. The State Government is responsible to maintain law and order in State. It gives the power to State Government to create and maintain its own police force. The constitutional position of the police is almost the same as it was in pre-independent time.

IV. POLICE ADMINISTRATION UNDER THE POLICE ACT, 1861

The Police Act of 1861 imposes a homogeneous police system which replaced the innumerable forces of infinitely varying composition and efficiency that had in the past grown up in the absence of any uniform police policy in India. The Act regulated organisation, recruitment, training and other allied provisions concerning the imperial as well as the provincial police force.

(A) Constitution of the Force

The entire police-establishment under the State Government shall, for the purposes of this Act, be deemed to be one police-force and shall be formally enrolled; and shall consist of such number of officers and men, and shall be constituted in such manner as shall from time to time be ordered by the State

---

53. Report of National Police Commission, 1977.
54. See, Constitution of India.

Government. [Subject to the provisions of this Act, the pay and all other conditions of service of members of the subordinate ranks of any police-force shall be such as may be determined by the State Government.]

(B) Superintendence in the State Government

The superintendence of the police throughout a general police-district shall vest in and shall be exercised by the State Government to which such district is subordinate, and except as authorised under the provisions of this Act, no person, officer or Court shall be empowered by the State Government to supersede or control any police functionary.

(C) Inspector-General of Police, etc.

The administration of the police throughout a general police-district shall be vested in an officer to be styled the Inspector-General of Police, and in such Deputy Inspectors-General and Assistant Inspectors-General, as the State Government shall deem fit.

The administration of the police throughout the local jurisdiction of the Magistrate of the district shall, under the general control and direction of such Magistrate, be vested in a District Superintendent and such Assistant District Superintendents as the State Government shall consider necessary.

(D) Powers of Inspector-General

The Inspector-General of Police shall have the full powers of a Magistrate throughout the general police-district but shall exercise those powers subject to such limitation as may, from time to time, be imposed by the State Government.

(E) Appointment, Dismissal, etc. of Inferior Officers

[Subject to the provisions of article 311 of the Constitution, and to such rules] as the State Government may, from time to time, make under this Act, the Inspector-General, Deputy

Inspectors-General, Assistant Inspectors-General and District Superintendents of Police may at any time dismiss, suspend or reduce any police-officer of the subordinate ranks] whom they shall think remiss or negligent in the discharge of his duty, or unfit for the same; [or may award any one of the following punishments to any police-officer [of the subordinate ranks] who shall discharge his duty in a careless or negligent manner, or who by any act of his own, shall render himself unfit for the discharge thereof, namely:

(a) Fine of any amount not exceeding one month's pay;
(b) Confinement to quarters for a term not exceeding fifteen days with or without punishment-drill, extra guard, fatigue or other duty;
(c) Deprivation of good-conduct pay;
(d) Removal from any office of distinction or special emolument].[5]

(F) Certificates to Police Officers

Every police-officer [appointed to the police force, other than an officer mentioned in section 4] shall receive on his appointment, a certificate in the form annexed to this Act, under the seal of the Inspector-General or such other officer as the Inspector-General shall appoint, by virtue of which the person holding such certificate shall be vested with the powers, functions, and privileges of a police officer, Surrender of Certificate. [Such certificate shall cease to have effect whenever the person named in it ceases for any reason, to be a police-officer, and on his ceasing to be such an officer, shall be forthwith surrendered by him to any officer empowered to receive the same.

A police officer shall not, by reason of being suspended from office, cease to be a police officer. During the term of such suspension the powers, functions and privileges vested in him as a police-officer shall be in abeyance, but he shall continue subject to the same responsibilities, discipline and penalties and to the same authorities, as if he had not been suspended.]

(G) Police-officers not to Resign without Leave or Two Months' Notice

No police-officer shall be at liberty to withdraw himself from the duties of his office unless expressly allowed to do so by the District Superintendent or by some other officer authorized to grant such permission, or without the leave of the District Superintendent, to resign his office, unless he shall have given to his superior officer notice in writing, for a period of not less than two months, of his intention to resign.

(H) Power of Inspector-General to make Rules

The Inspector-General of Police may, from time to time, subject to the approval of the State Government, frame such orders and rules as he shall deem expedient relative to the Organisation, classification and distribution of the police-force, the places at which the members of the force shall reside, and the particular services to be formed by them; their inspection, the description of arms, accoutrement and other necessaries to be furnished to them; the collecting and communicating by them of intelligence and information, and all such other orders and rules relative to the police-force as the Inspector-General shall, from time to time, deem expedient for preventing abuse or neglect of duty, and for rendering such force efficient in the discharge of its duties.

(I) Additional Police Officers Employed at Cost of Individuals

It shall lawful for the Inspector-General of Police or any Deputy Inspector- General or Assistant Inspector-General, or for the District Superintendent, subject to the general direction the Magistrate of the district, on the application of any person showing the necessity thereof, to depute any additional number of police-officers to keep the peace at any place within the general police-district and for such time as shall be deemed proper. Such force shall be exclusively under the orders of the District Superintendent and shall be at the charge of the person making the application:

Provided that it shall be lawful for the person on whose application such deputation shall have been made, on giving one month's notice in writing to the Inspector-General, Deputy Inspector-General or Assistant Inspector-General, or to the District Superintendent to require that the police-officers so deputed shall be withdrawn; and such person shall be relieved from the charge of such additional force from the expiration of such notice.

(J) Appointment of Additional Force in the Neighborhood of Railway and Other Works

Whenever any railway, canal or other public work, or any manufactory or commercial concern, shall be carried on or be in operation in any part of the country and it shall appear to the Inspector-General that the employment of an additional police force in such place is rendered necessary by the behaviour or reasonable apprehension of the behaviour of the persons employed upon such work, manufactory or concern, it shall be lawful for the Inspector-General, with the consent of the State Government, to depute such additional force to such place, and to employ the same so long as such necessity shall continue, and to make orders, from time to time, upon the person having the control or custody of the funds used in carrying on such work, manufactory or concern, for the payment of the extra force so rendered necessary, and such person shall, thereupon, cause payment to be made accordingly.

(K) Quartering of Additional Police in Disturbed or Dangerous Districts

(1) It shall be lawful for the State Government, by proclamation to be notified in the Official Gazette, and in such other manner as the State Government shall direct, to declare that any area subject to its authority has been found to be in a disturbed or dangerous state, or that, from the conduct of the inhabitants of such area or of any class or section of them, it is expedient to increase the number of police.

(2) It shall, thereupon, be lawful for the Inspector-General of Police, or other officer authorised by the State Government in this behalf, with the sanction of the State Government, to employ any police force in addition to the ordinary fixed complement, to be quartered in the area specified in such proclamation as aforesaid.

(3) Subject to the provisions of sub-section (5) of this section, the cost of such additional police force shall be borne by the inhabitants of such area described in the proclamation.

(4) The Magistrate of the district, after such enquiry as he may deem necessary, shall as aforesaid, liable to bear the same apportion such cost among the inhabitants who are such and who shall not have been exempted under the next succeeding sub-section. Such apportionment shall be made according to the Magistrate's judgment of the respective means within such area of such inhabitants.

(5) It shall be lawful for the State Government, by order, to exempt any persons or class or section of such inhabitants from liability to bear any portion of such cost.

(6) Every proclamation issued under sub-section (1) of this section shall state the period for which it is to remain in force, but it may be withdrawn at any time or continued from time to time for a further period or periods as the State Government may, in each case, think fit to direct.

Explanation. For the purposes of this section, "inhabitants" shall include persons who themselves or by their agents or servants, occupy or hold land or other immovable property within such area; and landlords who themselves or by their agents or servants, collect rents direct from raiyats or occupiers in such area, notwithstanding that they do not actually reside therein.]

(L) Awarding Compensation to Sufferers from Misconduct of Inhabitants or Persons Interested in Land

(1) If, in any area in regard to which any proclamation notified under the last preceding section is in force, death or grievous hurt, or loss of, or damage to, property has been caused by or has ensued from the misconduct of the inhabitants of such area or any class or section of them, it shall be lawful for any person, being an inhabitant of such area, who claims to have suffered injury from such misconduct, to make, within one month from the date of the injury or such shorter period as may be prescribed, an application for compensation to the Magistrate of the district or of the sub-division of a district within which such area is situated.

(2) It shall, thereupon, be lawful for the Magistrate of the district, with the sanction of the State Government after such enquiry as he may deem necessary, and whether any additional police force has or has not been quartered in such area under the last preceding section to:

(a) Declare the persons to whom injury has been caused by or has ensued from such misconduct;

(b) Fix the amount of compensation to be paid to such persons and the manner in which it is to be distributed among them; and

(c) Assess the proportion in which the same shall be paid by the inhabitants of such area other than the applicant who shall not have been exempted from liability to pay under the next succeeding sub-section:

Provided that the Magistrate shall not make any declaration or assessment under this sub-section, unless he is of opinion that such injury, as aforesaid, had arisen from a riot or unlawful assembly within such area, and that the person who suffered the injury was himself free from blame in respect of the occurrences which led to such injury.

(3) It shall be lawful for the State Government, by order, to exempt any persons or class or section of such inhabitants from liability to pay any portion of such compensation.

(4) Every declaration or assessment made or order passed by the Magistrate of the district under sub-section (2) shall be subject to revision by the Commissioner of the Division or the State Government, but save as aforesaid, shall be final.

(5) No civil suit shall be maintainable in respect of any injury for which compensation has been awarded under this section.

(6) *Explanation*: In this section, the word "inhabitants" shall have the same meaning as in the last preceding section].

(M) Special Police Officers

When it shall appear that any unlawful assembly or riot or disturbance of the peace has taken place, or may be reasonably apprehended, and that the police force ordinarily employed for preserving the peace is not sufficient for its preservation and for the protection of the inhabitants and the security of property in the place where such unlawful assembly or riot or disturbance of the peace has occurred, or is apprehended, it shall be lawful for any police-officer, not below the rank of Inspector, to apply to the nearest Magistrate, to appoint so many of the residents of the neighbourhood as such police-officer may require, to act as special police-officers for such time and within such limits as he shall deem necessary, and the Magistrate to whom such application is made shall, unless he sees cause to the contrary, comply with the application. Every special police-officer so appointed, shall have same powers, privileges and protection and shall be liable to perform the same duties and shall be amenable to the same penalties and be subordinate to the same authorities, as the ordinary officers of police. If any person, being appointed as special police-officer as aforesaid, shall without sufficient excuse, neglect or refuse to serve as such, or to obey such lawful order or direction as may be given to him for the performance of his duties, he shall be liable, upon conviction before a Magistrate, to a fine not exceeding fifty rupees for every such neglect, refusal or disobedience.

(N) Village Police Officers

Nothing in this Act shall affect any hereditary or other village police officer, unless such officer shall be enrolled as a police officer under this Act. When so enrolled, such officer shall be bound by the provisions of the last preceding section. No hereditary or other village police officer shall be enrolled without his consent and the consent of those who have the right of nomination.

(O) Duties of Police Officers

It shall be the duty of every police-officer promptly, to obey and execute all orders and warrants lawfully issued to him by any competent authority; to collect and communicate intelligence affecting the public peace; to prevent the commission of offences and public nuisances; to detect and bring offenders to justice and to apprehend all persons whom he is legally authorised to apprehend, and for whose apprehension sufficient ground exists; and it shall be lawful for every police-officer, for any of the purposes mentioned in this section, without a warrant to enter and inspect, any drinking-shop, gaming-house or other place of resort of loose and disorderly characters.

(P) Police-officers Always on Duty and may be Employed in any Part of District

Every police officer shall, for all purposes in this Act contained, be considered to be always on duty, and may, at any time, be employed as a police officer in any part of the general police-district.

(Q) Police-officer may Lay Information

It shall be lawful for any police officer to lay any

information before a Magistrate and to apply for a summon, warrant, search-warrant or such other legal process as may, by law, be issued against any person committing an Offence. It shall be the duty of every police-officer to take charge of all unclaimed property and to furnish an inventory thereof, to the Magistrate of the district.

The police officers shall be guided as to the disposal of such property such orders, as they shall receive from the Magistrate of the district.

(R) Magistrate may Detain Property and Issue Proclamation

The Magistrate of the district may detain the property and issue a proclamation, specifying the articles of which it consists, and requiring any person who has any claim thereto, to appear and establish his right to the same, within six months from the date of such proclamation.

(S) Confiscation of Property if no Claimant Appears

(1) If no person shall, within the period allowed, claim such property, or the proceeds thereof, if sold, it may, if not already sold under sub-section (2) of the last preceding section, be sold under the orders of the Magistrate of the district. (2) The sale-proceeds of property sold under the preceding sub-section and the proceeds of property sold under section 26 to which no claim has been established shall be [at the disposal of the State Government].

(T) Penalties for Neglect of Duty

Every police-officer who shall be guilty of any violation of duty or wilful breach or neglect of any rule or regulation of lawful order made by competent authority, or who shall withdraw from the duties of his office without permission, or without having given previous notice for the period of two months, [or who, being absent on leave shall fail, without reasonable cause, to report himself for duty on the expiration of such leave] or who shall engage without authority in any employment other than his police-duty, or who shall be guilty of cowardice, or who shall offer any unwarrantable personal violence to any person in his custody, shall be liable, on conviction before a Magistrate, to a penalty not exceeding three months' pay, or to imprisonment, with or without hard labour, for a period not exceeding three months, or to both.

(U) Regulation of Public Assemblies and Processions and Licensing

(1) The District Superintendent or Assistant District Superintendent of Police may, as occasion required, direct the conduct of all assemblies and processions on the public roads, or in the public streets or thoroughfares, and prescribe the routes by which, and the times at which, such processions may pass.

(2) He may also, on being satisfied that it is intended by any persons or class of persons to convene or collect an assembly in any such road, street or thoroughfare, or to form a procession which would, in the judgment of the Magistrate of the district, or of the sub-division of a district, if uncontrolled, be likely to cause a breach of the peace, require by general of special notice, that the person convening or collecting such assembly or directing or promoting such procession shall apply for a licence.

(3) On such application being made, he may issue a licence, specifying the names of the licensees and defining the conditions on which alone such assembly or such procession is to be permitted to take place, and otherwise giving effect to this section:
Provided that no fee shall be charged on the application for, or grant of any such licence.

(4) Music in the streets. He may also regulate the extent to which music may be used in streets on the occasion of festivals and ceremonies.]

(V) Powers with Regard to Assemblies and Processions Violating Conditions of Licence

(1) Any Magistrate or District Superintendent of Police or

Assistant District Superintendent of Police or Inspector of Police or any police-officer in charge of a station may stop any procession which violates the conditions of a licence granted under the last foregoing section, and may order it or any assembly, which violates any such conditions, as aforesaid, to disperse.

(2) Any procession or assembly which neglects or refuses to obey any order given under the last preceding sub-section, shall be deemed to be an unlawful assembly].

(W) Police to Keep Order on Public Roads

It shall be the duty of the police to keep order on the public roads, and in the public streets, thoroughfares, ghats and landing-places, and at all other places of public resort, and to prevent obstruction on the occasions of assemblies and processions on the public roads and in the public streets, or in the neighbourhood of places of worship, during the time of public worship, and in any case when any road, street, thoroughfare, ghat or landing-place may be thronged or may be liable to be obstructed. Every person opposing or not obeying the orders issued under the last [three] preceding sections, or violating the conditions of any licence granted by the District Superintendent or Assistant District Superintendent of Police for the use of music, or for the conduct of assemblies and processions, shall be liable, on conviction before a Magistrate, to a fine not exceeding· two hundred rupees. Nothing in the last [four] preceding sections shall be deemed to interfere with the general control of the Magistrate of the district over the matters referred to therein.

(X) Punishment for Certain Offences on Roads

Any person who, on any road or in any [open place or] street or thoroughfare within the limits of any town to which this section shall be specially extended by the State Government, commits any of the following offences, to the obstruction inconvenience, annoyance, risk, danger of damage of the [residents or passengers] shall, on conviction before a Magistrate, be liable to a fine not exceeding fifty rupees, or to imprisonment [with or without hard labour] not exceeding eight days; and it shall be lawful for any police-officer to take into custody, without a warrant, any person who, within his view, commits any of such offences, namely:

> *First*—Slaughtering cattle, furious riding, etc. Any person who slaughters any cattle or cleans any carcass; any person who rides or drives any cattle recklessly or furiously, or trains or breaks any horse or other cattle;
>
> *Second*—cruelty to animal. Any person who wantonly or cruelly beats, abuses or tortures any animal;
>
> *Third*—Obstructing passengers. Any person who keeps any cattle or conveyance of any kind standing longer, than is required, for loading or unloading or for taking up or setting down passengers, or who leaves any conveyance in such a manner as to cause inconvenience or danger to the public;
>
> *Fourth*—Exposing goods for sale. Any person who exposes any goods for sale;
>
> *Fifth*—Throwing dirt into street. Any person who throws or lays down any dirt, filth, rubbish or any stones or building materials, or who constructs any cowshed, stable or the like, or who causes any offensive matter to run from any house, factory, dung-heap or the like;
>
> *Sixth*—Being found drunk or riotous. Any person who is found drunk or riotous or who is incapable of taking care of himself;
>
> *Seventh*—Indecent exposure of person. Any person who wilfully and indecently exposes his person or any offensive deformity or disease, or commits nuisance by easing himself, or by bathing or washing in any tank or reservoir, not being a place set apart for the purpose;
>
> *Eighth*—Neglect to protect dangerous places.—Any person who neglects to fence in or duly to protect any well, tank or other dangerous place or structure.

(Y) Power to Prosecute under Other Law not Affected

Nothing contained in this Act shall be construed to prevent any person from being prosecuted under any other Regulation or Act for any offence made punishable by this Act, or from being liable under any other Regulation or Act or any other or higher penalty or punishment than is provided for such offence by this Act. Proviso. Provided that no person shall be punished twice for the same offence.

(Z) Limitation of Actions

All actions and prosecutions against any person, which may be lawfully brought for anything done or intended to be done under the provisions of this Act, or under the general police powers hereby given shall be commenced within three months after the act complained of shall have been committed, and not otherwise; and notice in writing of such action and of the cause thereof shall be given to the defendant, or to the District Superintendent or an Assistant District Superintendent of the district in which the act was committed, one month, at least before the commencement of the action.

Tender or amends. No plaintiff shall recover in any such action, if tender of sufficient amends shall have been made before such action brought, or if a sufficient sum of money shall have been paid into Court after such action brought, by or on behalf of the defendant, and though a decree shall be given for the plaintiff in any such action, such plaintiff shall not have costs against the defendant, unless the Judge before whom the trial is held shall certify his approbation of the action:

Proviso. Provided always that no action shall, in any case, lie where such officers shall have been prosecuted criminally for the same act.

(AA) Plea that Act was done under Warrant

When any action of prosecution shall be brought or any proceedings held against any police officer for any act done by him in such capacity, it shall be lawful for him to plead that such act was done by him under the authority of a warrant issued by a Magistrate.

Such plea shall be proved by the production of the warrant directing the act, and purporting to be signed by such Magistrate and the defendant shall, thereupon, be entitled to a decree in his favour, notwithstanding any defect of jurisdiction in such Magistrate. No proof of the signature of such Magistrate shall be necessary, unless the Court shall see reason to doubt its being genuine:

> Proviso. Provided always that any remedy which the party may have against the authority issuing such warrant shall not be affected by anything contained in this section.

(BB) Police-officers to Keep Diary

It shall be the duty of every officer-in-charge of a police-station to keep a general diary in such form as shall, from time to time, be prescribed by the State Government and to record therein, all complaints and charges preferred, the names of all persons arrested, the names of the complainants, the offences charged against them, the weapons or property that shall have been taken from their possession or otherwise, and the names of the witnesses who shall have been examined.

The Magistrate of the district shall be at liberty to call for and inspect such diary.

(CC) State Government may Prescribe Form of Returns

The State Government may direct the submission of such returns by the Inspector-General and other police officers as to such State Government shall seem proper, and may prescribe the form in which such returns shall be made. The State Government may direct the submission of such returns by the Inspector-General and other police officers as to such State Government shall seem proper, and may prescribe the form in which such returns shall be made.

(DD) Authority of District Superintendent of Police over Village Police

It shall be lawful for the State Government in carrying this Act into effect in any part of the territories subject to such State Government, to declare that any authority which now is or maybe exercised by the Magistrate of the district over any village-watchmen or other village police-officer for the purposes of police, shall be exercised subject to the general control of the Magistrate of the district, by the District Superintendent of Police.

Apart from this Act, Police have to perform many functions and duties under other Acts. Under Criminal Procedure Code, 1973, they have to register FIR, arrest person, seek police remand, conduct investigation, submit charge sheet and help courts to prosecute offender/accused.

V. ROLE OF POLICE IN PERFORMING THEIR DUTIES

The fundamental principle for any criminal justice system is the law of the lands, especially in democratic country. The very process of evaluation of laws in a democratic society, ensures a measure of public sanction for the law through consent expressed by their elected representatives. The entire criminal justice system in our country, therefore, revolves around law passed by the Union Parliament and State Legislature. The durability and reliability of criminal justice system will, in the first place, depend upon the inherent strength of witnesses of various laws enacted from time to time. After laws are made by the legislative bodies their enforcement taken by. Various agencies set-up for that purpose by the Government.

Police come at this stage as the primary law enforcement agency available to the State. Enforcement by the police is primarily as exercise of taking due notice of an infraction of law as soon as it occurs in ascertaining the connected facts, thereof including the identity of the offender. Thereafter the matter goes for trial before the judiciary where the facts ascertained by the enforcement agencies are presented by the prosecuting agency and the accused person gets a full opportunity to present and argue the side of the case. If the trial results in the accused person being found guilty, he is made to suffer penalty either by being held in custody for a special period or by being made to pay up an amount of money as fine to the State exchequer and or compensation to the victim of crime. Even in the cases where the convicted person is to be sentenced to imprisonment, there are legal provisions for exempting him from such physical custody in such circumstances and keeping him under special observation[55] by correctional agencies with the avowed object of facilitating is reform and smooth return in the society.

The criminal justice system covers the entire scenario from the occurance of crime, i.e. any deviatory conduct punishable by law, investigation into the facts thereof by the enforcement agency, adjudicating proceedings in the court added by the prosecuting agency (prosecuting counsel as well as the defence counsel). The performance of the correctional services if facilitating the quick return of the delinquent person to normal behviour and finally the administration of jails with ultimate object of re-socialising the criminal apart from deterring him from repeating the crime. Police, prosecution, advocate, judges, functionaries in the correctional services and jails form the different distinct organized wings of this system. The ultimate object of the system is to secure peace and order in the society. The success of the system, therefore, depends largely on a proper understanding of the objectives of the criminal justice system by all wings put together and their coordinated functioning to secure this objective. The role, duty, power and responsibility of the police with special reference to prevention of control and crime and maintenance of public order cannot be defined in isolation in absolute term, but has to be fitted in the overall requirements for the success of criminal justice system as a whole.

(A) Duties and Responsibilities of Police

Broadly speaking there are three principle functionaries in administration of criminal justice system viz., the police, the judiciary and the correctional services. Each compliments to the other to reach the common goal. Of necessity, the police, specially the investigating agency, comes for most in our system as it discharge certain function in the matter of investigation and collection of evidences over which the court adjudicate at later stage.

Though the duty and responsibility of the police has not been codified in the comprehensive way in any place, various provisions of Indian Police Act, the Police Acts of various states

---

55. For more details see Probation of Offenders Act, 1958.

and the Code of Criminal Procedure 1973 spell out the duty of the police.

(i) Prevention of crime
(ii) Investigation of crime
(iii) Maintenance of public order
(iv) Collection of intelligence
(v) Security
(vi) Traffic
(vii) Other duties, like:

    (a) Service of summon/warrants
    (b) Escort of prisoners
    (c) Guarding of vital installations
    (d) Duties are airport, ports, railways
    (e) Emergency duties during national calamity
    (f) Work relating to court.

Apart from these duties police have to perform many more duties as, Highway patrolling, border meetings, intelligence, verification of antecedents, VIP duties, etc.

VI. SUM-UP

In the domain of criminal justice administration, police remains as the only agency that is constant touch with the people. In case of violation of law the first agency that gets involved in initiating the process of criminal justice, is the police. The role of police in the administration of criminal justice in India is paradoxically central as well as peripheral. The law assigned to it the major responsibility of law enforcement, which includes prevention of crime in society and maintenance of public order whenever and wherever it is threatened.

The police remain central agency of criminal justice administration in all societies by virtue of nature of its functions. The other agencies can do a thorough and cautious review by the real quality of criminal justice in its ultimate depends and is determined by the quality of commitment and performance of the police. Hence, the police as the first and the foremost agency of criminal justice administration has to be in the forefront and this role is very much implicit in the functions which assigned to police by law.

CHAPTER

7

Conclusion and Suggestions

The quality of justice determines the quality of society and governance. Just as pollution poison the atmosphere, the poor justice system poisons the social atmosphere. Equal and fair justice is the hall mark of the society. The quality of justice in civilized society largely depends on a quality of investigation, investigation agency, judges, magistrate and lawyers. Unfortunately, the justice in India seems to be almost completely dominated by lawyers and their vested interests. In total exclusion of other wings of administration justice system. Most of the people who are arrested even for serious offences are not tried promptly and were release at the first appearance by on the spot decision by unscrupulous argument submitted by the defence lawyers.

In every civilized society, the primary role of criminal justice system is to protect the member of that society. Justice system in this respect is a formal instrumentally authorized by the people of the nation to protect both their collective and individual rights. Another duty of any administration of criminal justice is the maintenance of law and order. Since crime and disorder disrupt stability in the society. Therefore, we have vested the criminal justice system with the authority to act as means by which the existing order is maintained.

Criminal justice dispensation is as old as the mankind. It is oftenly said that the crime and man were born together. With the development of the society the criminal law, like other laws has undergone tremendous change. The concept of crime therefore, involves the idea of a public as opposed to a private wrong with the consequent intervention between the criminal and the injured party by an agency representing the community or public as a whole. In this view the crime is the intentional commission of an act or omission deemed socially harmful or dangerous and specifically defined, prohibited and punishable under the criminal law, which shall be in force for the time being.

In the modern civilized society only the violation of rules, regulations proclaimed and enforced by agencies of the government technically are crime. Although crime is sometime viewed in a very broad way as the violation of any important group standard of as the equivalent of anti-social, immoral and sinful behaviour, much immoral behavior is not covered by the criminal law and violation of some laws included in the criminal code are not regarded as immoral or even anti-social, or are so regarded only by a small portion of the population. No matter how immoral, disgusting of harmful an act may be it is not legally a crime unless it is covered by a law which prohibits it and prescribes punishment for it.[1]

The criminal justice system exists because society has deemed it appropriate to enforce the standards of human conduct so necessary to protecting Individuals and the community. It seeks to fulfil the goal of protection through enforcement by reducing the risk of crime and apprehending, prosecuting, convicting and sentencing those individuals who violate the rules and laws proclaimed by the society. The offender finds that the criminal justice administration shall punish him for his violation by removing him from society and simultaneously will try to dissuade him from repeating a social act through rehabilitation.

---

1. For more details see Chapter I of the study.

The criminal justice administration is comprised of police, court and correctional machinery. The police is responsible for controlling crime, maintaining law and order and act as an investigating agency. The courts are prosecuting agencies in criminal justice system. Finally, the aim of the correction is institutionalizing the activity of the offender and rehabilitating into full and useful participation in the society

The *Dharamshastras* are the earlier literature of Sanskrit in which some detail of the law in the modern sense is available. During this period it is interesting to observe that for the habitant the crime principally meant an evil act done with certain degree of violent attitude. The criminal was said to be a persons who without minding the spiritual efforts of his acts was promoted by the absolute spirit of violence and openly engaged himself in causing suffering to others. All such acts were punished with fine and imprisonment. The punishment varied according to whether the offence was against the king or ruling authority or against a person.

Kautilya also dealt with crime in his *Arthashastra*. Robbery has been defined by Kautilya as sudden and direct seizure of person or property. Kautilya specify a very sound theory that each complaint must be judged by the proper consideration of the evident authority available. Fine were to be imposed even for doing mischief to plants and trees. The views of Kautilya in all these matters of criminal intent were very scientific and up-to-date.

The *Manu Smriti* contains twelve chapters, in which he has attempted to bring out a co-ordinated growth of society, religion and polity. During this period King have to simply execute the law and he himself was bound by it and if he goes against it he becomes *adharmic* (he should be disobeyed). *Puranas* are full of instances where the kings were de-thrown and be-headed when they went against the established principles of laws at that time. According to this divine theory, the State is created by God. The king was given the power to control and governs people by divine authority and power.

Yajnavalkya's *Smiriti* is more systematic than Manu. He divided his work in three parts, i.e. *Achara* (conduct), *Vyavhara* (law), *Prayaschitta* (expiration). During this period the king was primarily responsible for the administration of justice with the help of learned and virtuous assessors. He further said that the king should inflict punishment for those who deserve the same after ascertaining and taking note of the nature of the offence, the strength, age, a vocation and the wealth of the culprit.

Criminal justice administration during the Medieval period witnessed a sea change. Muslim, they invade and some of them finally settled in India, as a result of this, they imposed an Islamic justice system in India. Muslim rulers who ruled during 16th and 17th century showed a remarkable tolerance to the Hindu religion. They did not accept the Hindu law for themselves.

During the Muslim rule only the criminal laws was largely common to Muslim with the exception of application of oath and ordeal. Crime under the Islamic law was considered to be an offence against God or the ruler or a private citizen, and as such it was a private affair between the offender and his God.

The king, the representative of God on earth was consider as "fountain of justice". He was supposed to exercised general supervision over all the courts within his territory. *Qazi* was most important person in the criminal justice system. Muslim rulers were very particular in appointing persons to these offices. The ruler alone had a power to appoint a person as a *Qazi* and he was invested with both civil and criminal power.[2]

In the course of time, Muslim society was confronted with new problems and the existing laws were inadequate to solve them. This gave a birth to the principal of *Ijma* and *Qias*. *Ijma* (universal consent) was accepted as a right solution. The *Qias* and *Haddis* were the analogous inferences based on the *Quran*. The punishment during this period was broadly classified as *Hadd*, *Quisa*, *Diya* and *Tazir*.

The administration of justice established by Muslim rulers was inherited by the Britishers during the East India Company period. The charter of 1633 issued by James-I in order to strengthen the hands of the company, in enforcing its laws and punishing the persons, subject to a jury trial. The Charter of 1661 conferred very wide powers on the company to administer justice in its settlement. This charter has two main features. Firstly, the judicial powers were granted to the governor and

---

2. For more details see, Chapter II of the study.

council of a company and secondly, justice was required to be administered according to English law.

The Charter of 1726 established for the first time three mayor's court in three presidency towns on uniform basis. The mayor's court had no criminal jurisdiction. The governor and five senior members of the council were appointed as a justice of peace in each presidency for the administration of criminal justice. They were empowered to arrest and punish for petty criminal offences. The charter of 1753, put mayor's court under the governor and council. These courts could try civil suits between European and natives

In 1772, a new judicial plan was introduced by Warran Hastings. A court of criminal judicature called the *Faujdari Adalat* was established in each district for the trial of murder, robbery, theft, forgery, felonies, assault, quarrels, adultery, etc. These *Faujdari Adalats* placed under the *Sadar Nizamat Adalat*. *Sadar Nizamat Adalat* was presided over by *Daroga* appointed by *Nizam* and assisted by chief *Qazi*. The chief *Mufti* and three *Molvis* supervise the proceeding of the provincial *Faujdari Adalat*.

The Regulating Act of 1773 established the Supreme Court of Calcutta. The Supreme Court of Calcutta consisted of Chief Justice and three puisne judges. Chief Justice and other judges were appointed by His Majesty. The Indian High Courts Act of 1861 makes one of the most important changes of the development in the judicial system of India. This Act empowers the Crown to establish the High Court in the North-West region. These High Courts have both the original and appellate jurisdiction in all civil and criminal matters.

The Charter Act of 1833 played an important role in shaping and moulding the criminal system in Modern India. Lord Macaulay was appointed the member of the council under the Charter. Sec. 53 of the Act made provisions for the establishment of the Law Commission for the purpose of the codification of the Indian laws. The First Law Commission was appointed in 1834 and Lord Macaulay was appointed as its chairman. The first Law Commission made a very comprehensive proposal that an Act should be passed making the substantive law of England as the law of the land. The Second Law Commission made a recommendation for the amalgamation of the Supreme Court and *Sadar* Court. As a result of these recommendations the Civil Procedure Code in 1859, Indian Penal Code in 1860 and Criminal Procedure Code in 1861 were enacted.

The Government of India Act, 1935 conferred a dignified position to the High Courts. This Act changed the structure of Indian government from Unitary Government to Federal. This necessitated the creation of federal court, as an independent court to decide the future dispute between the units. The Federal Court was set-up in the Delhi in 1937. It consists of chief justice and six other judges. It had the original jurisdiction in the matters involving the interpretations of the Act of 1935 or of the federal laws or the determination of rights and obligations arising thereunder. The Federal Court was not a court of criminal appeal. The appeal can be brought only if the court concern gives a certificate. Otherwise, the Privy Council remained the highest court to which appeals from High Courts in criminal cases can be taken.

After independence some reports submitted by Law Commission and recommended reforms in Judicial Administration in India. In 1973, old Criminal Procedure Code of 1898 was replaced by new Criminal Procedure Code, 1973.

The Criminal Procedure Code of 1973 and the Police Act, 1861 conferred various powers to the police, these include the registration of First Information Report, conduction of investigation, arrest of person, grant of a bail, seek police custody, submit a formal charge sheet, maintain police diary, produce a person before a magistrate and maintain law and order in the society.

The Criminal Procedure Code also provides a provision for the constitution of criminal courts and other offices. Code further makes a provision that besides the High Courts and courts constituted under any law other than this Code, there shall be, in every State the following classes of criminal courts namely Court of Session, Judicial Magistrate of the first class and, in any metropolitan area, Metropolitan Magistrate, Judicial Magistrate second class, and Executive Magistrate. The Criminal Procedure Code gives to the High Court various powers including those relating to reference, appeal, revision and transfer of cases. The Code also recognizes the inherent powers of the High Court to prevent the abuse of the process of any court, or to secure the ends of justice.

The Supreme Court is primarily a court of appeal and an extensive appellate jurisdiction has been conferred. Articles 132 and 136 of the constitution deal with the appellate jurisdiction of the Supreme Court in constitutional, civil and criminal matters. In criminal matters the Constitution of India for the first time set-up a court of criminal appeal over the High Court and creates a right of second appeal. Article 134 of the Constitution for the first time, provide for an appeal to the Supreme Court from any judgment, final order and sentence in the criminal proceeding of a High Court as of right where the High Court has on an appeal reverse an order of an accused and sentence him to death. An appeal may lie to the Supreme Court in the criminal case if the High Court certifies that the case is fit one for appeal to the Supreme Court.[3]

The Criminal Procedure Code, 1973 also provides a detail provisions for the grant of bail and bond. High Court and the Court of Session also empowered to grant anticipatory bail when any person has a reason to believe that he may be arrested on an accusation of having committed a non-bailable offence and if the High Court and Court of Session may think it fit, direct that in the event of such arrest, person shall be released on bail. In all the trial under the Criminal Procedure Code the accused is to be informed to the accusation in the form of charge, then the charge to be read and explain to the accused person. Every charge shall state the offence with which the accused is charged. If the law which created the offence gives it any specific name the offence may be describe in the charge by that name only and if the law does not give only specific name so much of the definition of the offence must be stated as to give the accused notice of the matter with he is charged.

Separate provision has been made for the offences of serious nature and the Court of Session conferred with the powers to try these offences. Offences less serious in the nature are triable by the Magistrates of different categories. Judicial Magistrate of first class is also empowered to try petty offences as summery trial. After considering the offences put forth by the

---

3. For more details see Chapter III of the study.

prosecution and the defence, the judgement to be deliver by the courts. In case of sentence, person sent to the prison. During his stay in the prison, prison administration to take care of him.

The accused person may be release on parole and probation. This release from prison is a conditional subject to his conduct and behaviour in the society and his acceptance to live under the guidance and supervision of parole and probation officer. In case a accused person is juvenile than he is to be prosecuted and punished under Juvenile Justice (Care and Protection) Act, 2000 and almost in all the cases he is to be send to various type of correctional institutions under the Act for his further rehabilitation and re-socialization.

In our constitutional scheme, Indian judiciary has been assigned the role of insuring social justice and envisaged in the Preamble, Fundamental Rights and the Directive Principles of the State Policy. Indian judiciary led by the Supreme Court has exhibited a judicial activism in clearing the misconceptions about the concept of the criminal trial under the procedure prescribed in the country which has resulted in the weakening of the criminal justice system.[4] Realising such misconception, the Hon'ble Supreme Court in the *State of Punjab* v. *Jagir Singh*[5] observed :

> a criminal trial is not like a fairy tale where in one is free to give flight to one's imagination and fantasy. It concerns itself with the question as to whether the accused assigned at the trial is guilty of the crime with which he is charged. Crime is an event in real life and is the product of inter-play of different human emotions. In arriving at the conclusion about the guilt of the accused charged with the commission of a crime, the court has to judge the evidence by the yardstick of probabilities, its intrinsic birth and animus of witness. Every case in the final analysis would have to depend upon its own facts. Although the benefit of every reasonable doubt should be given to the accused, the court should not at the same time reject evidence which is *ex-facie* trustworthy on the grounds which are fanciful of in the nature of the conjectures.

---

4. For more details see Chapter IV of the study.
5. AIR 1973 SC 2407.

Again in *State of H.P.* v. *Lekh Raj and Sons*[6] the Supreme Court observed that, criminal trial cannot be equated with a mock scene from a stunt film. The trial is conducted to ascertain the guilt or innocence of the accused arraigned. In arriving at a conclusion about the truth, the courts are required to adopted rational approach and judge the evidence by its intrinsic worth and the animus of the witnesses.

Justice P.N. Bhagwati in *Hussainara Khatoon* v. *Home Secretary, Bihar*[7] emphasized that:

> When an under-trial prisoner is produced before a Magistrate and he has been in detention for 90 days or 60 days, as the case may be, the Magistrate must, before making an order of further remand to judicial custody, point out the under-trial prisoner that he is entitled to be released on bail. If there are adequate grounds to Magistrate may extend the period—not excluding 60 days, for detention of an accused in the police custody. On the expiry of the period person should be released on the bail.

In the cases of arrest the Supreme Court in *Joginder Kumar* v. *State of U.P. and others*[8] held that :

> No arrest can be made because it is lawful for the Police Officer to do so. The existence of the power to arrest is one thing. The justification for the exercise of it is quite another. The Police Officer must be able to justify the arrest apart from his power to do so. Arrest and detention in police lock-up of a person can cause incalculable harm to the reputation and self-esteem of a person. No arrest can be made in a routine manner on a mere allegation of commission of an offence made against a person.

After all, function of criminal court is administration of criminal justice and not to count errors committed by the parties or to find out and declare who among the parties performed better.

---

6. Judgment Today, 1999(9)SC 43.
7. AIR 1979 SC 1377.
8. AIR 1994 SC 1349; 1994 CrLJ 1981.

In *Babulal Das v. State of West Bengal*,[9] Krishna Iyer, J. however struck a discordant note and adopted the observations made by the Calcutta High Court and observed:

It is fair that persons kept incarcerated and embittered without trial should be given some chance to reform themselves by reasonable recourse to the parole power under S. 15. Calculated risks by release for short periods may, perhaps, be a social gain, the beneficent jurisdiction being wisely exercised.

The term police is derived from the Greek word *'polis'* of its Latin equivalent *'politia'*. The Latin word *'politia'* stand for State and administration. Ernest Pround defined the police power as, *"the power of promoting public welfare by restraining and regulating the use of property and liberty."* In every state there are number of laws, rules and regulations clearly lay down the power of the police. These powers have been given to the law enforcement agencies so that society can be saved and safeguarded from the forces of lawlessness and disorder. In enforcing law, police can exercise discretion in the several fields i.e., in making arrest, search, detention, submission of charge-sheet, etc.

The history of police administration is as old as the history of organized human society. When the groups were small, it was possible for each person to do all that was needed for the existence. He could hunt, roast meat, draw water, cut trees, lit the fire, etc. But, when it came a controlling force of nature, more specialized skill was necessary and people had to be kept at particular jobs to develop special skills. Then it became necessary to develop codes and conventions of conduct in the society. The ability of society to tackle successfully, the innumerable challenges every day from nature and from internal and the external sources entirely dependent on its power to maintain its internal order, in this way police performed its functions.

Police system was also available during the ancient period in the form of spies. During the Medieval India Muslim put all the provinces under the control of *Subedar*. They were

---

9. (1975) 3 SCR 193; AIR 1975 SC 606.

responsible for the criminal justice system and keeping law and order within their respective jurisdiction. As Mughal Empire declined this system begin to disappear. The Britishers took over the charge and control of province after province. In 1816 Madras Regulation XI was passed. It established uniform pattern of village police throughout the presidency. This regulation also created the office of Superintendent of Police.[10]

Madras Government appointed the Torture Commission in 1858 to examine the existing organization of Madras Police. The Commission recommended that the Superintendent of Police should be appointed in each district and appointment of Commissioner of Police Operation through a centralized administrative agency. Another Police Commission was appointed in 1860 and recommendations of this Commission were incorporated into the Police Act, 1861. This Act is still in operation throughout India. Act made a numerous provisions for police powers, duties, responsibilities and functions.

Suggestions

Therefore, in view of the above observations, the following suggestions deserve for the consideration:

For implementing speedy criminal justice large number of courts are to be established in those areas where large number of the cases are instituted, for early disposal of cases this is necessary because it will be an extra ordinarily work load on the part of judicial magistrate to dispose large number of criminal cases, where more courts are necessary. Retired judges, jurists, law teachers, eminent lawyers, shall be invited to deliver lectures on special skills, tactics for speedy disposal of the criminal cases. This will be of enough help to the learned judicial magistrate expediting the criminal trial.

For effecting speedy criminal justice in respect of trial of summons and warrant procedure cases, a time limit must be fixed for conclusion of trial with a condition that all sorts of

---

10 . For more details see Chapter V of the study.

dilatory and notorious tricks by either side for defeating the purpose of the fair·trial by adjournment petitions or other petitions for hampering the progress of the trial shall be severely dealt with by inflicting heavy cost and in such circumstances the trial period shall be expended.

A separate independent authority, by whatever name called fully insulated from political interference comprising a chairman and at least two members (with the Director General of police of the concerned State or Union Territory as ex-officio member), should be created in each State or Union Territory to supervise the progress of investigation and regulate the flow of cases to court by examining if the case is *prima facie* strong enough to be put up for trial before the report under Sec. 173 of the Criminal Procedure Code, 1973 is submitted. The appointment of the Chairperson and members should be made with the concurrence of the Chief Justice of the State. This will also reduce the number of under-trial prisoners and avoid their association with hardened criminals. This will help to reduce the volume of weak cases being carried to court.

An independent investigation agency should be established, under the exclusive control of the authority contemplated in the previous paragraph, which should impart intensive and extensive training in scientific investigation that would eschew partiality, bias and third degree practices and be answerable for posting, promotions and the transfer of said authority only. Such agency should have facility at all the major police stations in the city for providing immediate finger print, forensic and pathological assistance to the investigation officer, while awaiting the official report to arrive from the established laboratory and finger print bureau.

The concern government should work out a time table for equipping the investigation machinery with the skills and tools needed for the scientific investigation.

The sections 13 and 18 of the Criminal Procedure Code provide for the appointment of special judicial magistrate and special metropolitan magistrate respectively, upon receipt of a request from the concern government. The person to be appointed should be one "who holds or has held any post under the government" provided he or she possesses such qualification or experience in relation to legal affairs as the High

Court may, by rules, specify. The empowerment may depend on the experience of each person so appointed. Researcher is of the view that the traffic cases and such of the cases falling within the table under Sec. 320(1) of the Code of Criminal Procedure, 1973 can be dealt with by such appointees. The procedure is that they would follow would be out lined by the High Court, depending on the extent of power conferred on them. This would lessen the burden of the regular Magistrates. If the experiment is successful, powers can be enlarged from time to time.

In the scheme of the trial of the criminal case, the appearance of the accused is the first stage, the second stage is the framing of the charge, the third stage is the recording of the evidence, fourth stage is the examination of the accused under Sec. 313 of the Code of Criminal Procedure, 1973, fifth stage is the hearing of the argument, and last stage is the judgement. It is necessary that short adjournments are given till the case reaches the stage of the framing of the charge. After framing the charge, there is no point in recycling the case in calling once in a month or two.

The categorization of majority of offences as non-bailable appears to be for name sake only. The content and text of the provisions of the section 437 of Criminal Procedure Code, 1973, on a careful reading makes almost all offences bailable. If the offence is punishable with the imprisonment for more than seven years a discretion is endowed in the court to grant bail on conditions, which by converse implication could be interpreted to mean that rest of the offences are bailable without any condition. To categorises majority of offences as non-bailable in the present context of the court is very irrational. Keeping in view the public and social interest, only grave and select offences have to be categarised as non-bailable and rest of the offences to be identified and made bailable as a matter of right.

The provision of the anticipatory bail gives a very confusing projection of the objective of the law. Before the Incorporation of Sec. 438 of the Criminal Procedure Code, 1973, the absconding of an accused was a serious negative point for obtaining bail. However, Sec. 438 in its practical use encourages the accused to abscond and keep him away from the process of investigation. The guidelines and the test applicable in the grant of the bail should be made invariably applicable for the grant of bail under Sec. 438 also. The system on the subject on bails by and large functions by the precedent. There are divergent conflicting precedents projecting confusing picture to the trial judiciary in exercise of discretion. Therefore, to obviate the confusions, a legislative exercise is very much necessary in this behalf as suggested above.

Bail should normally be the rule and the jail an exception and the legislature should not restrict the discretion of the court in the matter of the grant of bail by imposing difficult and impossible conditions to be met, as in case of POTA and MACOCA.

In most of the courts of Judicial Magistrates (particularly in the Metropolitan cities) large number of criminal cases is pending for execution of warrant and proclamation against the accused persons. These cases hamper the progress of new cases in the criminal courts. After a considerable period of time, these criminal cases must be "filed for the present", otherwise these cases will create an obstacle in the speedy disposal of cases.

A more liberal (pro-active) role should be allowed to the Magistrate and the presiding judge than enjoyed at present, to get to the truth by putting question through court.

If and only if, all the existing safeguards provided by the Criminal Procedure Code and the Evidence Act in favour of the suspect or the accused continue and are not diluted through adverse presumption and exceptions built into the law, the degree of proof required could be "preponderance of probabilities". However, the presumption of innocence should apply and the onus of proof should, throughout the trial, rest on the prosecution.

Since the accused has a right to be defended by lawyer of his choice or through the legal aid system, he should be informed his right immediately on arrest and his counsel should be permitted to advise him during investigation. This would also act as a restraint on the use of third degree method.

Legal aid to be provided to the accused should be of a high order, particularly in cases where the sentence provided is of five years or above. It must be remembered that the legal aid is the matter of right under Article 39-A of the constitution and should not be reduced to a mere formality by providing an inexperienced or incompetent advocate. So also, in sensitive matters, where highly reputed or senior lawyer represent the defence, it may be advisable to engage a reasonable competent lawyers as special public prosecutor to present the prosecution case.

The term of the employment of the public prosecutor should be liberalized and their emoluments should be revised upward to attract the good talent to match competent defence lawyers, and similarly, the lawyers of reasonably good talents should be engaged to defend the accused under the legal aid scheme or as required under Sec. 304 of the Criminal Procedure Code, 1973.

It is necessary that very strong measures should be taken to stop the growing tendency of lawyer's strike. The subordinate courts shall not take cognizance of any resolution passed by Bar Association to strike, and to stop judicial work. The presiding judge concerned should not entertain or circulate any such resolutions amongst the judicial officers in his judgeship. The Judges/Magistrates should sit in court during court hours and should pass orders in cases listed before them, whether the lawyers are present or not. The judicial officers must strictly adhere to court hours and perform the entire judicial work on the dais, and should not accept any request to rise, or to stop judicial work on the request of lawyers or litigants. In case lawyers do not attend to work the judicial officer should proceed to work, heard the parties personally and pass necessary orders in cases requiring no further evidence.

It is also suggested to separate the investigation agency from the law and order police, such separation can be made in the urban area in all States as beginning. In the State of Uttar Pradesh this separation has already been put in to effect. The investigation officer of the crime police should be at least of the rank of ASI and must be graduate, preferable with the Law degree and having five year experience in the police work

In most of the prison today, one-third are remand prisoners and under-trials, one-third are short-terms and only the remaining one-third are long-term prisoners, cases alone the correctional process has some meaning. One of the earliest and most compelling needs of the prison reforms, therefore will surely be to convert this distressing heterogeneity in the prison population to some reasonable measure of homogeneity facilitating appropriate treatment.

Releasing on the probation, with or without supervision, is the most important and about the most practical of the alternatives to imprisonments. This has been conclusive demonstrative by the benefits that have accrued to the effected subjects and to the community at large, during the past few decades when the probation system has been vague in our country. It is also considerably cheaper to the state than maintaining the prisoners in the custody. It is thus not for nothing that the probation has been universally acclaimed as the trusted remedy for the problem of short-term prisoners. The Probation of Offender Act, 1958, is a comprehensive measure and provides ample scope for utilizing admonition, probation and compensation in lieu of imprisonment.

The purposeful administration of criminal justice can not be effectively implemented with out proper orientation at all levels and the coordinated functioning of all three agencies involved in this process i.e., the police, the criminal courts and the correctional administration consisting of the prison service, the probation service and the correctional agencies only when this vital coordination is secured at all stages and all levels, will it be possible to achieve the real purpose of the crime prevention by the reformation and the rehabilitation of the criminal.

In order to make people aware of court procedure regarding the posting of the case for evidence or other stages, wide visual media publicity should be given, so that people also aware of the significance of the posting of the cases and the importance of attending the proceeding at the relevant stages.

Finally, it is suggested that every State government should enact their own Police Act because the Police Act 1861 is already 145 years old and it also required amendments or new look

The administration of justice is already heading towards a paralyzed coma stage and if urgent steps are not taken in the above lines it will collapse totally and forever on its own weight of delay.

Table of Cases

Bibliography

A. Books

A.K.R. Kiralfy, Potter's Historical Introduction to English Law, Sweet and Maxwell Ltd., London, (1958)
————, Potter's Historical Introduction to English Law, Sweet and Maxwell, (1970).

A.S. Altekar, State and Government in Ancient India, Motilal Banarsidas, (1984).

Ahmad Siddique, Criminology, Eastern Book Company, (2005).

Alan C. Bent, Police, Criminal Justice and the Community, Harper and Row, London, 1976.

Andrew Ashworth, Principles of Criminal Law, Oxford University Press, (1999).

B.L. Verma, Development of Indian Legal System, Deep and Deep Publications, (1987).

B.N. Mani Tripathi, Jurisprudence Legal Theory, Allahabad Law Agency, (2001).

B.S. Jain, Administration of Justice in Seventeenth Century India, Metropolitan Book Co. Pvt. Ltd. (1970).

B.S. Sinha, Legal History of India, Central Law Agency, Allahabad, (1976).

Baldwin John (ed.), Criminal Justice, Martin Robertson, London, 1978

Cemellin, Neil C. and Kenneth R. Evans, Criminal Law and Policemen, Prentice Hall, New Jersey, 1976.

Chandradhar Jha, History and Sources of Law in Ancient India, Ashish Publishing House, New Delhi, (1987).

Charles F. Hemphill, Criminal Procedure : The Administration of Justice, Good Year Publishing Co. Inc. (1978).

Chifford E. Simonsen and Marshall S. Gordon III, Juvenile Justice in America, Glencol Criminal Justice Series.

Cross and Jones, Introduction to Criminal Law, Butterworths, (1972).

D.P. Varshni, How to Form a Charge, Eastern Book Company, (1994).

Damayanti Doongaji, Law of Crime and Punishment in Ancient Hindu Society, Ajanta Books International, (1986).

David Duffee, Frederick, Hussey and John Karmer, Criminal Justice : Organization, Structure and Analysis, New Jersey Preventive, 1978.

David Duffer, Frederik Hussey and John Karmer, Criminal Justice : Organisation Structure and Analysis, Prentice Hall, (1978).

David J. Bardua, Police : Six Sociological Essays, John Willy, New York, 1967.

Dostoyersky Fyodor, Crime and Punishment, Pengwin, New York, 1977.

Durga Das Basu, Criminal Procedure Code, 1973, Prentice Hall of India, Pvt. Ltd. (1997).

Frank R. Prassel, Introduction to American Criminal Justice, Harper and Row Publications, (1975).

George T. Gelkenes, Criminal Law and Procedure, Prentice Hall Inc. (1976).

Gerald D. Robin, Introduction to the Criminal Justice System, Harper Row Publishers, New York, (1980).

Giri Raj Shah, Encyclopaedia of Crime, Police and Judicial System, Anmol Publishing Pvt. Ltd., New Delhi, 1999.

Granville Williams, Text Book of Criminal Law, Universal Law Publishing Co. Pvt. Ltd. (1999).

H.L. Kapoor, Police Investigation Law and Procedure, Ess. Ess. Publications, New Delhi, 1989.

H.M. Seervai, Constitutional Law of India, N.M. Tripathi, Pvt. Ltd., Bombay, (1984).

H.V. Sheeniwasa Murthy, History of India, Eastern Book Company, (2003).

H.V. Sreenivasa Murthy, History of India, Part II, Eastern Book Company, (2003).

Harihar Prasad Dubey, The Judicial System of India, N.M. Tripathi, Pvt. Ltd., Bombay, (1968).

Harihar Prasad Dubey, The Judicial Systems of India and Some Foreign Countries, N.M. Tripathi Private Limited, (1968).

Harry W. More, Principles and Procedures in the Administration of Justice, John Willey and Sons, Inc. (1975).

J.C. Madan, Indian Police, Uppal Publishing House, New Delhi, 1980.

J.D. Mcclean, Criminal Justice and the Treatment of Offenders, Sweet and Maxwell, (1969).

J.K. Mittal, Indian Legal History, Central Law Agency, (2004).

J.P.S. Sirahi, Criminology and Criminal Administration, Allahabad Law Agency, 1983.

James Vadackumchery, Police Enforcements, Crime and Injustice, Gyan Publishing House, New Delhi, 2001.

Joginder Singh, Inside Indian Police, Gyan Publishing House, 2002.

K.D. Gaur, Criminal Law and Criminology, Deep and Deep Publications Pvt. Ltd., (2002).

K.I. Vibhute, Criminal Justice, Eastern Book Company, (2004)

K.K. Mishra, Police Administration in Ancient India, Mittal Publication, 1987.

K.K. Sharma, Law and Order Administration, National Book Organisation, New Delhi, 1985.

Krishan Mohan Agrawal, Kautilya on Crime and Punishment, Shree Almora Book Depot, (1990).

Lord Cross of Chelsea, Radcliffe and Cross the English Legal System, London, Buttersworth, (1971).

M.J. Sethna, Society and the Criminal, N.M. Tripathi Pvt Ltd., (1971).

M. Ram Jois, Legal and Constitutional History of India, N.M. Tripathi Pvt. Ltd., Bombay, (1984).

M. Rama Jois, Ancient Indian Law Eternal Values in Manu Smriti, Universal Law Publishing Co. Pvt. Ltd. (2004).

M. Rama Jois, Legal and Constitutional History of India, Deep and Deep Publications, (1990).

M.S. Pandit, Outlines of Ancient Hindu Jurisprudence, N.B. Tripathi Pvt. Ltd., (1989).

M.S. Parmar, Problems of Police Administration, Reliance Publishing House, New Delhi, 1992.

M.P. Jain, Outlines of Indian Legal History, Wadhwa and Company, Nagpur, (2005)

Mehraj-ud-din-Mir, Crime and Criminal Justice System in India, Deep and Deep Publications, (1984)

Michael Zander, Cases and Materials on the English Legal System, Weidenfeld and Nicolson, (1973).

Mohammad Farajina, Police Protection to Victims of Crime Ghazarni, Deep and Deep, New Delhi, 2002.

Mohd. Farajina Ghazvini, Police Protection to Victims of Crimes, Deep and Deep Publication, New Delhi, 2002.

Monica David, Indian Legal and Constitutional History, Allahabad Law Agency, (1981).

N.D. Basu, Code of Criminal Procedure, Ashoka Law House, New Delhi, (2002).

N.J. Coulson, A History of Islamic Law, Universal Law Publishing Co. Pvt. Ltd. (1964).

N.V. Paranjape, Indian Legal and Constitutional History, Central Law Agency, (2004).

N.V. Pranjape, Criminology and Penology, Central Law Publications, (2005).

Neil C. Chamelin, Vernon B. Fox and Paul M. Whisenand, Introduction to Criminal Justice, Prentice Hall Inc. (1975).

O.P. Motiwal, Changing Aspects of Law and Justice in India, Chugh Publications (1979).

P.D. Sharma, Police Polity and People of India, Uppal Publishing House, New Delhi, 1981.

P.D. Sharma, Police, Polity and People in India, Uppal Publishing House, 1981.

P.S. Bawa, K. Krishnamurthi's Police Diaries, Lexis Nexis Butterworths, (2002).

P.J. Fitzgerald, Salmond on Jurisprudence, Univeral Law Publishing Co. Pvt. Ltd., (2002).

Police Hand Book, Delhi Law House, (1981).

Priya Nath Sen, Tagore Law Lectures, General Principles of Hindu Jurisprudence, Allahabad Law Agency, (1984).

R.K. Bag, Supreme Court on Criminal Justice, Asia Law House, (2003).

R.M. Jackson, The Machinery of Justice in England, Cambridge University Press, (1967).

R.V. Kelker, Criminal Procedure, Eastern Book Company, (2002).

Rajender Prashar, Police Administration, Deep and Deep Publications, New Delhi, 1986.

Rajender Saran Agarwal, Crime and Punishment in New Perspective, Mittal Publication, 1986

Ram Avtar Sharma, Justice and Social Order in India, Intellectual Publishing House, (1984).

Ram Jois, Seeds of Modern Public Law in Ancient Indian Jurisprudence, Eastern Book Company, (2000).

Ram Lal Gupta, Guide to Police Laws in India, Eastern Book Company, 1961.

Ratanlal and Dhirajlal, The Code of Criminal Procedure, Wadhwa and Company, Nagpur, (2002).

Rober D. Pursle, Introduction to Criminal Justice, Glencol Publishing Co. Inc., London, (1977).

Roscoe Pound, Justice according to Law, Yale University Press, (1952).

Russel R. Wheeler and Howard R. Whitcomb, Judicial Administration : Text and Readings, (1977).

S.C. Sarkar, Sarkar on The Law of Criminal Procedure, Indian Law House, (2004).

S.K. Ghosh, Police in Ferment, Light and Life, New Delhi, 1981.

S.K. Puri, Indian Legal and Constitutional History, Allahabad Law Agency, (2003).

S. Meharaj Begam, District Police Administration, Anmol Publication Pvt. Ltd., 1996.

S.N. Misra, Indian Penal Code, Central Law Agency, (2004).

S.R. Myneni, Indian History, Allahabad Law Agency, Faridabad, 2004.

Sen, Sanker, Police Today, Ashish Publishing, New Delhi, 1986.

Shraddhakar Supakar, Law of Procedure and Justice in Ancient India, Deep and Deep Publications, (1986)

Sir James Fitzjames Stephen, A History of the Criminal Law of England, Burt Franklin, New York (1983).

Suresh Chandra Pant, Hindu Polity, State and Government in Ancient India, Prakashan Kendra, Lucknow, (1971).

Syed Samshul Huda, The Principles of the Law of Crimes in British India, Eastern Book Company, (1982).

T. Ramanujam, Prevention and Detention of Crimes, Madras Book Agency, (1968).

U.C. Sarkar, Epochs in Hindu Legal History, Vishyeshvaranand Vedic Research Institute, Hoshiarpur, (1958).

U.C. Sarkar, Legal Research Essays, Allahabad Law Agency, (1984).

V.D. Kulshreshtha, Landmarks in Indian Legal and Constitutional History, Eastern Book Company, (1995).

V.K. Gupta, Kautilyan Jurisprudence, B.D. Gupta, Delhi, (1987).

V.K. Krishna Iyer, Indian Justice : Perspectives and Problems, Vedpal Law House, (1984).

V. Mitter, Police Diaries Statement, Allahabad Law Publishers, 1970

V.N. Shukla, Constitution of India, Eastern Book Company, (2001).

V.R. Krishna Iyer, Minorities, Civil Liberties and Criminal Justice, People's Publishing House, (1980).

Vijay K. Jindal, New Punjab Jail Manual, 1996, Chawla Publications Pvt. Ltd. (1998).

Walker and Walker, The English Legal System by R.J. Walker, Butterworths, (1980).

B. Articles and Journals

A.H. Mandal, Crime, Victims and Their Treatment in the Administration of Criminal Justice, *Central India Law Quarterly*, Vol. 14, Jan.-Mar. 2001.

A.M. Ahmadi, Reform of the Criminal Justice System of India, *Religion and Law Review,* Vol. 10-11, 2000-01.

Ananda Chandra Pradhan, Crime-Control and Criminal Justice System, *Cuttack Law Times,* Vol. 90, 2000.

Anu Saxena, Prisons and State Institutions, *Civil and Military Law Journal,* (2000).

Arun Bhagat, Policing *versus* Politicking, *Civil and Military Law Journal,* Vol. 37, Nos. 2 and 3, April-Sept. 2001.

Arvind Tiwari, Crime Prevention and Criminal Justice System, *CBI Bulletin,* Vol. 12, Jan. 2004.

Arvind Verma, Human Rights in Criminal Justice System, *Indian Journal of Criminology and Criminalistics,* Vol. 16, July-Dec. 1995.

B.B. Pande, Human Rights and Criminal Justice Administration in India : Rhetoric and Reality, *Delhi Law Review*, Vol. 17, 1995.

B.D. Agarwal, Criminal Justice System : Is Lie Oriented, *Criminal Law Journal*, Vol. 99, Dec 1999.

B.D. Shourie, Crime and Justice, *Civil and Military Law Journal*, Vol. 35, No. 4, Oct.-Dec. 1999.

B.K. Karkra, Police and Law and Order : Police Should not be Militarised, *Civil and Military Law Journal*, Vol. 33, 1977.

B.N. Chattoraj, Citizen Voice in Criminal Justice Administration, *Indian Journal of Criminology and Criminalistics*, Vol. 14, Jan. 1993.

B.N. Chattoraj, Training Needs of Criminal Justice Functionaries with Special Emphasis of Police Training, *Indian Journal of Criminology and Criminalistics*, Vol. 15, Jan-Dec. 1994.

B.P. Singh, Human Rights in the Administration of Criminal Justice System in India, *MDU Law Journal*, Vo. 7, 2002.

B.R. Sharma and Vandna Kashyap, Prison System in India : A Historical Retrospection, *Civil and Military Law Journal*, Vol. 30, No. 2, April-June, 1994.

B.R. Sharma, Constitutional Rights of Prisoners, *Civil and Military Law Journal*, Vol. 21, 1985.

B.S. Sherawat, Criminal Courts and Justice Delivery System, *Indian Bar Review*, Vol. 28, Jan.-Mar., 2001.

Baidyanath Chaudhary, Right to Fairness : An Humanising Element for Pre-trial Process in the Administration of Criminal Justice, *Criminal Law Journal*, Vol. 106, Oct. 2000.

Baidyanath Choudhary, Victims' Rights against Terrorism and the Administration of Criminal Justice, *Criminal Law Journal*, Vol. 108, Mar. 2002.

Bharat B. Das and Swagata Patnaik, Victims Perception of Criminal Justice System, *Central India Law Quarterly*, Vol. 6, Apr.-Jun., 1993.

C.L. Anand, Oversolicitous Homage to the Criminal Defendant's Liberty and Cause of Public Justice, *Civil and Military Law Journal*, Vol. 26, April-June, 1990.

C.S. Dharmadhikari, Criminal Justice System and Tribes in India, *Central Inda Law Quarterly*, Vol. 1, July-Sept., 1988.

D. Banerjee, Criminal Justice System and Police : The Whole and a Part, *CBI Bulletin*, Vol. 6, Nov. 1998.

D.P. Sharma, Speedy Justice and Indian Criminal Justice System, *Indian Journal of Public Administration*, Vol. 45, July 1999.

D.R. Singh, Evolution of Indian Criminal Justice System : Influence of Political and Economic Factors, *Indian Journal of Public Administration*, Vol. 40, July-Sept. 1994.

Dharam Pal Sharma, Delay in Criminal Trials, *CBI Bulletin*, Vol. 25, August 1991.

Durga Das Pada, Some Suggestions for Revamping the Criminal Justice System, *Criminal Law Journal*, Vol. 108, March, 2002.

Durga Das Pada, Study on the Causes of Failure of Criminal Cases in India, *Calcutta High Court Notes*, Vol. 2, 2001.

Ed. Cape and Lee Bridges, Criminal Justice or Social Exclusion, *Lawyers' Collective*, Vol. 15, Nov. 2001.

F.V. Arun, International Criminal Police Organisations, *CBI Bulletin*, Vol. 10, Jan. 2002.

Faizan and Talib Javed Mustafa, Influence of Public Interest Litigation on Administration, *Aligarh Law Journal*, Vol. 11, 1996.

G.S. Bhargawa, Flashback on 1975 and Jayalalitha's Administration of Criminal Justice, *Mainstream*, 2001.

G. Sadasivan Nair, Processual Criminal Justice and Human Rights, *Cochin University Law Review*, Vol. 20, Mar.-June, 1996.

Gulab Gupta, Social Justice Perspective of Criminal Justice, *Central India Law Quarterly*, Vol. 1 August, 1987.

Gurbachan Singh Nayyar, Civil and Criminal Justice under Maharaja Ranjit Singh, *Civil and Military Law Journal*, Vol. 28, Jan.-Mar. 1992.

H. Suresh, Human Rights and Criminal Justice Functionaries, *Economic and Political Weekly*, Vol. 31, 1996.

Hendrik Kaptein, Just Criminal Lawyers, Professional Ethics and Problems of Punitive Justice : Restorative Perspectives, *Indian Socio-Legal Journal*, Vol. 29, 2003.

Hira Singh, U.N. Crime Prevention and Criminal Justice Programme, *Social Defence*, Vol. 31, Oct. 1991.

Hruda Ballav Das, Study on the Prospect of Reformative Criminal Justice with Special Reference to Probation of Offenders' Act : Law Relating to Victimology, *Criminal Law Journal*, Vol. 97, June 1991.

Hrudaya Ballav Das, Introduction of the Concept of Plea Bargaining in Criminal Administration of Justice, *Cuttack Law Times*, Vol. 70, 199.

Hrudaya Ballav Das, Introduction of the Concept of Plea-bargaining in Criminal Administration of Justice, *Criminal Law Journal*, Vol. 96, Sept. 1990.

Indira Jaisingh, British Criminal Justice System, *Lawyers' Collective*, Vol. 6, 1991.

Iqbal Ali Khan, Human Rights and Criminal Justice : A Pathetic State, *Aligarh Law Journal*, Vol. 13, 19998

J.N. Chandrasekharan Pillai, Criminal Justice Administration : A Balance Sheet, *Academy Law Review*, Vol. 18, 1994.

Jagmohan Singh, Law and Justice in Jammu and Kashmir, *Civil and Military Law Journal*, Vol. 27, No. 4, Oct.-Dec. 1991.

Justice V.R. Krishna Iyer, Beyond Human Justice, *Civil and Military Law Journal*, Vol. 16, No. 1, Jan.-March, 1980.

Justice V.R. Krishna Iyer, Consciousness, Criminal Behaviour and Crime, *Civil and Military Law Journal*, Vol. 19, No. 4, Oct.-Dec. 1983.

Justice V.R. Krishna Iyer, Crime and Correctional Processes Key Issue in Contemporary Criminology, *Civil and Military Law Journal*, Vol. 28, No. 4, 1982.

Justice V.R. Krishna Iyer, Crime and Correctional Processes— Key Issues in Contemporary Criminology, *Civil and Military Law Journal*, Vol. 28, No. 4, Oct-Dec. 1992.

Justice V.R. Krishna Iyer, The Pathology of Indian Criminology and its Prognosis, *Civil and Military Law Journal*, Vol. 17, No. 1, Jan.-March, 1981.

K. Madhavan, Criminal Justice System, *CBI Bulletin*, Vol. 26, July 1992.

K.N. Goyal, Criminal Justice Reform, *Criminal Law Journal*, Vol. 107, April 2001.

K.N. Goyal, Human Rights and Criminal Justice, *Criminal Law Journal*, Vol. 108, Oct., 2002.

K. Rama Joga, Use of Criminal Law Machinery for Environment Protection, *Supreme Court Cases*, Vol. 7, 2001.

K. Ramachandra Reddy, Suggestions for Speedy Justice in Criminal Trials, *Supreme Corut Journal*, Vol. 3, 1990.

K.S. Srinivasan, Dharma and Violence, *Civil and Military Law Journal*, Vol. 33, 1997.

K. Shreedhar Rao, Criminal Justice System : Required Reforms, *Journal of Indian Law Institute*, Vol. 43, Apr.-Jun. 2001.

K. Sreedhar Rao, Criminal Justice System—Required Reforms, *Criminal Law Journal*, Vol. 108, Jan. 2002.

K. Venkataraman, Delay in Criminal Justice Delivery System : Cause Effect Remedy, *Criminal Law Journal*, Vol. 106, June 2000.

Kishore Chandra Patnaik, Review of Laws and Criminal Justice System to Deal with Corruption Cases, *Cuttack Law Times*, Vol. 91, 2001.

Latha Krishnamurthi, Role Conflicts and Tensions of Women Police in Criminal Justice Administration, *Indian Journal of Social Work*, Vol. 57, 1996.

M.G. Mukherji, Thoughts on Human Rights and Criminal Justice System, *Central India Law Quarterly*, Vol. 14, Apr.-Jun. 2001.

M.L. Sharma, Role and Function of Prosecution in Criminal Justice, Part II, *CBI Bulletin*, Vol. 5, Oct. 1997.

M.S. Rahi, Fresh Look on Administration of Criminal Justice (Relating to Offences under (NDPS) Act : A Necessity or a Mere Academic Probe, *Criminal Law Journal*, Vol. 105, July 1999.

M. Venkateswara, Need to Amend Section 482, Criminal Procedure Code to Enable the Subordinate Judiciary to Administer Justice Effectively, *Criminal Law Journal*, Vol. 98, Nov. 1999.

M.R.A. Khan, Theories of Punishment, *Civil and Military Law Journal*, Vol. 19, No. 1, Jan.-March, 1993.

Madhu Sudan, Role of Public Prosecutor in Administration of Criminal Justice, *Criminal Law Journal*, Vol. 103, Sept. 1997.

Mahesh T. Pai, Delay in the Criminal Justice System : Common Cause Evaluated, *Cochin University Law Review*, Vol. 20, Sept.-Dec. 1996.

Modh. Ashraf, Police and Administration of Criminal Justice in India : An Appraisal, *Civil and Military Law Journal*, Vol. 36, April-June, 2000.

Mohd. Ashraf, Need to Reform Indian Judicial System, *Civil and Military Law Journal*, Vol. 39, No. 4, Oct.-Dec. 2003.

N.K. Chakravartty, Decision Making Process in the Criminal Justice System and the Law of Probation, *Criminal Law Journal*, Vol. 97, Nov. 1991.

N.K. Chakravartty, Victim Assistance and Compensations to Crime Victims Under Indian Criminal Justice System, *Criminal Law Journal*, Vol. 105, 1999.

N.K. Chakravartty, Criminal Justice Policy of Humanitarian Law : Theories, *Aligarh Law Journal*, Vol. 11, 1996.

Nalini Kanta Dutta, Criminal Justice in Tradition of Hindu Society, *Gauhati University Journal of Law*, Vol. 4, 1990.

Neeta Sharma, Modernising Police Force, *Civil and Military Law Journal*, Vol. 36, No. 3, July-Sept. 2000

Nikhil Jaiprakash, Criminal Justice System in India : Whither Commitment, *CBI Bulletin*, Vol. 12, Jan. 2004.

Nirman Arotra, Custodial Torture in Police Stations in India, *Journal of Indian Law Institute*, 1999.

P.C. Sharma, Criminal Justice System and the Fight Against Corruption : Challenges Ahead, *CBI Bulletin*, Vol. 11, Dec. 2003.

P.M. Bakshi, Continental System of Criminal Justice, *Journal of Indian Law Institute*, Vol. 36, Oct.-Dec 1994.

P.V. Indiresan, Restructuring the Criminal Justice System, *CBI Bulletin*, Vol. 8, Feb. 2000.

Prakash Singh, Police and Law and Order : Police and the Question of Accountability, *Civil and Military Law Journal*, Vol. 33, 1997.

Priyabrata Ghosh, Songs in the Criminal Justice System of India, *CBI Bulletin*, Vol. 101, Nov. 1995.

Promila Kalhan, Indian Judicial System, *Civil and Military Law Journal*, Vol. 23, No. 1, Jan.-March, 1987.

Qaiser Hayat, Human Rights and Criminal Justice System in India : A Study or Pre-trial Detainees, *Aligarh Law Journal*, Vol. 13, 1998.

R. Damodar, Participation of Accused in Criminal Justice, *Criminal Law Journal*, Vol. 99, Dec. 1993.

R. Deb, Need for Judicial Activism in Administration of Criminal Justice, *Criminal Law Journal*, Vol. 99, Feb. 1999.

R. Deb, Police and Administration of Criminal Justice, *CBI Bulletin*, Vol. 26, Feb. 1992.

R.K. Bag, Perspective in Victimology in Context of criminal Justice System, *Criminal Law Journal* Vol. 105, Oct. 1999.

R.K. Raizada, Role of Public Prosecutor in Criminal Justice in India, *Aligarh Law Journal*, Vol. 9, (1998).

R.P. Sethi, Criminal Justice System : Problems and Challenges, *Aligarh Law Journal*, 1999-2000.

R.S. Saini, Custodial Torture in Law and Practice with Reference to India, *Journal of Indian Law Institute*, 1994.

Rajiv Gupta, Salient Features of Memorial Lecture of Hon'bleMr. Justice K.T. Thomas on New Trends in Criminal Law, *All India Reporter*, Vol. 89, April 2002.

Ramesh P. Vaghela, Human Rights in Criminal Justice System : Conflicting Priorities, *Gujarat Law Herald*, No. 2, Vol. 17, 19997.

Ranjit S. Mooshahary, Cirminal Justice System : The Quest for Truth, *Indian Police Journal*, Vol. 50, Oct.-Dec. 2003.

Ranjit S. Mooshahary, Criminal Justice System-I : Truth and Its Judicial Interpretation, *CBI Bulletin*, Vol. 12, March 2004.

Ranjit S. Mooshahary, Criminal Justice System-II : Courts Must become Party to the Quest for Truth, *CBI Bulletin*, Vol. 12, March, 2004.

Ranjit Sinha, Administration of Criminal Justice—Need for Co-ordination Between Police and Correctional Process, *CBI Bulletin*, Vol. 7, Sept. 1999.

Roscoe Pound, The Limits of Effective Legal System, *Civil and Military Law Journal*, Vo. 16, No. 1, Jan.-March, 1980.

S.K. Dubey, Gender Issue Criminal Justice and Women, *Central Indian Law Qaurterly*, Vol. 9, Oct.-De. 1996.

S.M. Afzal Qadri, Police Role in Administration of Criminal Justice, *Kashmir University Law Review*, Vol. 6, 1999.

S.M. Afzal Qadri, Women Victims and Criminal Justice, *Social Defence*, Vol. 31, 1991.

S. Muralidhar, Rights of Victims in the Indian Criminal Justice System, *Journal of the National Human Rights Commission*, Vol. 2, 2003.

S.P. Srivastava, Human Rights and Administration of Criminal Justice in India, *Indian Journal of Criminology and Criminalistics*, Vol. 19, Jan.-April 1998.

S.R. Sankhyan, Criminal Justice System : A Framework for Reforms, *Economic and Political Weekly*, Vol. 34, 1999.

S. Ratnavel, Criminal Justice System in India, *Indian Journal of Criminology and Criminalisitcs*, Vol. 16, July-Dec. 1995.

S. Subramaniam, Police and Society, *Civil and Military Law Journal*, Vol. 31, 1995.

S. Subramanian, Police and Society, *Civil and Military Law Journal*, Vol. 31, No. 3, July-Sept., 1995.

Sabasachi Mukherji, Indian Legal and Judicial System Problems and Challenges, *Civil and Military Law Journal*, Vol. 26, No. 1, Jan.-March 1990.

Sanjay Malik, Justice Through Inherent Powers of the Court, *Civil and Military Law Journal*, Vol. 36, No. 1, Jan.-March, 2000.

Sneh Lata Singh, Human Rights and Administration of Criminal Justice in India, *Journal of Constitutional and Parliamentary Studies*, July-Dec. 2001.

Sree Priyabrata Ghosh, New Dimensions of Indian Criminal Jurisprudence, *Criminal Law Journal*, Vol. 105, June 1999.

Subhash Chandra Singh, Criminal Justice : An Overview, *Criminal Law Journal*, Vol. 105, March, 1999.

Subhash Chandra Singh, Participation of Victim in the Criminal Justice Process, *Criminal Law Journal*, Vol. 104, May 1998.

Subhash Chandra Singh, Role of Public Prosecutor in the Administration of Criminal Justice, *Criminal Law Journal*, Vol. 106, Jun 2000.

Surinder Kumar, Crime : Its Causation, Diagnosis and Treatment, *Civil and Military Law Journal*, Vol. 36, No. 4, 2000.

T.C. Surya Rao, Police *vis-a-vis* the Criminal Justice System, *Andhra Law Times*, Vol. 95, Nov. 1998.

Vijay Karan, Moribund State of Criminal Justice System and Urgency of Total Reforms, *Indian Journal of Public Administration*, Vol. 40, July-Sept. 1994.

Vijay Kumar, Human Rights and the Criminal Justice System in India, *Central India Law Quarterly*, 2003, Vol. 16, Oct.-Dec. 2003.

Vineet Agarwal, Recasting Criminal Justice System Using Electric Curent Model, *CBI Bulletin*, Vol. 8, Sept. 2000.

Wing Commander U.C. Jha, Summary Court-Martial in U.K. and USA, *Civil and Military Law Journal*, Vol. 39, No. 4, Oct.-Dec. 2003.

Zubair Ahmad, History of Criminal Justice System in India : A View of Mughal and British Period, *Aligarh Law Journal*, 1999-2000.

C. Journals

All India Reporter
American Journal of International Law
Civil and Military Law Journal
Civil Services Chronicle
Criminal Law Journal
Economic and Political Weekly
Frontline
India Today
Journal of the Indian Law Institute
Journal of Legal Education
Mainstream
Organiser
Outlook
Seminar
Socio Legal Journal
The Competition Master
The competition Wizard
Yojana
Indian Police Journal
Delhi Law Review
Central India Law Quarterly
Academy Law Review
CBI Bulletin
Journal of the National Human Rights Commission
M.D.U Law Journal
Religion and Law Review
Aligarh Law Journal
Journal of the Constitutional and Parliamentary Study
Supreme Court Journal
Cuttack Law Times
Gauhati University Journal of Law

Social Defence
Kashmir University Law Review
Indian Journal of Public Administration
Cochin University Law Review
Indian Association of Social Science Institutions Quarterly
Gujarat Law Herald
Indian Journal of Criminology and Criminalistics
Andhra Law Times
Lawyers' Collective
Delhi Law Review
Indian Journal of Social Work
Indian Bar Review
Calcutta High Court Notes

(D) Newspapers

Amar Ujala (Hindi Daily)
Employment News (Weekly)
Indian Express
Sahara Time (Weekly)
The Hindu
The Hindustan Times
The Times of India
The Tribune

(E) Dictionaries and Encyclopaedia

A New Survey of Universal Knowledge, Encyclopaedia Britannica, William Benton Publisher, Chicago (1996).

David M. Walker, The Oxford Companion of Law, Clarendon Press, London, (1980).

Elizabeth A. Martin, A Concise Dictionary of Law, Oxford University Press, Great Britain, (1983).

H.W. Fowler and F.G. Gowler, The Concise Oxford Dictionary of Current English, Oxford University Oress, Calcutta (1974).

J. Voulson, The Oxford Illustrated Dictionary, Oxford at the Clarendon Press, (1978).

The New Encyclopaedia Britannica, (15th Ed.) Encyclopaedia Britannica Inc., Chicago, (2002).

Sanford, H. Kadish, Encyclopaedia of Crime and Justice, Vols. 1, 2, 3 and 4, The Free Press, New York, (1983).

(F) Websites

www.internationalstudies.ilstu.edu
www.ojp.usdoj.gov.
www.indiatogether.org.
www.countercurrents.org
www.vedamsbooks.com
In.dir.yahoo.com/government/law/criminaljustice
www.frontlineonnet.com.
faculty.ncwc.edu
www.indian.edu/crimjust/faculty/verma/him
pib.nic.in
www.hindu.com
www.icj.org/img/po16/india

(G) Acts and Manuals

The Police Act, 1861
The Prisons Act, 1894
The Constitution of India, 1950
The Probation of Offenders' Act, 1958
The Code of Criminal Procedure, 1973
The Juvenile (Care and Protection) Act, 2000
Jail Manual
Punjab Jail Manual

(H) Commissions and Committees

Mallimath Committee Report on Criminal Justice System
National Police Commission Report
Himachal Pradesh Police Annual Administrative Reports
Law Commissions Reports

Index